A Thoughtful Faith for the 21ˢᵗ Century

A Thoughtful Faith for the 21ˢᵗ Century

EDITED BY PHILIP L. BARLOW

FaithMatters

FM

Faith Matters Publishing
2929 W Navigator Drive, Suite 400
Meridian, ID 83642
faithmatters.org

ISBN: 978-1-953677-24-2 (paperback)
       978-1-953677-25-9 (ebook)

LIBRARY OF CONGRESS NUMBER: 2025934052

10 9 8 7 6 5 4 3 2 1

For **KATE HOLBROOK** (1972–2022),
lovely in soul and mien,
who died before she could write
here of her thoughtful faith,
but lived to inscribe it in every act.

And for her companion in
calling and radiance,
MELISSA INOUYE (1979–2024),
who lived to write here of
her thoughtful faith,
Jesus shining boldly in
her countenance.

CONTENTS

PREFACE

A cherished friend of mine experienced in his thirties a "dark night of the soul"—at least in the phrase's modern sense of a personal crisis. This bleak season lasted several years, during which the things he had most trusted in life no longer seemed dependable. Like me, he had studied religion formally in graduate school, which raised all manner of questions about his personal religion. This brought strain, but his trial entailed additional dimensions as well: occupational, financial, marital, and existential ones. It included a sense of betrayal and abandonment in both professional and personal spheres. Suddenly he was broke, jobless, wifeless, and navigating a fractured faith. His life seemed caught, he said, "in the vortex of an abyss." How to survive and move forward? Among other things, he needed to decide what his fundamental disposition would be toward The Church of Jesus Christ of Latter-day Saints. He eventually resigned his membership.

I have known a darkness not unlike my friend's—a lonely and imperiled time. I empathize with him, respect him, and love him. In my case, however, prayer, thought, study, grace, patience, and discussion with wise souls at length persuaded me of the depth and permanence of my faith and my commitment to the institutional church as I came to understand them. This, despite their necessarily human entanglements. I emerged from my own season of anguish and learning a more humble, more rooted, less naïve, and slightly scarred disciple. I am grateful for the path I have walked.

Seeing, decades ago, that the sorts of difficulties that assaulted my friend's faith were not rare among my people, I decided publicly to articulate "the reasons for the hope that was in me." I recruited a cluster of allies I admired to similarly convey the grounds for their enduring life in the church. The published result was *A Thoughtful Faith: Essays on Belief by Mormon Scholars* (1986), which included the ruminations of a sampling of Latter-day Saints versed in history, psychology, literature, law, philosophy, science, and political science. In other words, people who understood at a professional level, from different angles of vision, the sorts of questions with which many struggled. These were informed Saints, unwilling to forfeit either their intellect or their heart. ⚜

Feedback over the course of the generation that followed suggests readers found nourishment in these voices. One early reviewer said the collection disabused her of the notion that "the ways of God spell ruin for the aspiring artist or intellectual." She had previously been led to suppose that in striving to obey God's laws, one's individuality must be "lopped off little by little, that she or he might conform to more universal standards of godliness." "'Losing your life to gain it' meant

⚜ Years later, a friend borrowed our book's title for a podcast he was launching. This enterprise, however, soon went its own way and evolved into a forum for complaint, independent of our book's spirit, title, and purpose in thoughtfully exploring faith. The book and the podcast are not otherwise related and should not be confused.

trading individuality for eternity in the company of your duplicates." The *Thoughtful Faith* authors allowed her more space. There is "nothing depersonalized or duplicate about these twenty-two seasoned saints or their essays."[1] In their variety, in their humanity, in their quest for goodness and a faith sturdy enough for the rigor of thought and experience, they give us a glimpse of the rich variety of God's wisdom.

The world has turned some since the essays were published and the volume has long been out of print. Strands of some essays may seem dated, hence the need for the present volume, *A Thoughtful Faith for the Twenty-First Century*, a collection of fresh perspectives from a new generation. Yet the original book retains worth. Older and younger generations have things to learn from one another: the hearts and minds of the fathers and mothers must be turned to their children, and vice versa.

We have addressed this need in two ways. First, we have made the original volume, *A Thoughtful Faith: Essays on Belief by Mormon Scholars*, available online, courtesy of the Harold B. Lee Library at Brigham Young University, through the Scholar's Archive:

https://scholarsarchive.byu.edu/books/33/ ⟿

Second, we have incorporated a half-dozen samples of the earlier essays into the present tangible volume. The faithful wisdom of such disciple-scholars as Laurel Thatcher Ulrich, Leonard Arrington, and Richard Bushman should make the intergenerational value immediately apparent to younger

---

⟿ The 2016 edition of that work, which includes postscripts from a number of the authors commenting on how their thinking had evolved or endured over the thirty years since the book first appeared, is available (also courtesy of BYU's library) here: **https://scholarsarchive.byu.edu/books/35/**.

readers. Complementing these classic authors, the present collection speaks immediately to our time, includes more women, more scientists, more perspectives from outside the United States, and additional attention to social issues contested among us in the twenty-first century. In several instances, by request, a newer author is directly paired with one of the classic authors whose essays are reprinted in this volume: Spencer Fluhman comments on Richard Bushman's adjacent chapter; Melissa Inouye comments on Laurel Ulrich; Terryl Givens comments on Eugene England. In another instance, Joseph Spencer comments here on Richard L. Anderson, whose essay is available in the original *Thoughtful Faith* collection, available online through the Harold B. Lee Library at BYU, as noted on page XIII.

Scholar Saints are sometimes called upon to defend the faith. The contributors to this book have naturally done so in their own ways, both in their writing and by their lives. It is rather a different matter, however, when some observers construe a metaphorical call to arms as license to become fundamentally defensive in orientation. Sometimes such defensiveness becomes aggressive, which often backfires, inciting rather than disarming critics, contravening the spirit of Jesus, and embarrassing the church. Indeed, it is not unheard of for us as a people to show signs of an autoimmune disease (call it rheumatoid religion) in which, with excess zeal, we stir contention, attacking fellow believers. We sometimes fail to recognize our real friends, perhaps because they have been honest enough to acknowledge historical, conceptual, or social challenges in the course of their faithful scholarship. When church members turn on fellow Saints whose efforts are trying to inoculate less experienced compatriots against real historical or social difficulties, we may detect in our collective selves such an autoimmune response. As with Job's friends, it is possible to offend God by a flawed, presumptuous, or distorted attempt to defend God.

The people assembled between these covers incline to candor rather than to a public relations blitz while expressing their faith and loyalty to the church. Such informed honesty may raise occasional eyebrows among those unaccustomed to working through rather than avoiding difficulties, but they will relieve many others who sense they can trust the process of authentic dialogue. The contributors gathered here defend the faith not by skirting tough issues, but by acknowledging them while emphasizing and unpacking the richness and redeeming glories of the gospel, often in original, highly personal ways. I cannot speak for all of them, but many would agree with an assertion taken from the Preface to the original *Thoughtful Faith*: the phenomenon of revelation is real, yet the church is made up entirely of human beings, who in their imperfect ways are trying to respond to the divine with which they have been touched. Both things can be true at once. This leaves room for—this demands—a great expanse of charity as together, and by covenant, we pursue the noble aims of the kingdom.

And they *are* noble, these aims of Zion and Eternal Life. So too is their divine author, whom Jesus counseled us to love with all that we are: "with all thy *heart*, and with all thy *soul*, and with all thy *mind*" (Matt. 22:37). To attempt to submerge any of these parts of ourselves does not render devotion more pure, but only more partial and vulnerable.

PHILIP BARLOW

Lusterware

LAUREL ULRICH

Reprinted from the 1986 collection,
A Thoughtful Faith: Essays on Belief by Mormon Scholars.

 **have been thinking lately** about an Emily Dickinson poem I first heard twenty-five years ago in an American literature class at the University of Utah. I remember feeling intrigued and somewhat troubled as the professor read the poem since he was reported to be a lapsed Mormon. "Was that how it felt to lose faith?" I thought.

> It dropped so low—in my Regard—
> I heard it hit the Ground—
> And go to pieces on the Stones
> At bottom of my Mind—
> Yet blamed the Fate that flung it—less
> Than I denounced Myself,
> For entertaining Plated Wares
> Upon my Silver Shelf.—

Since then I have lost faith in many things, among them Olympia typewriters, *New York Times* book reviews, and texturized vegetable protein; and yes, like most Latter-day Saints, I have had to reconsider some of my deepest religious beliefs. I have always been a somewhat skeptical person. I can remember raising my arm in Beehive class in the Sugar City Ward and telling my teacher that regardless of what she said I did *not* think that polygamy was sent by God. That kind of behavior may have had something to do with the palm reading I received from another teacher at an MIA gypsy party. She traced the lines on my upturned hand and told me my "head" line was longer and better developed than my "heart" line. For a while I worried about that.

As I have grown older, I have become less fearful of those "stones at the bottom of my mind." In fact, I am convinced that a willingness to admit disbelief is often essential to spiritual growth. All of us meet challenges to our faith—persons who fail to measure up, doctrines that refuse to settle comfortably into our minds, books that contain troubling ideas or disorienting information. The temptation is strong to "blame the fate that flung it" or to ignore the crash as it hits the ground, pretending that nothing has changed. Neither technique is very useful. Though a few people seem to have been blessed with foam rubber rather than stones at the bottom of their minds (may they rest in peace), sooner or later most of us are forced to confront our shattered beliefs.

I find Emily Dickinson's little poem helpful. Some things fall off the shelf because they did not belong there in the first place; they were "Plated Wares" rather than genuine silver. At first I didn't fully grasp the image. The only "Plated Wares" I knew anything about were made by Oneida or Wm. Rogers. Although less valuable than sterling, that sort of silverplate hardly falls to pieces when dropped. Then I learned about lusterware, the most popular "Plated Wares" of Emily Dickinson's time. In the late eighteenth century, British manufacturers developed a technique for decorating ceramic ware with a gold or platinum film. In one variety, a platinum luster was applied to the entire surface of the object to produce what contemporaries called "poor man's silver." Shiny, inexpensive, and easy to get, it was also fragile, as breakable as any other piece of pottery or china. Only a gullible or very inexperienced person would mistake it for true silver.

All of us have lusterware as well as silver on that shelf we keep at the top of our minds. A lusterware Joseph Smith, for instance, is unfailingly young, handsome, and spiritually radiant; unschooled but never superstitious, persecuted but never vengeful, human but never mistaken. A lusterware image fulfills our need for an ideal without demanding a great deal from us. There are lusterware missions and marriages, lusterware friendships, lusterware histories, and yes, lusterware visions of ourselves. Most of these will be tested at some point on the stones at the bottom of our minds.

A number of years ago I read a letter from a young woman who had recently discovered some lusterware on her own shelf. "I used to think of the Church as one-hundred percent true," she wrote. "But now I realize it is probably ten percent human and only ninety percent divine." I gasped, wanting to write back immediately, "If you find any earthly institution that is ten percent divine, embrace it with all your heart!" Actually ten percent is probably too high an estimate. Jesus spoke of grains of salt and bits of leaven, and He told His disciples that "the kingdom of heaven is like unto treasure hid in a field; the which when a man hath found, he hideth, and for joy thereof goeth and selleth all that he hath, and buyeth that field" (Matthew 13:44). Thus a small speck of divinity—the salt in the earth, the leaven in the lump of dough, the treasure hidden in the field—gives value and life to the whole. Now the question is where in the Church of Jesus Christ of Latter-day Saints do we go to find the leaven? To the bishop? To the prophet? To the lesson manuals? Do we find it in Relief Society? In sacrament meeting? And if we fail to discover it in any of these places shall we declare the lump worthless? Jesus's answer was clear. The leaven must be found in one's own heart or not at all: " . . . the kingdom of God is within you" (Luke 17:21).

Many years ago a blunt bishop countered one of my earnest complaints with a statement I have never forgotten: "The Church is a good place to practice the Christian virtues of forgiveness, mercy, and love unfeigned." That was a revelation to me. The Church was not a place that exemplified Christian virtues so much as a place that required them. I suppose I had always thought of it as a nice cushion, a source of warmth and comfort if ever things got tough (which they seldom had in my life). It hadn't occurred to me that the Church could *make* things tough.

Eliza R. Snow expressed it this way in a hymn that seems to be missing from the new book:

> Think not when you gather to Zion,
> Your troubles and trials are through,
> That nothing but comfort and pleasure
> Are waiting in Zion for you:
> No, no, 'tis designed as a furnace,
> All substance, all textures to try,
> To burn all the "wood, hay, and stubble,"
> The gold from the dross purify.

Probably the hymn deserved to be dropped from the book. The third stanza suggests that the author, like more than one Relief Society president since, had made too many welfare visits and had listened to too many sad stories. Her charity failing, she told the complainers in her ward to shape up and solve their own problems:

> Think not when you gather to Zion,
> The Saints here have nothing to do
> But to look to your personal welfare,
> And always be comforting you.

In the Church, as in our own families, we have the worst and the best of times.

A young missionary on a lonely bus ride somewhere in Bolivia thinks he is equal to what lies ahead. He can endure hard work, strange food, and a confusing dialect. But nothing in the Mission Training Center has prepared him for the

filthiness of the apartment, for the cynicism of his first companion, or for the parakeet who lives, with all its droppings,
under the other man's bed.

A young bride, ready to enter the temple, feels herself spiritually prepared. By choosing a simple white gown useable
later as a temple dress she has already shown her preference
for religious commitment over fantasy. She has discussed the
covenants with her stake president and she feels she understands them. Yet sitting in the endowment room in ritual
clothing no one had thought to show her, saying words she
does not understand, she turns to her mother in dismay. "Am
I supposed to enjoy this?" she says.

An elder's quorum president, pleased that his firm has won
the contract for the ward remodeling project, prepares for the
hard work ahead. He knows the job will be demanding. He
expects some tension between his responsibilities as project
manager and his commitment to the Church, but he is ready
to consecrate his time and talents for the upbuilding of the
Kingdom. What he doesn't expect is the anger and the humiliation that follow his year-long encounter with the Church
bureaucracy. "I wonder how far up this sort of thing goes?" he
asks, and contemplates leaving the Church.

A middle-aged woman reads deeply in the scriptures,
sharing her insights with friends individually and in a small
study group. She feels secure in her quest for greater light
and truth until she begins to examine certain troubling episodes in Church history. The discrepancy between the official
accounts and the new accounts distresses her. Has she been
lied to? And if in one issue, why not many? Confiding her
doubts to her friends, she feels them back away.

"And the rain descended, and the floods came, and the
winds blew, and beat upon that house; and it fell not: for it
was founded upon a rock" (Matthew 7:24–25). What rock can

secure us against such storms? Occasionally some gentle soul, perhaps as puzzled as my Beehive teacher by my outspoken ways, will ask, "What keeps you in the Church?" "My skepticism," I answer, only half in jest. Over the years I have noticed that Saints with doubts often outlast "true believers." But of course the answer is inadequate. I don't stay in the Church because of what I don't know, but because of what I do.

The Church I believe in is not an ascending hierarchy of the holy. It is millions of ordinary people calling one another "brother" and "sister" and trying to make it true. Not so long ago I had one of those terrible-wonderful experiences that I have been talking about. It started in an innocuous way, then built to a genuine crisis—a classic Liahona-Iron Rod conflict between me and my bishop. After a week of sleepless nights I went into his office feeling threatened and fragile. What followed was an astonishingly open and healing discussion, a small miracle. As I told a friend later, "If we hadn't been Mormons, we would have embraced!" Our opinions didn't change much; our attitudes toward one another did. I give him credit for having the humility to listen, and I give myself credit for trusting him enough to say what I really felt. The leaven in our lump was a common reaching for the Spirit.

I am not always comfortable in my ward. There are weeks when I wonder if I can sit through another Relief Society lesson delivered straight from the manual or endure another meandering discussion in Gospel Doctrine class. Yet there are also moments when, surprised by my own silence, I am able to hear what a speaker only half says. Several months ago, as I was bracing myself for a Fast and Testimony meeting, a member of the bishopric approached me and asked if I would give the closing prayer. I said, "Yes," feeling like a hypocrite, yet at the same time silently accepting some responsibility for the success of the meeting. Were the testimonies really better? When I stood to pray I was moved to the point of tears.

For me the issue is not whether the Church of Jesus Christ of Latter-day Saints is the One True Church Upon the Face of the Earth. That sounds to me like a particularly Zoramite brand of lusterware:

> Now the place was called by them Rameumptom, which, being interpreted, is the holy stand. Now, from this stand they did offer up, every man, the self-same prayer . . . We thank thee, O God, for we are a chosen people unto thee, while others shall perish. (Alma 31:22,28)

The really crucial issue for me is that the Spirit of Christ is alive in the Church, and that it continues to touch and redeem the lives of the individual members. The young man survived his mission, returning with a stronger, more sober sense of what it meant to serve. The bride returned to the temple and enjoyed it more. The elder's quorum president, though still struggling with his anger, knows it is his problem to face and to solve. The middle-aged woman grew through her loss of faith into a richer, deeper spirituality.

As I study the scriptures very few contemporary problems seem new. I wonder how men in tune with the divine can appear to be so complacent and self-righteous in their dealings with women. Then I read Luke's account of the visit of the angel to the women at the tomb on the first day of the week: "It was Mary Magdalene, and Joanna, and Mary the mother of James, and other women that were with them, which told these things unto the apostles. And their words seemed to them as idle tales, and they believed them not" (Luke 24:10–11). I wonder how a church purportedly devoted to eternal values can invest so much energy in issues that strike me as unimportant. Then I read the nineteenth chapter of Leviticus and find the second greatest commandment, "thou shalt love thy neighbor as thyself," side by side with a sober command that "neither shall a garment mingled of linen and woolen come upon thee" (Leviticus 19:18–19). Every dispensation has had its silver and its lusterware. God speaks to His children, as Moroni taught us, in our own language, and in our own narrow and culture-bound condition.

To me that is a cause for joy rather than cynicism. I love Joseph Smith's ecstatic recital in Doctrine and Covenants 128:

> Now, what do we hear in the gospel which we have received? A voice of gladness! a voice of mercy from heaven; and a voice of truth out of the earth . . .

> A voice of the Lord in the wilderness of Fayette, Seneca county . . .

> The voice of Michael on the banks of the Susquehanna . . .

> The voice of Peter, James, and John in the wilderness between Harmony, Susquehanna county, and Colesville, Broome county . . .

> And again, the voice of God in the chamber of old Father Whitmer, in Fayette, Seneca county, and at sundry times, and in divers places through all the travels and tribulations of this Church of Jesus Christ of Latter-day Saints! (D&C 128:19–21)

Joseph's litany of homely place names, his insistence that the voice of God could indeed be heard on the banks of an ordinary American river or in the chamber of a common farmer, gives his message an audacity and a power that cannot be ignored. For me Joseph Smith's witness that the divine can strike through the immediate is more important than any of the particulars enshrined in the church he established. If other people want to reduce D&C 128 to a data processing program for handling family group sheets, that's fine. I am far more interested in that "whole and complete and perfect union, and welding together of dispensations" that Joseph wrote about.

Two or three years ago I attended a small unofficial women's conference in Nauvoo. The ostensible purpose was to celebrate the founding of the Relief Society, but the real agenda was to come to terms with the position of women in the contemporary Church. The participants came from many places; a few of us known to each other, many of us strangers, the only common bond being some connection with the three organizers, all of whom remained maddeningly opaque as to their motives. I cannot describe what happened to me during those three days. Let me just say that after emptying myself of any hope for peace and change in the Church I heard the voice of the Lord on the banks of the Mississippi River. It was a voice of gladness, telling me that the gospel had indeed been restored. It was a voice of truth, assuring me that my concerns were just, that much was still amiss in the Church. It was a voice of mercy, giving me the courage to continue my uneasy dialogue between doubt and faith. I am not talking here about a literal voice, but about an infusion of the Spirit—a kind of Pentecost that for a moment dissolved the boundaries between heaven and earth and between present and past. I felt as though I were reexperiencing the events the early Saints had described.

I am not a mystical person. In ordinary decisions in my family I am far more likely to call for a vote than a prayer, and when other people proclaim their "spiritual experiences" I am generally cautious. But I would gladly sift through a great trough of meal for even a little bit of that leaven.

The temptations of skepticism are real. Sweeping up the lusterware, we sometimes forget to polish and cherish the silver, not knowing that the power of discernment is one of the gifts of the Spirit and that the ability to discover counterfeit wares also gives us the power to recognize the genuine.

A Church That is Real

MELISSA WEI-TSING INOUYE

As a youth I always had questions about faith, but did not dwell on them seriously until I went to university. At Harvard College, I wandered happily in the library stacks, surrounded by books analyzing events, ideas, and problems that had never before crossed my mind. I learned to interrogate an idea and poke hard at its soft spots. This was mostly fun. However, when I poked at my own beliefs, especially in the light of new things I was learning about my church's history, I felt tender and a bit at a loss.

At Harvard, I became acquainted with Laurel Thatcher Ulrich, a renowned professor and beloved mentor for Latter-day Saint students. When I read her 1986 essay, "Lusterware," reprinted in this volume, it made a deep impression on me. "Lusterware," Laurel explained, was a type of ceramic dishware popular in the late eighteenth century. It was plated with a platinum film so as to resemble solid silver, but if you dropped it, it would fall to pieces like ordinary crockery. In an Emily Dickinson poem, lusterware was a metaphor for disillusionment—a shining, supposedly solid thing which fell and unexpectedly shattered on "the stones at [the] bottom of my mind." Warning against a "lusterware" view of what we then called Mormonism, Laurel recalled one time in which a distressed young person in the middle of a faith crisis came to her worrying that the Church was perhaps only ninety percent (instead of one-hundred percent) divine. To this, Laurel responded, "If you find any earthly institution that is ten percent divine, embrace it with all your heart."

This idea sent shockwaves across my mind. Growing up, the gospel message drummed into my head was the message of the hundred percent. To my young self the stock phrases, "I know the Church is true" and "the fulness of the gospel" referred to my church's complete sufficiency and comprehensiveness. Church leaders were always divinely directed, whether it was a bishop giving dating advice or a general-level leader criticizing the theory of evolution. This hundred-percent outlook meant that there was no room for error, no possibility of contradiction, and no need to improve. In this view, the Church was the best of all possible worlds. Everything was as it should be, and should have been.

This is why Laurel's suggestion to treasure a venture that was less than "one-hundred percent divine" was both provocative and lifesaving. As a university student, the "all or nothing" framework left me with a faith crisis as I learned about church history, including past church leaders' flaws and fallibility. Clearly, there were times when Latter-day Saints had made mistakes with long-lasting and harmful repercussions. As I struggled to readjust my worldview, Laurel's example of embracing both divine direction and human limitation was a lifeline.

The Church that is true is a Church that is real, and a Church that is real is a Church that embodies contradictions and contrasts, which characterize the nature of reality itself. God's plan does not call on us to escape life's messiness by retreating to a bubble free of doubt and conundrum. Instead, our Heavenly Parents have given us the opportunity to struggle mightily with life's puzzles, thereby exercising our divine capacity. We reason and rage. We stumble, and correct course. We learn to be unshaken. We learn to bend.

The Church that is real is a Church that is patriarchal, hierarchical, and USA-centric. It is a Church with a history that, like its wider host society, includes racism, sexism, and nationalism.[1] It is a Church that shapes a distinctive "culture region" in the American Intermountain West known for conspicuous consumption and religious elitism. It is a Church in which some men in positions of ecclesiastical power have used that power to abuse others emotionally or sexually, in egregious violation of the Lord's instructions for righteous authority. It is a Church founded by Joseph Smith, Jr., who instituted a radical new system of marriage, and who likely concealed some of his additional marriages from his first wife Emma, for whom plural marriage was an excruciating ordeal.[2]

The Church that is real is also a Church that engaged in radical redistribution of wealth and communitarian economics. It teaches a theology of humankind's literal divine nature as beloved children of a Heavenly Father and Mother. All over the earth it facilitates the formation of local communities with their own distinctive cultures. It is a Church that unites rich and poor, North and South, women and men in sacred covenants to take upon themselves the name of Christ and mourn with those that mourn. It is a Church that calls people to serve, regardless of their caste or occupation, and obliges them to develop their capacities and become blessings in the lives of others. It is a Church whose founder, Joseph Smith, Jr., had a radical new vision of eternity and humankind's limitless potential to make enduring connections and bring forth good fruits.

Looking at the previous two paragraphs, if some were to read only the first they might conclude that I am an "anti-Mormon" being critical. If some were to read only the second they might call me an "apologist" pushing a rosy ideal. But there are not two Churches and I am not divided. There is one Church, and I claim it as my own, ashamed of what is shameful and proud of what is praiseworthy. My loyalty does not arise out of a calculation that the pros outweigh the cons, but out of reciprocity. In addition to the gift of Christ's atonement, which he gives freely to all, I owe a debt to my sisters and brothers.

Fellow Latter-day Saints have taught me to want to be good, protected me from danger, and helped make real the things I wanted to be true but could not see.

For me, one significant cost of this repayment is not merely time, money, meals, and mileage, but cognitive and emotional effort. Why must I labor to contextualize the racist language sometimes recorded in the Book of Mormon, our precious and holy book of scripture? When will the fundamental truth that women and men are spiritual equals created in the image of a Heavenly Mother and Heavenly Father, with the same potential to lead, teach, and bless the lives of their fellow beings, be meaningfully reflected in institutional Church decision-making structures? How do I maintain my faith in living prophets and apostles when history shows that over time, teachings sometimes change and contradict themselves? At one time in our early history plural marriage was elevated above monogamous marriage, but now it is grounds for discipline (unless it is for time and all eternity in the temple). At one time, using birth control would damn you and your posterity to the third and fourth generations, but now it's not a problem. At one time, some Church leaders wrongly depicted Black people as "fence-sitters" in the pre-existence, but as of 2015 this is officially disavowed (though it lingers on some Church-members' family bookshelves). If the Church is true, why can't it be "right" all of the time? Sometimes I grow weary of always having to explain! To compensate! To wait patiently! To put things "on the shelf"! The—damn—shelf—is—full!

For me, the long-term solution to these frustrations is not to abandon thoughtful reflection by compartmentalizing spiritual life. Some feel that critical thinking and deep faith do not mix. But for me, life with God in it comes as a whole package. If I can't make sense of my Latter-day Saint belief and practice in relation to all experience and all knowledge, then it isn't worth the effort. True, there are many things which we cannot know. But some basic paradigm should be reliable and worthy of wholehearted trust.

Nor do I feel that I personally would be happier, in the long run, abandoning the Church with the intent of moving on to a dissonance-free lifestyle. In today's world, nearly all of the institutions, organizations, and global structures within which we make our lives are ethically compromised, devilishly complex, and muddied by human error and apathy. To thrust in one's sickle in any of these places, cultivating a good harvest and eradicating weeds, is not only to improve that part of God's vineyard but also to develop capacity and experience for acting in the wider world. Time and again, my Latter-day Saint sisters and brothers have lent me inspiration and strength to bring to pass what I want, and need, to accomplish in my community, profession, country, and planet.

When someone asked Jesus what was most important, he responded: first, love God with all your heart, soul, mind, and strength; second, love your neighbor as yourself. On these two commandments, he said, hang all the law and the prophets.

I am thankful that Jesus included "mind" and "strength" as ways to love God. To engage the mind in the project of faith is not a slippery deviation, but a consecrated contribution to God's kingdom. Such intellectual engagement requires effort (strength). Here Jesus is putting this kind of effort on par with humans' other capacities of emotional, spiritual, and intellectual power. Perhaps effort is valuable in and of itself. As we seek to obey the two great commandments within the Church, we practice unselfishness and persistence. We never get it just right, but it is honest work.

Honest intellectual work sometimes leads to cognitive dissonance. That is to say, when one becomes aware of contradictions in what Latter-day Saints believe and do, particularly when these contradictions uniformly invoke divine authority, a murmur develops in the mind which is hard to ignore. For me, at one point, this cognitive dissonance was a deal-breaker. To my way of thinking, I was a smart, rational person who could not belong to an incoherent, irrational religion. Now, however, I have come to believe that cognition is not the most important aspect of being human. Like digestion, cognition is an essential process. Without it we would die. Yet in order to live in accordance with the reality of who we are as children of God (i.e., in accordance with truth), what is most vital is for us to pursue being good, as God is.

The Apostle Paul argued that even if someone had tremendous spiritual power, enough to prophesy, but had not charity, that person's utterances would be empty as a "tinkling cymbal." Even someone who understood all mysteries and knowledge, but had not charity, he said, was "nothing." Spiritual and intellectual power are not substantial in and of themselves, but only in relation to others. They help us to love God, but unless we also employ them to love our neighbors and "our strangers" they are for naught.

When I ask, "Which is harder: to say something smart and critical about Latter-day Saint practice, or to care for others as much as I care for myself?" the answer is clear. When I ask, "With what do I need more divine help: with becoming smarter and more knowledgeable, or with becoming kinder and more able to help others?" the answer is clear. When I ask, "Am I better positioned to accomplish God's work by myself, or in the company of fellow-travelers?" the answer is clear. For me, being a Latter-day Saint and participating in the mission of the Church is an opportunity to be more: to develop greater capacity to love; to know and serve; to enlist help. It is an opportunity to do something difficult but worthwhile.

I have friends who have decided to do good as individuals, without an organized religious community. Sometimes I envy their escape from the constant struggle to sort between divine fiat and tyrannical culture, godly practice and rote process. More often, however, I rejoice in my many sisters and brothers, in our humble collective search for the divine.

I also have friends who have left the Latter-day Saints and joined another religious community unencumbered by the "baggage" peculiar to our own faith and history. I respect their sense of integrity and feel that God consecrates their worthy work. In my professional study of religious traditions, particularly Buddhism, I have learned profound spiritual truths. I have also learned that all religious traditions have their own human histories, contradictions, and reasons for regret.

For myself, I choose to be a Latter-day Saint because I love our covenants: to God, to each other, and to the world. I love the baptismal covenant to bear one another's burdens, the sealing covenant to make human love everlasting, the temple covenant to consecrate our time and talents in establishing a Zion in which there are no poor among us. I rejoice in the power of these covenants to bind us across the world, to make us equal as we stand before God, to convert hope into solemn promises. I believe that these Latter-day Saint covenants are true, which is to say I believe God's power truly inhabits them, and through this power things which were otherwise impossible become possible.

In early 2017 I was diagnosed with colon cancer. I had surgery to remove the tumor in June. During the weeks of recovery, I remained home by myself in New Zealand while my husband and children went to the United States to visit our family. One night a sister from Relief Society, Sister Samuelu, ✦ knocked on the door. She was a Samoan woman

✦ I've used a pseudonym.

who spoke English as a second language. She stepped into my kitchen with a bunch of flowers. Her face, with its wrinkles and sags, and her voice, worn-down with use, reminded me of my Chinese grandmother. She chatted genially about the new investigator from Brazil, and her granddaughter who is on a mission in Australia, and how once the missionaries lived in a haunted house but how "they've just got to be brave." I thanked her for the time she had spent with my two younger children when she was their Primary teacher. She replied that in truth, she had been getting tired of Primary, but felt that it was important for the kids to have a teacher who showed up. She gave me her phone number and told me to text her anytime.

As her visit seemed to be coming to a close, I thanked her and gave her a hug. Then, surprising me, she asked: "Can I leave you with a prayer?" "Sure, thank you," I said, sitting down again. For some reason, I didn't close my eyes all the way, but stared down at the floor. I felt as if I were an observer. At that time of anxiety and pain, I didn't really know what to expect from prayers. I was afraid that beyond "Thy will be done," there was nothing to say.

Sister Samuelu said: "Bless Melissa so that she can live to take care of her kids." With great eloquence, she invoked blessings on my body, my spirit, the house, my children and husband far away. The specific words escape me, but I remember a feeling of deep, settling calm. I felt as if I could feel my blood vessels widening and my lungs expanding. This is what the presence of the Holy Spirit feels like to me. Sister Samuelu hadn't laid her hands on my head, but she had indeed blessed me, as did our Latter-day Saint foremothers in the nineteenth and twentieth centuries.

At this lonely juncture in my life, I was blessed by an older Samoan woman who has never made an academic argument, who but for the Church would never have come into my life to teach my children and minister to me. Her prayer said what I had been afraid to say and asked what I had been afraid to ask. It is frightening to face a life-threatening illness and wonder whether God intends for you to make it to the other side. You feel foolish pleading for your life, because it's quite possible that God has already seen that this will go nowhere. But if someone else makes this plea on your behalf, you feel not presumptuous, but grateful, and receiving. Through Sister Samuelu, I felt God's power and care in my mind, my heart, and my body.

Sometimes we need others to plead with God alongside us. This is not because God responds to popularity contests, but because sometimes individuals wrestling with mortality are just not up to the task. The Church's many structures, some of which I have experienced as teeth-gnashingly bureaucratic and subject to patriarchal control, are nevertheless designed to facilitate this sort of potentially transformative human interaction and intercession. Here, in the spaces between us, spring up fountains of living water.

Although they are irreducible to neat percentages, we can embrace both the human and the divine within the Church. We, Latter-day Saints all over the world who labor to build Zion, are ordinary people with ordinary shortcomings. We regularly fail to live up to the measure of our divine callings. Nevertheless, God is real, and patient, and among us.

It is genuinely painful to encounter un-Christlike behavior not only "in the world" but also within one's own Church and its history. But since I myself am a regular source of un-Christlike behavior, this pain is something I must own. I must have the integrity to take responsibility for what needs fixing and put my shoulder to the wheel. Just like volunteering to vacuum carpets and empty trash in the meetinghouse, there are ways to volunteer time and energy to repair and renew the living structures of my Church.

The work of living with contradiction and tension is also something I must own. While it can be a relief to associate only with like-minded individuals with "correct" educational backgrounds, political views, class values, and theological inclinations, it is also a sort of prison—a sanitized separation from the fecund soil of humanity in which God wants us to spread our roots. If our Heavenly Parents had intended for everyone to think alike and to follow the same path back to them, they could have endorsed Lucifer's plan. Instead they gave us the power of agency, which is the power to make terrible mistakes and cause lasting damage. But it is also the power to be brave, to be wise, to extend the self, and to be a true healer.

The fundamental reality of humanity is that our values and assumptions are rooted in the diverse circumstances into which we were born, and we disagree deeply about what is good and true. The Church is not a solution for the problem of diversity, but a preserve within which to practice diversity's values. It is a gritty sandbox within which we bump against each other and become more polished. It is a place with enemies to love, peace to make, and cause for meekness. In this our teacher is the Holy One who ministered in the shadow of imperial power, associated with tax collectors and centurions, met with despised outcasts, and taught people in their own lands and languages. His was always the path of most resistance.

The path as a Latter-day Saint in pursuit of Zion is not always an easy path, but ease is not its purpose. Here I have found people to love and people who love me. Here I have ample cause to rejoice, to grieve, to act, and to be still. Here I am becoming more than I was, and more as I hope Christ has invited me to be.

What the Church Means to People Like Me

RICHARD D. POLL

Reprinted from the 1986 collection,
A Thoughtful Faith: Essays on Belief by Mormon Scholars.

A natural reaction to my title might be, "Who cares?" Yet I believe I represent a type of Latter-day Saint found in most wards and branches in the Church. By characterizing the nature of my commitment to the gospel, I hope to contribute a little something of value, whether it turns out that you are "people like me" or not.

My thesis is that there are two distinct types of active and dedicated Latter-day Saints. I am not talking about "good Mormons" versus "Jack Mormons" who have surrendered their faith, nor about Saints in white hats and pseudo-Saints in black. No, I am talking about two types of *involved* Church members, each deeply committed to the gospel but also prone toward misgivings about the legitimacy, adequacy, or service-ability of the commitment of the other.

The purpose of my inquiry is not to support either set of misgivings, but to describe each type as dispassionately as I can, to identify myself with one of the types, and then to bear witness concerning some of the blessings which the Church offers to the type I identify with. My prayer is that this effort will help us all to look beyond the things which obviously differentiate us toward that "unity of the faith" which Christ set as our common goal.

For convenience, let me propose symbols for my two types of Saints. They are affirmative images, because I am talking only about "good" members. I found them in the Book of Mormon, a natural place for a Latter-day Saint to find good symbols and good counsel.

The figure for the first type comes from Lehi's dream—the Iron Rod. The figure for the second comes also from Lehi's experience—the Liahona. So similar they are as manifestations of God's concern for his children, yet just different enough to suit my purposes.

The Iron Rod, as the hymn reminds us, was the Word of God. To the person with his hand on the rod, each step of the journey to the tree of life was plainly defined; he had only to hold on as he moved forward. In Lehi's dream the way was *not easy*, but it was *clear*.

The Liahona, in contrast, was a compass. It pointed to the destination but did not fully mark the path; indeed, the clarity of its directions varied with the circumstances of the user. For Lehi's family the sacred instrument was a reminder of their temporal and eternal goals, but it was no infallible delineator of their course.

Even as the Iron Rod and the Liahona were both approaches to the word of God and to the kingdom of God, so our two types of members seek the word and the kingdom. The fundamental difference between them lies in their concept of the relation of man to the "word of God." Put another way, it is a difference in the meaning assigned to the concept "the fulness of the gospel." Do the revelations of our Heavenly Father give us a handrail to the Kingdom, or a compass only?

The Iron Rod Saint does not look for questions, but for answers, and in the gospel—as he understands it—he finds or is confident that he can find the answer to every important question. The Liahona Saint, on the other hand, is preoccupied with questions and skeptical of answers; he finds in the gospel—as he understands it—answers to enough important questions so that he can function purposefully without answers to the rest. This last sentence holds the key to the question posed by my title, but before pursuing its implications let us explore our scheme of classification more fully.

As I suggested at the outset, I find Iron Rods and Liahonas in almost every LDS congregation, discernible by the kinds of comments they make in gospel doctrine classes and the very language in which they phrase their testimonies. What gives them their original bent is difficult to identify. The Iron Rods may be somewhat more common among converts, but many nowadays are attracted to the Church by those reasons more appropriate to Liahonas which I will mention later on. Liahona testimonies may be more prevalent among born members who have not had an emotional conversion experience, but many such have developed Iron Rod commitments in the home, the Sunday School, the mission field, or some other conditioning environment. Social and economic status appear to have nothing to do with type, and the rather widely-held notion that education tends to produce Liahonas has so many exceptions that one may plausibly argue that education only makes Liahonas more articulate. Parenthetically, some of the most prominent Iron Rods in the Church are on the BYU faculty.

Pre-existence may, I suppose, have something to do with placement in this classification, even as it may account for other life circumstances, but heredity obviously does not. The irritation of the Iron Rod father confronted by an iconoclastic son is about as commonplace as the embarrassment of the Liahona parent who discovers that his teenage daughter has found comfortable answers in seminary to some of the questions that have perplexed him all his life.

The picture is complicated by the fact that changes of type do occur, often in response to profoundly unsettling personal experiences. The Liahona member who, in a context of despair or repentance, makes the "leap of faith" to Iron Rod commitment is rather rare, I think, but the investigator of Liahona temperament who becomes an Iron Rod convert is almost typical. The Iron Rod member who responds to personal tragedy or intellectual shock by becoming a Liahona is known to us all; this transition may be, but is not necessarily, a stage in a migration toward inactivity or even apostasy.

My present opinion is that one's identification with the Iron Rods or the Liahonas is more a function of basic temperament and of accidents than of premortal accomplishments or mortal choices, but that opinion—like many other views expressed in this sermon—has neither scriptural nor scientific validation.

A point to underscore in terms of our objective of "unity of the faith" is that Iron Rods and Liahonas have great difficulty understanding each other—not at the level of intellectual acceptance of the right to peaceful coexistence, but at the level of personal communion, of empathy. To the Iron Rod a questioning attitude suggests an imperfect faith; to the Liahona an unquestioning spirit betokens a closed mind. Neither frequent association nor even prior personal involvement with the other group guarantees empathy.

I have suggested that the essential difference between the Liahonas and the Iron Rods is in their approach to the concept "the word of God."

The Iron Rod is confident that, on any question, the mind and will of the Lord may be obtained. His sources are three-fold: Scripture, Prophetic Authority, and the Holy Spirit.

In the standard works of the Church Iron Rod members find far more answers than do their Liahona brothers or sisters, because they accept them as God's word in a far more literal sense. In scripture they find answers to questions as diverse as the age and origin of the earth, the justification for capital punishment, the proper diet, the proper role of government, the nature and functions of sex, and human nature. To the Liahona Saint, the Iron Rods sometimes seem to be reading things into the printed words.

In the pronouncements of the general authorities, living and dead, Iron Rod Saints find many answers, because they accept and give comprehensive application to that language of the Doctrine and Covenants which declares: "And whatsoever they shall speak when moved upon by the Holy Ghost shall be scripture, shall be the will of the Lord, shall be the mind of the Lord, shall be the word of the Lord, shall be the voice of the Lord, and the power of God unto salvation" (D&C 68:4). This reliance extends to every facet of life. On birth control and family planning, labor relations and race relations, the meaning of the Constitution and prospects for the United Nations, the laws of health and the signs of the times, the counsel of the "living oracles" suffices. Where answers are not found in the published record, they are sought in correspondence and interviews, and once received, they are accepted as definitive.

Third among the sources for the Iron Rod member is the Holy Spirit. As Joseph Smith found answers in the counsel of James, "If any of you lack wisdom, let him ask of God . . . ," so any Latter-day Saint may do so. Whether it be the choice of a vocation or the choice of a mate, help on a college examination or in finding "Golden Prospects" in the mission field, healing the sick or averting a divorce, prayer is the answer. The response may not be what was expected, but it *will* come, and it will be a manifestation of the Holy Spirit.

Implicit in all this is the confidence of the Iron Rod Latter-day Saint that our Heavenly Father is intimately involved in the day-to-day business of His children. As no sparrow falls without the Father, so nothing befalls a human being without His will. God knows the answers to all questions and has the solutions to all problems, and the only thing which denies us access to this reservoir is our own stubbornness. Truly, then, people who open their minds and hearts to the channels of revelation, past and present, have the Iron Rod which leads unerringly to the Kingdom.

Liahona Latter-day Saints lack this certain confidence. Not that they reject the concepts upon which it rests—that God lives, that He loves His children, that His knowledge and power are efficacious for salvation, and that He does reveal His will as the Ninth Article of Faith affirms. Nor do they reserve the right of selective obedience to the will of God as they understand it. No, the problem for Liahonas involves the adequacy of the *sources* on which the Iron Rod testimony depends.

The problem is in perceiving the will of God when it is mediated—as it is for almost all mortals—by "the arm of flesh." Liahonas are convinced by logic and experience that no human instrument, even a prophet, is capable of transmitting the word of God so clearly and comprehensively that it can be universally understood and easily appropriated by humans.

Because Liahonas find it impossible to accept the literal verbal inspiration of the standard works, the sufficiency of scriptural answers to questions automatically comes into question. If Eve was not made from Adam's rib, how much of the Bible is historic truth? If geology and anthropology have undermined Bishop Ussher's chronology, which places creation at 4000 B.C., how much of the Bible is scientific truth? And if our latter-day scriptures have been significantly revised since their original publication, can it be assumed that they are now infallibly authoritative? To Liahonas these volumes are sources of inspiration and moral truth, but they leave many specific questions unanswered, or uncertainly answered.

As for the authority of the latter-day prophets, Liahona Saints find consensus among them on gospel fundamentals but far-ranging diversity on many important issues. The record shows error, as in Brigham Young's statements about the continuation of slavery, and it shows change of counsel, as in the matter of gathering to Zion. It shows differences of opinion—Heber J. Grant and Reed Smoot on the League of

Nations, and David O. McKay and Joseph Fielding Smith on the process of creation. To Liahonas, the "living oracles" are God's special witnesses of the gospel of Christ and his agents in directing the affairs of the Church, but, like the scriptures, they leave many important questions unanswered, or uncertainly answered.

The Iron Rod proposition—that the Spirit will supply what the prophets have not—gives difficulty on both philosophical and experimental grounds. Claims that prayer is an infallible, almost contractual, link between God and mortals through the Holy Spirit find Liahona Mormons perplexed by the nature of the evidence. As a method of confirming truth, the witness of the Spirit demonstrably has not produced uniformity of gospel interpretation even among Iron Rod Saints, and it is allegedly by the witness of that same Spirit—by the burning within—that many apostates pronounce the whole Church in error. As a method of influencing the course of events, it seems unpredictable and some of the miracles claimed for it seem almost whimsical. By the prayer of faith one man recovers his lost eyeglasses; in spite of such prayer, another man goes blind.

All of which leaves Liahona Latter-day Saints with a somewhat tenuous connection with the Holy Spirit. They may take comfort in their imperfect knowledge from the portion of the Article of Faith which says that "God will yet reveal many great and important things. . . ." And they may reconcile their conviction of God's love and their observation of the uncertain earthly outcomes of faith by emphasizing the divine commitment to the principle of free agency, as I shall presently do. In any case, it seems to Liahona Latter-day Saints that God's involvement in day-to-day affairs must be less active and intimate than Iron Rod Latter-day Saints believe, because there are so many unsolved problems and unanswered prayers.

Are Iron Rod members unaware of these considerations which loom so large in Liahona members' definition of their relationship to the word of God? In some instances, I believe, the answer is yes. For in our activity-centered Church it is quite possible to be deeply and satisfyingly involved without looking seriously at the philosophical implications of some gospel propositions which are professed.

In many instances, however, Iron Rod Saints have found sufficient answers to the Liahona questions. They see so much basic consistency in the scriptures and the teachings of the latter-day prophets that the apparent errors and incongruities can be handled by interpretation. They find so much evidence of the immanence of God in human affairs that the apparently pointless evil and injustice in the world can be handled by the valid assertion that God's ways are not man's ways. They are likely to credit their Liahona contemporaries with becoming so preoccupied with certain problems that they cannot see the gospel forest for the trees, and they may even attribute that preoccupation to an insufficiency of faith.

As a Liahona, I must resist the attribution, though I cannot deny the preoccupation.

Both kinds of Latter-day Saints have problems. Not just the ordinary personal problems to which all flesh is heir, but problems growing out of the nature of their Church commitment.

Iron Rod members have a natural tendency to develop answers where none may, in fact, have been revealed. They may find arguments against social security in the Book of Mormon; they may discover in esoteric prophetic utterances a timetable for the Second Coming of which "that day and hour knoweth no man. . . ." Their dogmatism may become offensive to their peers in the Church and a barrier to communication with their own family; their confidence in their own insights may make them impatient with those whom they publicly sustain. They may also cling to cherished answers in the face of new revelation, or be so shaken by innovation that they form new "fundamentalist" sects. The Iron Rod concept holds many firm in the Church, but it leads some out.

Liahonas, on the other hand, have the temptation to broaden the scope of their questioning until even the most clearly defined Church doctrines and policies are included. Their resistance to statistics on principle may deteriorate into a carping criticism of programs and leaders. Their ties to the Church may become so nebulous that they cannot communicate them to their children. Their testimonies may become so selective as to exclude them from some forms of Church activity or to make them hypocrites in their own eyes as they participate. Their persistence in doubting may alienate their fellow Saints and eventually destroy the substance of their gospel commitment. Then they, too, are out—without fireworks, but not without pain.

Both kinds of Latter-day Saints serve the Church. They talk differently and apparently think and feel differently about the gospel, but as long as they avoid the extremes just mentioned, they share a love for and commitment to the Church. They cannot therefore be distinguished on the basis of attendance at meetings, or participation on welfare projects, or contributions, or faithfulness in the performance of callings. They may or may not be "hundred percenters," but the degree of their activity is not a function of type, insofar as I have been able to observe. It may be that Iron Rods are a little more faithful in genealogical work, but even this is not certain.

Both kinds of members are found at every level of Church responsibility—in bishoprics and Relief Society presidencies, in stake presidencies and high councils, and even among the general authorities. But whatever their private orientation, the public deportment of the general authorities seems to me to represent a compromise, which would be natural in the circumstances. They satisfy the Iron Rod by emphasizing the solid core of revealed truth and discouraging speculative inquiry into matters of faith and morals, and they comfort the Liahonas by reminding the Saints that God has not revealed the answer to every question or defined the response to every prayer.

Lacking the patience, wisdom, breadth of experience, or depth of institutional commitment of the general authorities, we sometimes criticize and judge each other. But usually we live and let live—each finding in the Church what meets our needs and all sharing the gospel blessings which do not depend on identity of testimony.

Although I have tried to characterize two types of Latter-day Saints accurately, I can speak with conviction only about one example from one group. In suggesting—briefly—what the Church offers to a Liahona like me, I hope to provoke all of us to reexamine the nature of our own commitments and to grow in understanding and love for those whose testimonies are defined in different terms.

By my initial characterization of types, I am the kind of Latter-day Saint who is preoccupied with questions and skeptical of answers. I find in the gospel—as I understand it—answers to enough important questions so that I can function purposefully, and I hope effectively, without present answers to the rest.

The primary question of this generation, I believe, is the question of meaning. Does life really add up to anything? At least at the popular level, the philosophy of existentialism asks, and tries to answer, the question of how to function significantly in a world which apparently has no meaning.

When the philosophy is given a religious context, it becomes an effort to salvage some of the values of traditional religion for support in this meaningless world.

To the extent that existence is seen as meaningless—even absurd—human experiences have only immediate significance. A psychedelic trip stands on a par with a visit to the Sistine Chapel or a concert of the Tabernacle Choir. What the individual does with himself—or other "freely consenting adults"—is nobody's business, whether it involves pot, perversion, or "making love, not war."

For me, the gospel answers this question of meaning, and the answer is grandly challenging. Meaning lies in three revealed propositions: (1) Humans are eternal; (2) humans are free; (3) God's work and glory is to exalt eternal free agents: people.

The central concept is agency. With a belief in the doctrine of agency I can cope with some of the riddles and tragedies cited in support of the philosophy of the absurd. In the nature of human freedom—as I understand it—is to be found the reconciliation of the concept of a loving God and the facts of an unlovely world.

The restored gospel teaches that the human essence is eternal, that a human being is a child of God, and that it is our destiny to become like our Heavenly Parents. But this destiny can only be achieved as we voluntarily gain the knowledge, the experience, and the discipline which godhood requires. This was the crucial question resolved in the council in heaven— whether we should come into an environment of genuine risk, where we would walk by faith.

To me, this prerequisite for exaltation explains the apparent remoteness of God from many aspects of the human predicament—my predicament. My range of freedom is left large, and arbitrary divine interference with that freedom is kept minimal, in order that I may grow. Were God's hand always upon my shoulder, or his Iron Rod always in my grasp, my range of choice would be constricted, and my growth as well.

This view does not rule out miraculous divine interventions, but it does not permit their being commonplace. What is seen as miracle by the Iron Rod Saints, my type tends to interpret as a coincidence, or a psychosomatic manifestation, or an inaccurately remembered or reported or interpreted event. The same attitude is even more likely with regard to the Satanic role in human affairs. Liahonas see the conflict between good and evil—with its happy and unhappy outcomes—more often as a derivative of human nature and environment than as a contest between titanic powers for the capture of human pawns. If God cannot, in the ultimate sense, coerce the eternal intelligences which are embodied in His children, then how much less is Lucifer able to do so? We may yield to the promptings of good or evil, but we are not puppets.

There is another aspect of the matter. If, with or without prayer, humans are arbitrarily spared the consequences of their own fallibility and the natural consequences of the kind of hazardous world in which they live, then freedom becomes meaningless and God capricious. If the law that fire burns, that bullets kill, that age deteriorates, and that rain falls on the just and the unjust is sporadically suspended upon petition of faith, what happens to that reliable connection between cause and consequence, which is a condition of knowledge, and what peril to faith lies in the idea that God can break the causal chain, that He frequently does break it, but that in my individual case He may not choose to do so? This is the dilemma of theodicy—reconciling God's omnipotence with evil and suffering—which is so dramatically phrased: "If God is good, He is not God; if God is God, He is not good."

From what has been said, it must be apparent that Liahonas like me do not see prayer as a form of spiritual mechanics, in spite of such scriptural language as "Prove me now herewith...," and "I, the Lord, am bound...." Prayer is rarely for miracles, or even for new answers. It is—or ought to be—an intensely personal exercise in sorting out and weighing the relevant factors in our problems, and looking to God as we consider the alternative solutions. (Many of our problems would solve themselves if we would consider only options on which we could honestly ask God's benediction.) We might pray for a miracle, especially in time of personal frustration or tragedy, but we would think it presumptuous to command God and would not suspend the future on the outcome of the petition.

This is not to say that Liahonas cannot verbalize prayer as proficiently as their Iron Rod contemporaries. One cannot be significantly involved in the Church without mastering the conventional prayer forms and learning to fit the petition to the proportions of the occasion. But even in the public prayers it is possible for the attentive ear to detect those differences which I have tried to describe. To oppose evil as we can, to bear adversity as we must, and to do our jobs well—these are the petitions in Liahona prayers. They invoke God's blessings, but they require human action.

To this Liahona Latter-day Saint, God is powerful to save. He is pledged to keep the way of salvation open to all and to do, through the example and sacrifice of His Son and the ordinances and teachings of His Church, what we cannot do for ourselves. But beyond this, He has left things pretty much up to me—an independent agent, a god in embryo who must learn by experience as well as direction how to be like God.

In this circumstance the Church of Jesus Christ performs three special functions for me. Without them, my freedom might well become unbearable. In the first place, the Church reminds me that what I do makes a difference. It matters to my peers because most of what I do or fail to do affects their progress toward salvation. And it matters to me, even if it has no discernible influence upon others. I reject the "hippie" stance, not because there is something intrinsically wrong with beards and sandals, but with estrangement and aimlessness. Even though life is eternal, time is short and I have none to waste.

In the second place, the Church suggests and sometimes prescribes guidelines for the use of freedom. The deportment standards of the Ten Commandments and the Sermon on the Mount, the rules for mental and physical well-being in the Doctrine and Covenants, the reminders and challenges in the temple ceremony—these are examples, and they harmonize with free agency because even those which are prescribed are not coerced.

There is a difference here, I think, between the way Iron Rods and Liahonas look at the guidelines. Answer-oriented, the Iron Rods tend to spell things out; Sabbath observance becomes no TV or movies, or TV but no movies, or uplifting TV and no other, or no studying, or studying for religion classes but no others. For Liahonas like me, the Sabbath commandment is a reminder of the kinship of free brothers and sisters and loving Heavenly Parents. What is fitting, not what is conventional, becomes the question. On a lovely autumn evening I may even, with quiet conscience, pass up a church fireside for a drive in the canyon. But the thankfulness for guidelines is nonetheless strong.

In final place comes the contribution of the Church in giving me something to relate to—to belong to—to *feel* a part of. Contemporary psychology has much to say about the awful predicament of alienation. "The lonely crowd" is the way one expert describes it. Ex-Mormons often feel it; a good friend who somehow migrated out of the Church put it this way the other day: "I don't belong anywhere."

For the active Latter-day Saint such alienation is impossible. The Church is an association of kindred spirits, a subculture, a "folk"—and this is the tie which binds Iron Rods and Liahonas together as strongly as the shared testimony of Joseph Smith. It is as fundamental to the solidarity of Latter-day Saint families, almost, as the doctrine of eternal marriage itself. It makes brothers and sisters of the convert and the Daughter of the Utah Pioneers, of the Hong Kong branch president and the missionary from Cedar City. It unites this congregation—the genealogists and the procrastinators, the old-fashioned patriarchs and the family planners, the eggheads and the doubters of "the wisdom of men."

This is the witness of the Spirit to this Liahona Latter-day Saint. When the returning missionary warms his homecoming with a narrative of a remarkable conversion, I may note the inconsistency or naïveté of some of his analysis, but I am moved nevertheless by the picture of lives transformed—made meaningful—by the gospel. When the home teachers call, I am sometimes self-conscious about the "role playing" in which we all seem to be engaged, yet I ask my wife often—in our times of deepest concern and warmest parental satisfaction— what might our daughters have become without the Church. When a dear friend passes, an accident victim, I may recoil from the well-meant suggestion that God's need for him was greater than his family's, but my lamentation is sweetened by the realization of what the temporal support of the Saints and the eternal promises of the Lord mean to those who mourn.

For this testimony, the Church which inspires and feeds it, and fellowship in the Church with the Iron Rods and Liahonas who share it, I express my thanks to God.

The Beauty of Holiness

KRISTINE HAGLUND

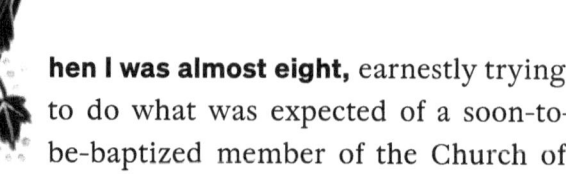

hen I was almost eight, earnestly trying to do what was expected of a soon-to-be-baptized member of the Church of Jesus Christ of Latter-day Saints, I decided I needed to participate in the customary fast on the first Sunday of the month. Skipping breakfast before church was easy, but not eating lunch left me cranky by two or three in the afternoon. My long-suffering but exasperated mother responded to my whining by suggesting a few distracting activities, all of which I pronounced "dumb." She finally said, not hopefully, "maybe you could read the scriptures. Maybe Psalms?" I liked the idea of Psalms—a beloved schoolteacher had given me a pocket-sized "Testament and Psalms," which I kept in my box of treasures, but hadn't really read. I took it down to my favorite basement reading spot—a remnant of green carpet laid next to the woodstove, where the comforting warmth from the stove generally made up for the annoyance of the splinters of wood that worked their way into the carpet and thence occasionally into a reclining reader's elbows.

I dutifully read for a while, interrupted occasionally by impressively loud stomach grumblings, and had almost given up when I got to Psalm 29 and was arrested by the phrase "worship him in the beauty of holiness." I knew from Joseph Smith's story that sometimes a scripture could leap from the page and change the world, and recognized this as my own Epistle of James moment, which would cleave my life into before and after. (This sounds very dramatic. I was a dramatic child. But it is also the truest way I know to tell the story). I did not cry, not then. But I did go and get my violin and start practicing the most beautiful thing I knew, and worked myself into tears with the little sighing grace notes in the third measure of the Brahms Waltz in Suzuki Book 2.

It is a strangely precise memory, perhaps because the details laid out the only nearly infallible mechanism for accessing the transcendent that I have discovered in my life: the recognition—often faint—of an idea, a "stroke of thought" that evokes a kind of longing that is not assuaged, but heightened and intensified by trying to capture the feeling in words or music. I know the details, because I have lived them, with slight variations of the carpet color and the text and the music involved, hundreds of times.

Curiously, I experienced that moment not as a revelation about God, but as a moment of *self* revelation. That is, I was aware more or less instantly that this would be both method and content of my testimony. What I know, and nearly all I have been given to know, is the aching, joyous longing for the beauty of holiness. I don't really believe Keats's famous couplet: "Beauty is truth, truth beauty,—that is all/Ye know on earth, and all ye need to know." There is plenty of truth in the world that is ugly, or harsh and bracing, and I have fallen for some beautiful lies. Nevertheless, the things I believe most deeply about God—the tiny list of things I am sure of—have come to me as traces of beauty tinged with a yearning something like homesickness. I am not convinced that beauty is always truth, but the entanglement of beauty and truth is, for me, a wellspring of joy.

The problem with this story is that it ought to be the back-story of a talented musician or composer or painter or sculptor, and I am none of those. I am a middling violinist with rusting skills, and a solid utility alto. It is also not a particularly promising origin story for someone who is going to be spiritually nurtured in the workaday, low church traditions of Latter-day Saint worship. My peculiar mode of access to the spiritual realm, combined with a notable lack of any evident artistic gifts, and the coincidence of being born into a cheerfully practical religious tradition that does not generally invest overmuch in artistic excellence in worship, is a recipe for restless frustration. I am saved by moments of unexpected grace and what at least one exhausted Primary teacher called "sheer cussedness."

I occasionally went back to the Psalms as I grew up, and I started to recognize the poetry in Isaiah, and felt its tug. But there was easier poetry to be captivated by—Edna St. Vincent Millay's Poems for Young People, then her sonnets; my mother's beloved Emily Dickinson; George Herbert, whose "Easter Wings" inspired a few attempts at shape poems that even at 15 I could see needed to be not merely discarded, but burned; Hopkins's "Pied Beauty," which was (in what I am happy to call a miracle) a handout on the Sunday I graduated from Primary into Young Women. My father warned me sternly, after yet another assignment as youth speaker which I fulfilled mostly by reading E. E. Cummings over the pulpit, that I should not get *all* my theology from poetry, to which I responded that Isaiah seemed to have been Jesus's major theological influence, so I didn't see what the problem was. (A prime example of the aforementioned cussedness.)

I went away to college, and had a freshman year straight out of a college brochure or an overwrought nineteenth-century novel about the delights of the mind. I took courses in Politics and Literature, German lyric poetry, philosophy, and music. I sang in a choir that went to New York to perform in Carnegie Hall on my eighteenth birthday. And I sang in the chapel choir, discovering the possibilities for creating beautiful, reverent worship services with professional organists and conductors and auditioned singers. On Sundays, I would spend the morning in the majestic chapel in the middle of campus, feeling my heart leap at the first chords of the Old Hundredth and the simple psalm paraphrase of John Kethe:

All people that on earth do dwell,
Sing to the Lord with cheerful voice!
Him serve with mirth, his praise forth tell;
Come ye before him and rejoice.

A service typically included three or four hymns, plus choral prelude and postludes, an anthem, and a choral benediction or amen, often some service music or a communion anthem. Always there were responsive readings of Psalms.

My senior year, a new conductor, freshly arrived from England, decided to teach us Anglican chant. It is hard to describe how I felt in that first rehearsal figuring out how to read the tune at the top of the page, and make the words fit with a series of instructions provided by a few simple symbols, mostly | , * , · , and an occasional — . The first attempts were awkward, but after a few minutes, I felt like I was speaking my native language for the first time. I didn't have words for the sense of joyous homecoming. I had felt that way in a Latter-day Saint service only once, fleetingly, when I was very small, and a fine organist opened up all the very big stops for the pedal as we sang "Far, Far Away on Judea's Plains."

Maybe, I thought, that's to be expected. After all, it's hard to know what coming home feels like if you have never left. I tried not to notice that the way I felt singing Psalms in this ancient tradition seemed akin to what many people describe when they convert to the Church of Jesus Christ of Latter-day Saints.

It wasn't that I didn't have a testimony of my own church. I did. I had had a few powerful experiences I couldn't explain away, and I wanted to be faithful to the truths I had received in Latter-day Saint contexts. But what to do with the sweetness of this recognition that felt like homecoming?

I would like to say that I have figured it out, or that my conviction of the truth of the Church of Jesus Christ of Latter-day Saints overwhelms every uncertainty. But that isn't true. I struggle to make sense of how like a fish out of water I feel at church sometimes, and I have to work hard to figure out how to contribute meaningfully in a church where so many people seem to connect to God in a different way than I do. Have I missed my calling because I stayed in my religious home? What does it mean that the gifts that seem most precious to me are seldom wanted where I have promised to offer everything?

I have no answers to these questions, or to the most painful question of all—why was I given the gift of loving music, and not the gift I have always wanted most—to be good at singing the praises I hear so clearly in my heart? The years seem only to bring more questions.

But some of the questions are gracious—big enough to stretch my understanding and make faith possible. One comes from a beloved Christmas carol, "In the Bleak Midwinter": What can I give him?

My chronic grief about not being a great musician makes me wonder earnestly about the disconnect between what I think God would like and what I can actually give. It occurs to me sometimes that *most* of what we bring to the altar is not nearly as valuable as we suppose. The difficulty of figuring out what the Lord wants from us is illustrated in Genesis by Cain's rejected sacrifice, articulated again in Samuel's insistence that "to obey is better than sacrifice," and the psalmist's recognition that "thou desirest not sacrifice; else would I give it: thou delightest not in burnt offering. The sacrifices of God are a broken spirit: a broken and a contrite heart, O God, thou wilt not despise." The Nephites are instructed that their "burnt

offerings shall be done away, for I will accept none of your sacrifices and your burnt offerings." And just before the Saints at
Kirtland are asked to give a tithe of money to build the temple,
a new kind of sacrifice, they're reminded that "all among them
who know their hearts are honest, and are broken, and their
spirits contrite, and are willing to observe their covenants by
sacrifice—*yea, every sacrifice which I, the Lord, shall command*—
they are accepted of me."[1]

Perhaps we need to be told exactly what to sacrifice because
we aren't very good at recognizing what is valuable. Maybe
Paul's description of gifts within the body of Christ isn't just
about other people's gifts that we wrongly think are less
worthy than our own, but about our estimation of what it is
we ourselves have to offer.

> Nay, much more those members of the body,
> which seem to be more feeble, are necessary:
>
> And those members of the body, which we think
> to be less honourable, upon these we bestow
> more abundant honour; and our uncomely parts
> have more abundant comeliness.
>
> For our comely parts have no need: but God hath
> tempered the body together, having given more
> abundant honour to that part which lacked. (I
> Corinthians 12:22–24)

Maybe artistic gifts, like all the others, are useful for bringing us to the place where we can offer all that we really have
to give—our brokenness, our need, our yearning to know
and be known.

And this brings me to the biggest and most helpful question for me: What is beautiful? Or, in Gerard Manley Hopkins's lovelier formulation, "To what serves mortal beauty?" and "What do then? How meet beauty?"

A lot of debates about Christian aesthetics worry through these questions, starting from the premise that the beautiful is costly, in money or time or unequally distributed talents, and that those resources ought to be used for more practical kinds of discipleship. Other askers of these questions are troubled by the possibility that art will draw attention to itself and away from God. Latter-day Saints seem to be nervous about the arts on both counts, in ways that are clear more from our practice than our doctrine: choir practice is never going to take precedence over ward council, and maintaining the floor of the basketball court is usually a higher priority than tuning the pianos. The art that is part of our worship is not chosen by artists or trained critics, but by men with ecclesiastical authority. Their appraisal of what kinds of art and music are suitable for Latter-day Saint worship carries more weight than the considered judgment of people who spend all their lives thinking about what is beautiful or true; we are, institutionally, wary of people who think that beauty could tell us something about God that authority cannot. I don't know any artists or musicians in the Church who don't chafe at these constraints.

And yet, on my more patient and charitable days, I am able at least to ask whether these constraints may tether us to what Hopkins calls "God's better beauty, grace." After all, the closest thing to an aesthetic theory for the Restoration presents itself in Section 42 of the Doctrine and Covenants, in a passing reference to beautiful garments in Zion:

And again, thou shalt not be proud in thy heart;
let all thy garments be plain, and their beauty the
beauty of the work of thine own hands. . . .

Thou shalt not be idle; for he that is idle shall
not eat the bread nor wear the garments of
the laborer.

And whosoever among you are sick, and have not
faith to be healed, but believe, shall be nourished
with all tenderness, with herbs and mild food,
and that not by the hand of an enemy.

Thou shalt live together in love insomuch that
thou shalt weep for the loss of them that die. . . .
(verses 40, 42–43, 45)

This is beauty not as aesthetic, but as *ethic*, part of the consecration of all human striving within a community committed to a tender regard for every member and for the labor
that sustains bodies and souls. And while it might be read to
minimize the importance of beautiful things, and certainly is
a warning against aesthetic snobbery, it also offers the possibility of sanctification for working to make things beautiful;
it insists that skillful handwork can matter deeply in God's
economy of time and effort, which makes me hopeful about
choir rehearsals in Zion.

It begins to answer the question "what is beauty" in a more
expansive way than our usual post-Enlightenment, post-Ro-
mantic theorizing. It situates the beautiful in the life of a community, insists that it is not only a matter of self-expression.

It recognizes, in a way that we sometimes fail to attend to in other contexts, that making things beautiful is WORK, not the magical efflorescence of "talent" or "passion" or any of the flimsier things we sometimes call "art." And it allows for the possibility that the beautiful will exist right alongside the terrible—idleness and pride, illness and disease, even death. It is a human and earthbound beauty that God commends to us.

Here finally is the truth of it for me: God wants to tell us, all the time, that creation is good, that this world and all that is in it is beloved. The stirrings I felt as a child by the woodstove and with my squeaky little violin were real and true, but they were not meant to pull me towards transcendence so much as to push me towards love. Beauty is an index to the divine not because it lifts us out of the earth, but because it lets us see the ways we are part of it, and lets us hear God whispering that "it is very good." God's love of the creation includes not only the rose, but the thorns and the dirt and the earthworms and even the aphids. What God calls beautiful is not only the expertly-performed Bach prelude, but the toddler running to his nursery teacher with arms outstretched, a loaf of bread baked for the sacrament by one of the high priests, that one Sunbeam yelling every song in the Primary program, the surreptitious passing of tissues during testimony meeting, a stack of variously shaded and wrinkled hands laid together to give a blessing, the endless passing of signup sheets to help with moves, rides to Girls Camp, chapel cleaning, the sacrament of ham and potato casseroles after funerals. We build our part of Zion with wood and stone and mud, and then God promises to restore our wastelands and make our feeble gifts worthy of his habitation—he will, in Isaiah's words, lay our stones with fair colours, and lay our foundations with sapphires, make our windows of agates, our gates Salvation and our walls Praise.

None of this makes me stop going to Evensong services and choir concerts, and loving them. It doesn't completely assuage the grief of not having enough time or talent to make the kind of music I long for. None of this is to say that I have become reconciled to bad music in our worship services, or that I don't believe God wants us to work more diligently at creating beauty. It is only to say that I am, ever so belatedly, beginning to understand that worshiping *God* in the beauty of holiness is a different thing than worshiping beauty, and that holiness is beautiful in both the poetry of the Psalms and in the homely prose of a dutiful life. Indeed, I may say that I follow the admonition of Zephaniah:

> "Sing, O daughter of Zion; shout, O Israel; be glad and rejoice with all the heart, O daughter of Jerusalem.
>
> The Lord hath taken away thy judgments, he hath cast out thine enemy: the king of Israel, even the Lord, is in the midst of thee: Fear thou not.
>
> The Lord thy God in the midst of thee is mighty; he will save, he will rejoice over thee with joy; he will rest in his love, he will joy over thee with singing."

Minerva & Muse, Pain & Imperfection, and an Abundance of Revelation

DAVID F. HOLLAND

I believe. Any account of my belief will necessarily be partial, as it derives from many sources, some of which lie beyond my powers of expression. I cannot do much more here than touch on a few constitutive elements of my faith.

Some of my conviction draws from historical women and men whose thinking I find compelling and whose impact on the world I admire. Some of it is fueled by the theologies of those who mean the most to me. And some rests on my own revelatory encounters with a God I love.

I start here with a pair of historical thinkers whose ideas have enriched my belief. Their sense of how one should search for divine light seems particularly appropriate for a volume on thoughtful faith.

Minerva & Muse

When the nineteenth-century Transcendentalist Margaret Fuller sought to capture the combination of traits that constituted a woman's full world-altering power, she picked two figures from Roman mythology: Minerva and Muse. The warrior goddess Minerva represented a being confident in her own independent capacity for reason and discernment. Muse signified poetic intuitions, a soul attuned to "joyous inspiration" and "incessant revelation." Fuller came to believe that these two personae, Minerva and Muse, lay within all of us and that they need to be harmonized for the sake of our own souls and for the flourishing of the world around us. Fuller's remarkable life flowed out from her conviction that the

combination of spiritual inspiration and independent thinking—however tumultuous their union—would ultimately lead
us into the redemptive power of eternal truth.[1]

Fuller's Transcendentalist contemporary, Theodore Parker,
invoked a somewhat similar set of complementary principles
in his search for true religious faith. He shared Fuller's conviction that many of the most important truths about human
existence could be felt intuitively, springing naturally from the
divine elements of the human conscience. He also believed that
these flashes of light come to us rough-hewn and in need of
refinement. To be a lasting source of illumination, Parker held,
our spiritual insights must wrestle honestly with the discoveries of science and history and the demands of hard thinking.
Lives of faith start with the inspirations of the soul, he insisted,
but only those intuited truths that could survive testing and
scrutiny, research and review, were worthy to be called true.
Our hearts provide the ore, our minds the refining fire.[2]

Though they had different ways of describing the process
of soul formation, Fuller and Parker each offered an account
of human faith that required a combination of spontaneous
spiritual creativity and critical thinking. Both believed this
dialectical process led to a God of beauty and goodness and
a world of greater justice. If either part of this pairing were
allowed to overwhelm the other, they contended, we would
surely fall short of the divinity for which we had been designed.
The ennobling interplay of inspiration and reasoning requires
our very best effort to nourish both capacities.

When I reflect on human history, the sorts of lives I most
admire and the kinds of contributions I most want to emulate
seem to rest on a balanced commitment to these two elements.
The fact that Fuller and Parker developed into truly courageous

champions of what I consider to be profoundly righteous causes (abolition, women's rights, civil liberty) strikes me as very weighty evidence in support of their theologies.

Pain & Imperfection

The impact of ideas like Margaret Fuller's and Theodore Parker's on my own understanding of a life of thoughtful faith has been profound. And yet, I radically part company with them on a number of key issues. For one, though they were aware of the message of the restoration, they chose not to embrace it, whereas I believe that the restored gospel is God's ultimate instrument for the redemptive gathering of his children. Relatedly, their thoughtful faith led them away from a sense of dependence on the grace of Jesus Christ whereas mine seems to bring me ever more fully into that core Christian truth. I have thought a lot about how and why I differ from them on this question of atonement. I have concluded that it has everything to do with the key concepts of two theologians who exercise even more influence on my thinking.

First, Patricia Terry Holland, my mother. Through both intuitive impulses of empathy and a view of the world shaped by generous listening and extensive reading, she developed a distinctive theology in which human suffering and divine goodness form the cross-braced foundations of an unshakable faith. I grew up watching her study the writings of two Teresas, one from Avila and the other of Calcutta, one who captured her belief in a God of inexpressible love and the other who reminded her of a humanity that cries out in collective agony. Patricia Holland called on me from my earliest memories to do what her theology posited as the essential things: to love God, to think carefully about a world in pain, and to see the covenanted community of my church as an indispensable place to live that love and address that pain. I hope I have risen to her charge. The Church she gave me, the Church of Jesus Christ of Latter-day Saints, has certainly offered me many opportunities to try.

Much of my adult life in the Church has been spent in callings that relentlessly educate me in the lasting consequences of trauma. I have watched members of my wards and stakes survive deep harm and live with its legacies. As I have observed—and often clumsily tried to support—their paths to healing, I have come to recognize that a survivor's journey necessarily wends through a complex mix of principles: truth and grace, appropriate trust and all due skepticism, justice and mercy, divine healings and human therapies, a cleared-eyed confrontation with the brutalities of the past and a steady look to the promise of the future. These things do not always easily coincide. Indeed, they sometimes violently repel each other. Bringing such disparate principles into a complete whole seems to stretch a soul to its farthest limits. I have seen women and men do this difficult work. I have seen them keep at it even as wounds seep and exhaustion overwhelms. It is a heart-wrenching and humbling and inspiring thing to behold.

As these Saints resolutely cling to these contrasting values, and as they rise toward healing on the tense interplay of their competing truths, I have seen an image of Jesus Christ, hands outstretched and nailed in opposite directions on the cross. He, too, was lifted on the tension of opposing forces. I have often thought of a gospel that points us toward a trauma-tized God, one willing to incur eternal wounds to ensure that justice will prevail and mercy will overflow, that life can be lived with both honesty and hope, that we can confront our histories without being bound by them.

Some Transcendentalists talked a lot about "self-reli-ance"; I am much more inclined toward a sense of sacred dependence. The more I consider this pain-pocked existence of ours, the more I understand the necessity of Jesus's atoning mission. The more I observe the sometimes mutually exclusive demands that human suffering makes of those who would heal, the more I appreciate a Savior who offered himself as the reconciler of the irreconcilable principles that we so desperately need. That is, my understanding of our wants as a species—an understanding based on observation and rational reflection—suggests the necessity of a force beyond human will and reasoning, one capable of bridging the chasms that fracture the whole we seek. I believe life requires a doctrine of atonement.

I don't claim to know exactly how Jesus Christ empowers us to live at the union of disunited things. Though I have preferences among various theories of atonement (I certainly prefer satisfaction theory to penal substitution, and moral influence to ransom), I confess to some degree of agnosticism on the importance of getting this exactly right. Rather, what I need is reason to believe that we have a gift of divine love beyond ourselves to accomplish what we clearly cannot do. Theodore Parker argued that the best way to know if God had provided something in the universe was to recognize humanity's need of it. We need food; food is available. Water likewise. So, too, with sunlight. Parker reasoned that the same must be true of spiritual needs. "The very wants themselves imply the satisfaction," he wrote.[3] For him that meant a palpable human hunger for divine revelation must have a means of satisfaction, hence he was a Transcendentalist. (This is the same reason, it turns out, why I am a Latter-day Saint; more on this below.) But even before we get to the logic that insists on the availability of revelation I would say humanity encounters an even greater need: Grace. Hence, I am a Christian. The more I think about reality, the more I believe in Jesus.

I owe much of that sense of reality to my mother. Its other essential element comes from another theologian of enormous impact on my doctrinal thinking: Jeanne Hansen Holland, my wife.

Minerva, the Roman goddess whom Fuller associated with independent thought, is often depicted with an owl and a spear; these would seem to be similarly fitting accoutrements for Jeanne. Her theology emphasizes the absolute importance of honesty and sincerity. I've actually never known her to do a disingenuous thing in the twenty-five years I have lived with her. She has no time for the façades or the flattery that so many of us have adopted in order to navigate life in a close-knit community. Jeanne seems to fear no human judgment. She is not fooled by whited sepulchers. She believes redemption is more likely to be found in the self-awareness of our failings than in the public performance of our virtues. After a quarter century of trying, I've realized I cannot argue with that.

Jeanne's commitment to a doctrine of transparency—with its accompanying skepticism toward illusions of perfection—has added to my awareness of the brokenness of all earthly things. Disinclined to the gauzy filters of sentimentality, she has clarified my vision. Just as my mother's attentiveness to the pain of the world has brought me to Jesus, so, too, has Jeanne's clear-eyed conception of fallen humanity. This doctrine has shaped her soul into one of the least judgmental I have ever encountered and it has opened my understanding to our profound dependence on a Savior. My careful thinking has brought me to this: Jesus Christ offers the best account of and the most compelling remedy for the truth my wife has helped me see.

These two theologies, one that attunes me toward the world's endemic pain and the other that highlights human imperfection, have kept Christ resolutely at the center of my faith when I might otherwise have been tugged by natural inclination toward the Transcendentalist's romantic confidence in humanity's capacity to make itself whole. I see that Patricia and Jeanne Holland have understood the world more fully than I have. I may seem to view these women in idealistic terms, but they have actually made of me a realist. And that has made me a Christian.

An Abundance of Revelation

What, then, makes me a Latter-day Saint? There are any number of answers to that question. Some of these answers point to conditioned emotions and cultural comforts, explanations that probably do not rise to the standard of "a thoughtful faith." My most meaningful answers, however, seem invariably rooted in my thinking about revelation.

The restored gospel emphasizes three primary sources of revealed truth: ancient scripture, living prophets and personal inspiration. It is distinctive in this regard. Many traditional Christians have placed their emphasis on the first. Transcendentalists—and a host of new age spiritualities—have had great confidence in the last. Latter-day Saints, often isolated and embattled on this point, rush to defend the middle. The Restoration actually asks us to embrace all three, not because they are perfect, but precisely because they are not. We need the tripart revelation that the restored gospel uniquely offers.

In this triangulation of revelatory media, I confess to some bias toward scripture. When I think of why I believe in the Church of Jesus Christ of Latter-day Saints, my mind usually turns toward texts.

Some of my scriptural reasons for believing are quite rationalistic. For instance, I am completely convinced that the biblical history of the Exodus, which so many Christian figures have declared to be a typological account of our journey toward redemption, uncannily supports the Latter-day Saint sense of the plan of salvation. This applies right down to the idea of a preexistence to which the fallen must return (Genesis 46:4), a fortunate fall based on a divinely anticipated sin (Genesis 45:5–8), a salvific combination of liberating divine grace (the blood of the lamb) and human choice (40 years' worth of agentive wandering), the centrality of a temple for the journey back home and the fact that the story of redemption is fundamentally related to families. When I see such striking scriptural parallels between the ancient stories and our restored theology—especially when those parallels seem to have escaped the founders of our faith—I am confirmed once again in my belief that there is a superhuman power at play in the restored gospel that is drawing God's family together across time and space.

Apropos of my theological training from Patricia and Jeanne Holland, my most meaningful engagements with the scriptures tend to occur at those intersections where human trauma and divine love coincide, for instance when the prodigal's father races to meet his estranged son in the road or when the Book of Moses depicts a Heavenly Father who weeps at a world riven by hate. (Undoubtedly these readings are informed by love and gratitude for my own earthly father.) Perhaps most significantly, the textual supports of my faith strengthen when the scriptures seem to deepen in shades of darkness and light just before bursting forth in living color to meet the most specific of personal needs. Many such occasions come readily to my mind. One remains especially vivid though it is now nearly two decades old.

The context of the experience was an inconsequential thing, really. At least it pales in comparison to the burdens others have borne. But it was mine.

In January of 2003 I sat alone in the empty ballroom of the Downtown Chicago Marriott. I was an advanced PhD student attending the annual meeting of the American Historical Association, the conference where hopeful academicians come to interview for faculty positions. Student participation in these professional conferences can be a rather demoralizing experience. Even mathematically-challenged humanities scholars can see at a glance that there are many more seekers than jobs on offer.

I was married with two children. I was running out of funding. I was running low on hope. I needed a job. I am not often given to panic, but I had been panicking as I walked the corridors of that conference. I'd had a very small handful of interviews and none of them seemed to go particularly well. So, as the day faded and the snow fell and I felt a long way from home, I had made my way into the cavernous silence of the lowly-lit hotel ballroom. I wandered over to a chair in the shadows of a far corner. As I tend to do in moments of silence and solitude, I instinctively began to pray. I set my backpack on the floor in front of me and reflexively reached in and pulled out the soft-cover copy of the Book of Mormon that always seemed to be in that bag. It was always in that bag because living prophets—witnesses who shaped my spiritual formation—had told me to make it a central feature of my devotional life.

I randomly opened the book to Alma 14. That chapter marks the climax to the story of Alma and Amulek in Ammonihah. They are bound by cords, watching the immolation of the innocent, verbally abused and physically assaulted by those in power, facing the imminent prospect of their own martyrdom.

This was trauma. I had read that story many times before, but on that night, in that ballroom, it did something remarkable to me. A verse to which I had previously paid little attention suddenly filled my heart with irresistible hope.

> And it came to pass that they all went forth and smote them, saying the same words, even until the last; and when the last had spoken unto them the power of God was upon Alma and Amulek, and they rose and stood upon their feet (Alma 14:25).

The first thing that occurred to me is that Alma and Amulek had to see the process through to the end. Their deliverance did not come until they had endured "even until the last." Through this text I felt a Heavenly Father whisper in my soul, "Persist." And then I read on, and at the moment when Alma and Amulek "stood upon their feet," I felt a Heavenly Father call to me, "Stand up!" I took the call literally and physically rose up out of my chair, standing on somewhat wobbly legs, sobbing in a way I had not wept for many, many years. I knew I had been spoken to. I knew I needed to stand and persist.

Though there were many more long, dark nights to endure— indeed, they continue—my Father had undeniably lifted me in my moment of despair. The Book of Mormon had been the medium of his message. Text and spirit and circumstance coincided with profound effect. In that ballroom I encountered, yet again, the God I love.

The instinct to pray, the conditioned impulse to read, and the ineffable experience of personal divine deliverance did not involve a great deal of careful thought that evening. But I have thought about that moment a thousand times since. One of the things I have thought about is the discrepancy between the God I experienced in that moment and the God described by Alma in the very passage that prompted the experience. Alma depicts the Almighty as allowing the innocent to suffer horribly in this life so he can punish the wicked justly in the next. That is not the God I personally encountered on that snow night in Chicago.

This is not the only place of misalignment between my experience of God and a textual representation of him. I experience something similar in Numbers 31 and section 132 of the Doctrine and Covenants and in any number of other places in our canon. These are the most striking examples of a general phenomenon. I have a settled sense that there are yawning gaps between God's true being and the words that appear on the page. This is undoubtedly as true in the passages I love as in the ones I don't. In the case of Alma 14, they are one and the same.

There are many things about that chapter that I don't know: I don't exactly know how well Joseph Smith's process of translation captured the meaning of what Mormon scratched into the plates. I don't know how precisely Mormon conveyed the content of whatever intermediate record he was working from. I don't know how faithfully that intermediate record described the experience as it occurred. I don't even know how accurately Alma's statement, uttered in a moment of incomprehensible distress, reflected a true and full understanding of God's actual work in the world. Given what I do know about the imperfection of everything human beings handle, I'm inclined to accept that this account bears the marks of the fallible people with whom it originated and of the many mortal hands through which it passed before it ever got to me. And that is to say nothing of my own considerable faults and folly as the reader.

Any image of God, as seen in any text, necessarily reflects off various mediating conveyances before it gets to me. I say

this as a lover of scripture: To take any passage as a definitive statement on the Father of us all is a profoundly fraught
endeavor. I believe that is one of the reasons we are called
upon to take seriously the three witnesses of revelation:
text, prophet, and individual inspiration. A hallmark of the
restored gospel is its veneration of all three. None of these is
a perfect conveyance, but in the concert and convergence of
them, we find something somewhat different than what any
one of them can offer on its own.

My moment in Chicago exemplified both the inadequacy
of any one revelatory source and the power of their conflu-
ence. My situation's fit with the text was far from perfect: I
did not, for instance, believe God was prolonging my relatively privileged experience of job-searching so that he could
rain brimstone upon the search committee from Bridgewater
State. The inclinations of my own soul were likewise insufficient; before encountering that text, they were prone to
an unseemly self-pity, a wallowing in the egotism of inner
feeling that was only arrested when the text reminded me that
others had suffered before me and beyond me. And both the
reading of text and the experiences of spirit were informed by
a prophetically established theology that had long made the
parental goodness of God the central feature of my faith, even
as the reading and the attending spiritual encounters gave his
divine character a kind of depth and complexity that often
goes unmentioned in general conference. When my God
lifted me, yet again, on that wintry evening, I caught another
glimpse of his nature as revealed by the convergence—greater
than the sum of the parts—of the Restoration's triangulated
sources of light. Together, they brought me briefly but irre-
futably into the direct presence of his love. These are the sorts
of experiences with the Church's distinctive abundance of
revelation that make me a Latter-day Saint.

Such moments remind me that I am, in fact, surrounded by a cloud of witnesses. None of them perfectly captures the essence of my faith, but all of them contribute something essential. I am grateful for their combined effect and I would be loath to lose any of them. To the extent that I can claim a thoughtful faith, I owe its thoughtfulness to the careful thinking of many others. Historical figures like Margaret Fuller and Theodore Parker have helped me know how I might thoughtfully believe. Thinkers like Jeanne and Patricia Holland have shown me that my thoughtful faith must center in Jesus. The ancient authors of a complex scriptural canon and their modern-day colleagues have forced me to grapple with intellectually challenging questions about sacred texts and their relationship to a living spirit. And with and through it all, I end up where this essay began. I believe.

Life Abundant

THOMAS McCONKIE

My conversion to the restored gospel didn't initially come through a testimony of the Book of Mormon or of Joseph Smith as prophet. It didn't come through a specific belief in my mind or a feeling in my heart. My conversion came unexpectedly and powerfully through the body. To this day my faith lives in me with increasing joy and potency. I'll tell you how it began.

I remember it was a dank winter in Salt Lake City. I'd caught a nasty flu virus that had my body convulsing in waves of hot and cold. It was the first time in my short life of twelve years that I could vaguely sense my own mortality. My mom, with her typical brightness of hope, asked if I wanted her dad to come give me a blessing. Her faith in his gift to heal was absolute.

As my granddad stepped in from the cold, dark night, my parents greeted him with the care and deference one pays to a genuinely holy man. He took off his coat without fanfare, like it was just another late night at the office.

We moved in procession to the middle of the living room where my parents set out a folding chair. As my dad poured consecrated oil on my head—a cool drop into the fiery lake—I sat with great anticipation, almost delirious with fever, believing I could be healed.

The moment my granddad began to pronounce a blessing it was as if a portal had opened; pure light seemed to pour into me and illuminate every tissue, every cell in my entire body. I felt incandescent, though the flame did not consume me. As power coursed through my whole being, I could only melt and give myself over to it.

This was the Spirit in which "we live and move and have our being."[1] I felt connected to family, connected to power from on high, connected to all of the richness of Heaven. I had never been so sick and afraid in my whole life. A few breaths later, I felt only God's grace infusing me. Like a burst of rain falling on hot summer pavement, the illness evaporated, leaving no trace.

Long after the blessing ended, the fire it left in me still crackled. I wasn't the same being after. I could never be the same.

I remember my granddad seeming quite stoic—ordinary—as I stood up. By any objective account, it was a miraculous healing he had just mediated. And yet, he carried it out with all the plainness of a man balancing a ledger or mopping the floor before closing up shop.

When he disappeared back into the night I remained in the afterglow of God. Young and immature, I couldn't contain all that energy in my small frame with the same dignity the patriarch did. I was giddily euphoric; a bubbling bliss floated up from my toes out through the crown of my head—effervescing away everything in me that felt solid and opaque. I remember bounding around the house that night like a gazelle on the open plains, overflowing with life. It was like I'd just been born, been given a new body to dance in.

I woke up the next morning with no memory of illness. That was a lifetime ago. There was no trace, no residue of anything but joy in my world now. I went skiing with my friends and floated through the mounds of freshly-fallen powder—weightless.

The experience could hardly have been more dramatic: a bona fide faith healing at the hands of one of God's elect witnesses. ✦ You might think that that single experience would be enough to infuse the rest of my life with an unwavering faith. And yet, not more than a year or so later, I found that my convictions, my identity as a Latter-day Saint all started to unravel, seemingly without warning.

In fact, the underlying conflict had been smoldering for years. I was the one of eight children who had a particular talent for drawing out all of my father's fierceness, all of his ire. He was a priesthood holder, a respected member of the community, and the man I feared more than anything else in the whole world.

How could I be safe at church? Somewhere in my child's mind, my father was the Church. Our relationship disturbed me. The more scared of him I became, the more repelled I felt by the Church.

At the same time I was nursing these doubts about the trustworthiness of the Church, my peers were starting to talk more about the peculiar history of "the Mormons": treasure seeking, polygamy, translation that was not literal but "inspired" (A peep stone? It can't be!). My impressionable mind was blown. "Why hasn't anyone ever told me about all this?" It began to feel like a great cover-up. *Things are not as they seem.*

Both the rift forming between me and my father and my growing suspicions toward an airbrushed history made for a clear decision to stop going to church. Which is not to say that the consequences for leaving weren't severe. My parents did everything that loving caregivers would do to look after my salvation—even if that involved some coercive discipline here and there. But the more resistance I encountered, the more determined I became to leave. The farther away I went, the more alienated I felt by their resistance. A death spiral ensued.

✦ My maternal grandfather, Joseph B. Wirthlin, was a member of the Quorum of the Twelve Apostles at the time.

Against some of my deepest instincts to take shelter in the village, I separated myself from family and tribe. Yesterday's salvation had become today's toxin. I knew in my bones that I had to leave. By the time I was eighteen years old, I had wandered far out of bounds into a spiritual desert, my body wracked with all the anxiety that isolation brings to a herd animal.

It's hard to express the dissonance I felt in my spiritual life at this time. I couldn't reconcile the divine power I'd *felt* as a child with the ideas and beliefs I was beginning to *think* as a young adult. What had felt true in my body was *untenable* in my mind. What's more, I didn't have any language at the time to express that these two realities—body and mind—were in conflict with one another. The battle waged on.

There was a time I went so far as to rationalize that my faith healing had been some great placebo effect. I was healed because I *believed* I could be healed. Even still, I felt dissatisfied with how hollow this perspective rang when I held it up to genuine spiritual experience. There was no recourse. I had to learn to build a home and take up residence in the contradiction I'd become.

I stumbled forward the best I knew how while a cocktail of adolescent hormones fomented my angst. My anger and distrust towards father and Father was a steady drip of poison in the bloodstream. Graduating from high school after a period of dropping out, I felt a great nothingness sprawl before me. I had no goals, no hope.

This new religion of doubt and disbelief I'd taken on unwittingly proved to be too demanding. Somewhere in my eighteenth year I began to let up on a corrosive skepticism just enough to become curious towards Mystery again. Once again I found myself sick, in need of a physician.

As it turned out, I didn't need to seek any farther than three blocks from my first college apartment in Salt Lake City, where I happened across the largest order of Zen Buddhism in the world outside of Japan. Something in me cried out for the spiritual innocence I'd known as a child. I wanted to believe again; to let the mind and body lie down with one another in green pastures, like lion and lamb. *Zen*—the literal meaning of which is "to manifest oneness"—resonated as an intuitive path for unlearning the mental divisions that seemed to be chopping me into little bits.

In many ways, I was well prepared for this new journey. I harnessed all the religious fervor I'd absorbed from growing up in a deeply devout family and poured it into studying the *Dharma*, (i.e. the Buddha's teachings). I channeled all the discipline that generations of scriptorians in my family had honed and directed it toward sitting still on my meditation cushion with a single-pointed mind. In short, I took what I could of the virtues my religious upbringing had gifted to me and applied them to a completely new spiritual path—a path that had yet to wound and betray me as I felt my former community had.

The setting of my initial attempt at meditation was in my first college apartment—a basement unit where I lived alone and lonesomely. Without the commotion of parents and siblings around me for the first time, I could better detect the contours of my suffering in the harsh silence. It quickly became clear that if I didn't figure out my mess of a life, nobody else was going to do it for me.

Trusting in *I-don't-know-what*, I settled myself on the carpeted floor of my bedroom. Once I let my body find its way into a posture where it could relax a little bit, I had a sudden experience of vast spaciousness that I had never felt before. As much as my awareness could handle or process at the time, I felt an impression of what "numberless worlds" must feel like to God.[2] It was as if I'd pulled back the curtain on the ordinary world and briefly glimpsed the eternities hidden behind a thin veil.

That was it: *love at first sit.* I'd struck a rich vein that somehow not only fed me but was simultaneously the umbilical cord of all the universe. All at once I had faith that there was nothing I needed to know that I wouldn't eventually know. All things hidden would be revealed.

It's a good thing my first experience of meditation was so profound—I might never have returned otherwise. During the next few years, sitting still and trying to meditate was not always or even often pleasant. Some days I would wring my hands, pace nervously and work myself up into a frenzy before I finally managed to sit myself down for just 30 minutes before going to bed. In many ways I dreaded the confrontation with silence, with my own misery. The more still I sat, the more everything hurt. But deeper down I could feel something working me. I started to sense into the part of me even beneath the suffering. The practice of stillness was *manna* to me from that day forward.

Development & Ongoing Progression

I carried on in this steady rhythm of daily practice and saw rather dramatic results over time. When I started meditating, I hoped it could help take the edge off my anxiety, alleviate my insomnia, and help me be a little less miserable in general. That was basically it. To borrow a phrase from Dan Harris, a popular mindfulness teacher, if meditation could make me 10% happier, I thought that would be more than enough.

In just the space of eight years, though, I went from dropping out of high school to graduating with honors at the university and spending four years abroad learning Mandarin and Spanish along the way. My mind was functioning at a different level than it ever had been. Emotionally, I felt resilient and confident. I didn't feel like the same person who'd started out on the contemplative path so long ago. Who I understood "myself" to be felt very different, even if I couldn't articulate how.

My meditation teacher at the time was exceptionally attuned to my metamorphosis and recommended I turn my attention from Eastern wisdom literature back to the western schools, especially in the direction of developmental psychology. In the developmental literature I gained new insights into how the mind, how *consciousness* can continue to change across the entire lifespan of a human being. Immediately I recognized myself in the transformations the research was describing. It felt a bit like looking into a mirror and seeing my once and future self.

At that point it had been about fourteen years since I had stopped going to church. When I started learning about adult development, my unguarded, spontaneous response was, "I can be Mormon again!"

Though developmental psychology and The Church of Jesus Christ of Latter-day Saints might not appear to have anything to do with one another on the surface, I saw a clear connection. ⟿ Essentially, adult development describes with painstaking precision how the adult mind makes meaning, *how we process experience, and who we understand ourselves to be at the deepest level.* It involves not so much the content of what we know but how we know it. It looks closely at the

⟿ I've written extensively about this in *Navigating Mormon Faith Crisis: A Simple Developmental Map* (Salt Lake City: Mormon Stages, 2015).

"knower" we take ourselves to be. What is more, it posits that our meaning making, processing and self-understanding can change dramatically over a lifetime.

As humans in the Modern era, many of us have adopted a belief that the objective world is simply given and that it's our job as sober little scientists to gather up the facts and form as accurate a picture of "reality" as we possibly can. Once we know the truth, whether about the laws of thermodynamics or the details of the plan of salvation, we can follow the rules and live reasonably happy lives, as the logic goes.

Now, developmental psychology does not deny there's such a thing as truth. But it does make tremendous trouble for the assumption that as humans, we're capable of clearly perceiving Truth without our perceptual filters bending or distorting it in any way. The field of adult development analyzes, categorizes and describes the different patterns of meaning-making we use to make sense of experience, even something as complex as religious experience—one's personal faith, for example.

It turns out that there are many, many *"styles of faith."* In other words, from the developmental point of view, there are coherent and patterned filters through which we adults naturally make sense of the restored gospel. As we grow in faith and maturity, the meaning we make of the gospel tends to become more nuanced and more capacious. Our ability to extend compassion toward ourselves and towards others who seem to be very different from us increases exponentially.

I sensed the possibilities immediately and realized, contrary to my previous assumption, that I had never stopped believing in the Restored Gospel *per se*. I had simply outgrown one particular meaning-making orientation to the faith, and was ready to grow into another—a hermit crab in search of a better-fitting shell. Development from that point on became for me a supplementary language for understanding the doctrine of *ongoing progression.* If we are to become gods and goddesses, I thought, we must *develop* into this stature: line upon line, from one stage to the next. Moreover, *we don't have to wait until after we die for the most exciting spiritual transformations to take place.*

My early obsession with patterns of adult development has given way to a fruitful career in research, writing and teaching others how these patterns can offer us life more abundant as disciples of Christ. In the following section I will outline a simple developmental pattern and offer a glimpse of what the gospel might look like through that lens. The progression unfolds in three parts: pre-rational, to rational, to postrational. ⚘

In the pre-rational stages, typically predominant into late adolescence, ⚘ we are immersed in the physicality and concreteness of life. We tend to accept things as they present to our senses. What you see is what you get.

Recall how at age twelve I marveled at the power of the blessing my granddad gave me. The power was *true.* It was *real,* physical. There was no more need to question it than to question if the snow falling outside the window that night was real.

⚘ This pattern, from "pre" to "post," is a long-established convention in developmental studies. One of the better known examples comes from Lawrence Kohlberg is his description of "preconventional," "conventional," and "postconventional" morality.

⚘ Research suggests that stage progression in adulthood is only loosely tied to chronological age. Still, I provide this information to help the reader intuit these particular stages from different times in their own lives.

There is a glorious quality of innocence present in these stages of development. ⚜ Experience pours in through our eyes, our ears, our hearts, and we receive it fully. Later on, we'll start to interrogate our own thinking, to consider cultural perspectives on how humans construct "truth." But for now, trusting as lambs, we allow ourselves to be led, taking in the experiences life offers. It is no wonder Jesus tells his disciples that we must become as little children to enter the Kingdom of Heaven. The challenge, we might say, is to remain a child as we grow into adulthood.

I do not mean to romanticize this phase of human life. There are challenges here that we need to navigate, even to outgrow. For example, typical of the pre-rational stages is a kind of perceptual confusion: we cannot yet clearly differentiate what happens in our mind and what is objectively playing out in the world. Our inner and outer worlds remain tangled up, *con-fused*. The implications for religious experience here are significant. In pre-rational spirituality, we tend to assume that what we experience—a rapturous feeling, a vision of angels—is true for all people, everywhere and at all times. We fail to see that our own perceptual biases and cultural contexts significantly shape the way we interpret raw experience.

It is not until later, at the rational stages of human development, that we start to ask if things *objectively* exist. At the pre-rational stages, if we experience it, then it exists. We are afraid of monsters in our closet because we can see them in our minds. We can't yet clearly separate the products of our imagination from the "external world." Essentially, as we move deeper into rational territory, we become more skilled

⚜ Researchers have discovered multiple sub-stages that fall under the category of "pre-rational." The details of these sub-stages exceed the scope of this essay.

at making distinctions between what is objectively real and what is subjective and personally *experienced*. We realize at the rational stages that not everything everyone experiences can be said to be objectively true. A "dark spirit" we think we sense in another person may reveal itself to be our own prejudice towards women, towards people with dark skin, towards Catholics.

A new class of inquiry arises in the rational mind: "Did Jesus really feed the multitudes with five loaves of bread and two fish? Did that actually happen?" Or in a more recent historical example, "Did an angel really visit Joseph Smith and show him where he could find golden plates buried in a mountain?" The rational mind cannot help but ask these questions because the rational mind thrives on objective, empirical evidence. ⚘ It naturally goes about disentangling subjective experience from verifiable, physical events.

A classic historical example of this shift in meaning making is that of Thomas Jefferson, who admired Jesus's moral teachings, but who rejected in large measure the supernatural elements of the gospels. He went so far as to compile a version of the Bible that largely omitted any miraculous or supernatural events in the life of Jesus, focusing primarily on the moral philosophy of Jesus's ministry.

Jefferson embodied a rational Christianity, one that *made sense* to the modern mind, as opposed to a pre-rational

⚘ The whole basis of the European enlightenment and ensuing scientific method that has come to revolutionize human civilization stems from this basic truth: that we can experiment with the natural world, see how it responds, and formulate laws that describe what is objectively true about it. Through experiment and reason, we can determine cause and effect. We can understand why things are the way they are. Muslims and Christians may disagree vehemently on whether or not Jesus is in fact their personal savior. But it makes no difference if they agree or disagree about the law of gravity. Jumping off a cliff as a daring act of faith, Christian and Muslim alike go splat.

Christianity that doesn't tend to object to historical accounts that openly defy the laws of physics. In point of fact, a record number of people throughout the world are disaffiliating with traditional religions precisely because the rational or objective evidence doesn't seem to support the truth claims upon which they hinge.[3]

Things can get quite messy when the rational and pre-rational worldviews collide. "True believers" tend to stress the virtue of believing and the necessity of believing it all—not picking and choosing what we find convenient. Moderns may respond condescendingly that there is nothing valiant about choosing to believe things that present to the senses as patently false. In the words of the satirist, Mark Twain: *Faith is believing what you know ain't so.*

This was certainly my predicament growing up as an exile from the faith. I could not will myself to believe what I was told to believe simply to be counted as a true believer. ⚜ There was much I just didn't believe, didn't care to believe. But I could still *feel*. After all those years cultivating and refining my sense of doubt, I could still feel the *living fire* dancing in my bones and all about me.

I didn't believe at that time that there was a man named Jesus who could walk on water and calm the seas. But I knew in the immediacy of my own body that my grandfather had rebuked my fever, calling on Christ, and that the "demon" had fled my body. I didn't necessarily have to believe that Christ quieted the winds on the Sea of Galilee. I already knew that what my grandfather called "Christ" had calmed the storms in

⚜ Joseph Smith had an eminently rational streak: "I never thought it was right to call up a man and try him because he erred in doctrine, it looks too much like Methodism and not like Latter-day Saintism. Methodists have creeds which a man must believe or be kicked out of their church. I want the liberty of believing as I please, it feels so good not to be trammeled."[4]

my own soul and body. The historical facts were blurry to me. Divine power was more clear than ever.

And so I groped for higher meaning. I couldn't deny what I knew in my heart. But I couldn't embrace truth claims that violated the dictates of my reasoning mind. Somewhere in me I believed that these different kinds of truths could be reconciled and circumscribed.

It was in this existential casserole I began to taste a new kind of *knowing* with the tip of my tongue—a postrational faith. The rational mind as the only trustworthy source of knowledge came to feel like a false god; an idol that could not hear my prayers or respond to my heart's longing. At a certain point, ironically, it felt irrational to trust rationality alone. Whoever said that our mind could know reality anyway? It was too narrow a sliver of the cosmos. My body, my heart, the fullness of my senses told me that I was living in a universe of a personal God, one who cared for me absolutely.

This is where my religious life was born again. Philosopher Paul Ricoeur beautifully captures the spirit of this new threshold of consciousness: "Beyond the desert of criticism, we wish to be called again!" For all that we can know with the mind, there tends to remain a nagging sense that we can't know everything *through* the mind and *by* the mind.

Skepticism at the rational stages offers us the gift of deeply examining the truths we previously accepted uncritically. It helps us to test truth, to temper it with the heat of the intellect. Truth is made truer when our rational faculties are fully firing. But eventually we run the risk of canonizing our rational beliefs and getting stuck in yet another unexamined belief system. To progress, we must learn to doubt the doubter too.[5]

I believe that if we remain open and humble, we come to learn that there are realities far beyond what the rational mind can comprehend. We learn that there are different ways to know what we know. Sometimes *unknowing* is the only way we can know. An anonymous fourteenth-century Christian mystic invited us into the "cloud of unknowing," where no belief can stand between us and full communion with God.[6] Somewhat counter-intuitively, the very beliefs that helped scaffold our life of faith now stand between us and a deeper intimacy with the Divine.

Jehovah speaks thunderously to Isaiah: *"My thoughts are not your thoughts, neither are my ways your ways . . . "*[7] Paraphrased for a new generation of spiritual seekers: *Don't be so sure you know what you think you know.*

I had a dream along this vein several years ago. I was on my hands and knees in a dark, dusty room, scratching at the bamboo floor, picking at the seams between the planks. Suddenly the floor opened up like a trap door, or better yet, a secret passageway.

I dropped into the room below and recognized it immediately as my grandma and granddad McConkie's dining room. I looked up toward the ceiling I had just fallen through and my great grandfather Oscar, whom I had never met, hovered above me. He was a risen angel, awesome in his glory. His arms were outstretched and palms opened towards me in a gesture that was at once fierce and grace-filled. He did not speak.

Throughout my entire body I felt a presence and power that was not of this world. The intensity of the encounter jolted me awake, where I felt the exact same presence and energy I'd communed with just then in the dream world.

An important piece of context to this dream is that I had had a painful falling out with my McConkie grandparents when I left the church, almost eighteen years before. I struggled to forgive them for what I experienced to be excessive harshness toward me based on a decision that I felt I'd come to honestly.

The message from the dream intuitively resonated throughout my entire body. In my great grandfather's sublime presence, I was made to know that God's children are all invincibly holy. It takes all of us time to grow into our callings. It takes time to smooth out our rough spots and imperfections. But never is there a moment we are not fully claimed by God and do not wholly belong to God's process of perfecting us.

In the dream I learned deep love and forgiveness for two people I'd struggled to forgive my entire adult life. It was a forgiveness too radical, too grand for my mind to understand.

Rationally, the dream was just a bunch of synapses firing in my brain, creating the illusion that I was seeing my great grandfather Oscar for the first time. But that's not what it *felt* like. I didn't experience him as an illusion. I experienced him as a being more real than the "real" people I meet in my waking life.

Experiences like these have given me an appreciation for Mystery. The materialistic view of the world insists that angels don't exist. But I have met them face to face.

After meditating daily for over a decade, something remarkable began to happen. After sitting still for 30 minutes or so, the meditation didn't abruptly end when I stood up from my cushion, but began to permeate my whole day the way the scent of fresh flowers wafts through the air in the springtime. No longer was meditation some delicate state I needed to carefully stack up like a house of cards. Metaphorically, I could now clearly see that meditation was the ground on which the house of cards stood. *Meditation was simply who I was.* Who we all are. If we have eyes to see, we cannot not see it. It's not some special state or place somewhere else, but right here. "The Kingdom is already so close!"[8] Jesus cried to his followers.

I became so much less interested in what I *thought* about life after this. What anybody said they thought about anything. In the words of the Sufi poet, Jalal ad-Din Rumi, "Think of who created thought! Why do you stay in prison when the door is so wide open?"[9] Joseph Smith acutely felt the prison of language too: "Oh Lord, God, deliver us in thy due time from the little narrow prison almost as it were total darkness of paper pen and ink and a crooked broken scattered and imperfect language . . . "[10]

From this new perspective I was beginning to see that belief, at best, acts as signage. It marks the path to ever more transcendent truths. At worst, we start to mistake the signs for the promised land itself. We stop progressing on the path because we think the sign that reads "Exaltation" is the destination itself.

As rich and rewarding as my spiritual life was at that point, it still felt imbalanced in some vague way. My meditation had become deep and abiding. It was a stabilized *samadhi* that accompanied me often throughout the day and even deep into the night of dreams and dreamless sleep. And yet, some yearning in my heart felt unmet.

That shifted one afternoon when I was sitting in meditation with my late teacher, Joshu Sasaki Roshi. During the final hour on the final day of an intensive week-long training (*sesshin* in Japanese), I had an experience that was as unexpected as it is indescribable.

There I was, sitting silently in the meditation hall one moment, and the next moment, without warning, everything was completely *gone*. The meditation hall, the monastery, the mountain, the entire world was gone. Even me; *I* was gone too. It was as if all the angels in heaven had fallen silent.

When I came back, when I realized I'd been gone, I was astonished to find that I had a body. I was completely stunned that there was a world around me. That I existed. That *I am*. Without a conscious thought going through my mind, I wept silently and could hear the delicate thud of tears falling on my black cotton robes. Beauty overcame me.

Coming down the mountain that evening, on my way to the airport to fly back to Salt Lake, I sensed that life would never be the same again. Somehow, my experience with the roshi on the mountain was an echo of the healing I'd felt as a young child at the hands of my grandfather. Once again, *I was not who I thought I was. The world was not what it seemed.*

It was much more grand.

The following Sunday morning I found myself gravitating to an LDS chapel down the street. It didn't seem to matter that I hadn't gone to church in 20 years. It was a new earth and a new day. My heart was called back to the place where I'd felt so much joy and so much sorrow as a young boy. I could not resist the call.

I sat in the chapel during sacrament meeting and just marveled at the energy I could feel coursing through the space. Light was streaming through the stained glass. Human hearts gathered around the sacrament table to drink in Christ's presence and call a greater measure of His power down to build Zion. Not least of all, I felt the profound integrity of my father who for so many years had done all he could to bring me to this banquet of Divine Love.

I knew myself to be a member of Christ's very body in that moment. My beliefs, my worldviews, all my life experiences since I first left the Church had gone through so many births and deaths. I was entirely different. I was utterly the same.

Over ten years from the day I stepped back into that chapel, I'm still an active member in my ward family. It feels like I've just barely begun to tap my potential to grow in the Restored Gospel—this living stream of Wisdom. The issues that initially tweaked by skeptic's nerve—Joseph Smith's character flaws, polygamy, golden plates, who gets to partake of temple blessings—those are still alive and well. I didn't simply make sense of them and put them to rest. If anything, I am more aware than ever that we as a faith community have a history to reckon with and a new story to tell.

But I am no longer confused about the *power* I feel when I worship. Whatever *grace* it was that healed me as a young boy is the same *power* that enlightens my mind, opens my heart and reveals the expanse of Eternity to me in this very moment. There are no words to describe this immense and boundless Love.

The belief I resonate with most at this time in my life is that there is no thought, no belief that can begin to express the goodness of the news that Christ embodied. Of course my mind still wants to make sense of it. Many of us so desperately want to capture the correct formula for salvation in order to be sure that we qualify for it. If Newton could develop a mathematical formula for gravity so precise that humans can chart the orbits of the planets, then why can't we know with the same certainty the means back to God's presence? We tell stories. We form credos. We render God lifeless by carving Him and Her into idols. The Israelites were tempted to worship Jehovah in the form of a golden calf. I wonder if our temptation to idolatrize our own beliefs is not still greater.

The sixteenth-century Spanish mystic known as Saint John of the Cross boldly states that "pure faith is a ray of darkness to the soul." This is troubling doctrine, indeed. What does the mind love more than to know the answers, after all? Faith to me is not just about what we know to be true, but also a cultivated willingness to strip off our cerebral vestments and stand naked before God once again as children, undisguised and undefended. Faith asks us to both know and *un-know*, again and again and again. *My thoughts are not your thoughts . . .*

As I reflect on my own spiritual path over the years, I am comically aware that truth is not what I once believed it was. When I sit down in ten years to read this very essay, I hope I haven't allowed my beliefs to become too precious. I hope I'll shake my head and laugh at what I thought I knew. "Today's enlightenment is tomorrow's mistake," they say in Zen. Isn't it so?

But what more do I have than these signposts, these *words*, to share my heart with you? From eternity to eternity, from Zion to Zion, we grow line upon line, here a little, there a little. God is truer than we can imagine. Truth is truer than we can possibly imagine.

Damned by Perfection

BONNIE YOUNG

his is the story of how my perfection almost damned me. That is, how my relentless quest for flawlessness undermined my happiness, my health, my orientation to the world, and my faith. It is a story, too, of a girl becoming a woman and in the process making room for grace.

I was barely twelve the first time I worked up the courage to see my bishop and confess. I'd learned that bishop-confessions were what you did when you committed particularly serious sins, but I never imagined that I would be the one in the bishop's office. I was so overcome by guilt immediately following my mistake that I confessed to my parents, but their reassurances weren't enough to quench the fire of condemnation that I felt so tortured by. (I'll elaborate, but for now, just understand that I feel guilt in an unusual way.) When I asked them if I needed to confess to the bishop, they were a bit surprised and told me that I could confess if it would help me feel better. Now I understand that they didn't think it was necessary for me to go, but they also must have felt discomfort at seeing their daughter in so much torment. I wanted to show God that I wanted to be good, and I desperately needed to know that he still accepted me. I needed someone who could tell me, with authority, that God forgave me and still loved me. I don't remember how the conversation went, other than that I wept and was met with overwhelming love and compassion from my dear bishop. When I walked out of his office, an immense weight had been lifted off my shoulders. I felt so free.

I remember similar feelings of distress-then-relief when I was baptized. I suspect most children don't worry much about their worthiness before being baptized, but I felt burdened by my childhood mistakes (what to my seven year-old brain felt like mortal sins), and I craved a fresh start. But at the same time, I worried that my wrongs made me unworthy to be baptized. If I didn't tell the bishop every detail of every mistake, would my baptism count? Adding to the question of my prepubescent worthiness, there were other uncomfortable moments on my baptismal day—my mother made me wear a floral dress with shoulder pads that I *really* did not want to wear, I worried about my underpants showing through my white baptismal jumpsuit (my activity day leader told me that she had accidentally worn pink ones on her baptismal day), and I felt embarrassed that all of the messages during the service were directed at me. But the relief that I felt as I emerged from the water—that I was all the way clean and totally forgiven—was powerful enough that if I meditate today on that moment, I can feel it again. It felt delicious to have a divinely-sanctioned fresh start.

As I rode home from the service, my wet hair dampening the despised shoulder pads of my dress, I lay horizontally across the back seat of our Dodge Grand Caravan with my hands behind my head and gazed out the window into the night sky. With the same innocent logic that led me to believe that if I tried hard enough I could dig to China from my backyard, I thought to myself, "I am *totally* clean, and if I try hard enough I can probably stay that way." I didn't want to feel the dread I'd felt before my baptism again, and I was naively but sincerely committed to putting in the work necessary to avoid needing repentance.

I took my spiritual journey, including the decision to be baptized and to remain clean, very seriously. I took a lot of things seriously as a child. Many of my day-to-day activities were touched—and often interrupted—by my carefulness and worries. Neither I nor my family understood how to make sense of my anxieties. I have some names and a couple of diagnoses for it now (one of which is "scrupulosity," a form of obsessive-compulsive disorder that is characterized by excessive fear of sin and reassurance-seeking rituals), but I remember it being called "a very sensitive spirit." My scrupulosity expressed itself in many ways—sometimes through repeated safety rituals or asking my mother for reassurance, but most often in the form of confession. I confessed everything, even if I was unsure if I had actually made a mistake. For example, if I had set an open pen on someone's floor, I confessed that I might have made a mark. I had an unusually low tolerance for dishonesty, uncertainty, and risk, and I felt guilt in a way that most of my peers and family couldn't relate to. I was much more careful than anyone else I knew and was much harder on myself than anyone ever was with me. The love and peace that the gospel could offer me were often replaced with guilt and fear about my standing before God.

Like most youngsters, my understanding of God as a child and adolescent was based on a transactional model of divine reward or retribution: I obey, he blesses. I disobey, he punishes. Although I held hope that God and Jesus loved me, my anxiety and developmental abilities made it difficult to emerge from my fear of doing something wrong and disappointing them. My perception of God's nature and my relationship with him was also complicated by contradicting teachings about him. My parents taught me that he was gentle and loved me always, but the Bible talked about a jealous and rageful God. How could I make sense of a God who was a hen gathering chicks in some verses and a wielder of a terrible and swift sword in others?[1] I was unsure of who was listening to my prayers. I feared how he felt about me, especially when I made mistakes, and was desperate to know I was enough in his eyes.

There were glimpses of transcendent love and light that burst through this transactional and fear-based God-view from time to time. My baptism, attending the temple, reading the scriptures, singing hymns, hearing the testimonies of my dear parents and trusted leaders—these were moments when I genuinely felt the Spirit and tasted God's mercy. When I wasn't worrying about my mistakes or experiencing disturbing intrusive thoughts, I felt happy when I attended church. My tight-knit ward family loved and supported me. But scrupulosity often lurked just beneath the surface, preying on my good desires and fanning the flames of uncertainty about my worthiness. The resulting unease propelled me to cling to the safety I was promised if I was exactly obedient.

My natural inclinations toward perfectionism found fertile soil to thrive within the programs and standards of the church. The need for reassurance that I was "enough" fueled my enthusiastic participation in my various classes. In many ways, my life held evidence that a simple transactional model of the divine order worked. I was following the rules, my home life was peaceful and stable, I attracted good friends with similar standards and goals, and together we avoided the consequences of mistakes that some of our peers struggled with. I attributed these successes—my happy, good life—to living the standards of the gospel with exactness. I could ignore the few times when the transactional model didn't work because there were so many times when it did ("work" meaning I saw myself blessed in obvious, outward ways). But there came a time when I couldn't ignore how poorly this model actually worked for me.

Anxiety and scrupulosity had been my regular companions during childhood and adolescence, but I had little awareness of them until they showed up in a way that made life hard to live. Before age twenty-one, I could engage in my compulsions (confessing, reassurance-seeking, repeated checking) somewhat freely. And while these compulsions didn't get rid of my anxiety, I could get by with the temporary relief they offered. Then I went on a mission to Chile, and things got really hard. In the missionary training center and in my first Chilean area, I experienced a deep darkness that surprised as much as it devastated me. It would be hard to imagine a young woman more excited about and dedicated to serving a mission than I was, and I certainly didn't expect my mission to feel like this. I had known sadness before, but this was different. I had been discouraged, confused, lonely, and even hopeless. This was different. Never before had I gone to bed at night wishing that I didn't have to wake up in the morning. Never before had I felt such dread and soul-crushing pain. Wasn't my obedience and sacrifice supposed to bring me joy? It did not make sense that I was being punished for disobedience—I literally didn't have any time to be disobedient, and I also didn't want to believe in a God who would "teach me a lesson" in this way. As questions about God's character began to surface, the transactional model of God that had sustained me during my earlier life began to crumble.

With time, the heaviest darkness lifted and I was able to experience manifestations of God's light. Yet striking moments of confusion continued for the remainder of my mission and after. Despite my sincere commitment to obedience, I sometimes felt emptiness and doubt as I prayed. I felt ashamed of this and kept these experiences to myself; it wasn't where I thought I would be spiritually at that stage of my life. I was obedient. I kept my covenants, I studied, I prayed, I served, I attended the temple, and I loved freely. Why did I feel so much uncertainty and despair when I was doing everything that I could to follow Christ? The added complexities of post-mission life, including my career and relationships, added more weight to my load of emotional and spiritual distress. I felt persistent fear that I would never be enough, and my response of "doing more" did little to help me find refuge and peace. Two years after my mission, I felt prompted to break off an engagement with a young man after previously feeling God's encouragement to marry him. This dealt another harrowing blow to my understanding of and relationship with the dependable, transactional God I had imagined. My view of God and my role in his plan weren't holding up.

During this time, I also began diving deeper into questions about him that had pricked my heart as a youth, especially surrounding how God felt about women. I asked these questions because I yearned to know how he felt about me—just me—a woman without a husband or children. From an early age, I observed the differences in how the church treated men and women. I think I could ignore the dissonance the differences caused because I had many opportunities that felt equal, or nearly equal, to those that my male counterparts had: I held important roles in ward and stake leadership as a youth, I served a mission, and I was even called to be an "asistenta"—a female assistant to the mission president for a stint. God was using me and my talents in meaningful ways to bless his children, and I felt that my voice and contributions were equal to the boys and men surrounding me. Then something changed.

Perhaps it was the effect of nearing a temple marriage and imagining myself in the role of wife and mother. In any case, the differences between women and men in the church began to pain me. I felt uneasy as I attended the temple. I fumed inside as I listened to rogue counsel given to wives and mothers over the pulpit; and I felt disoriented, even numb, as I discovered details about the church's polygamous past and present. I wondered if I was as important as men in God's plan. Would a man forever have authority over me? Even worse, would I be one of many women bound to one man eternally, unable to experience true reciprocated belonging and equality? I couldn't imagine a loving God who would command his daughters—his precious daughters—to live polygamously. It felt sad and scary to imagine that God might not care about my feminine fears and anxieties. I searched and searched for a more comprehensive understanding of God's character and how he felt about me.

In my sorrow and frustration, I promised him that I would stay near him and keep trying. I knew that I needed to be fed spiritually—I needed light and mercy and divine power to guide me. I also knew that focusing exclusively on the frustrations of my questions would not give me the nourishment I needed to feel connected to my true self and to heaven. I didn't need to have the answers to all of my questions before I could connect with heaven. Yet as I struggled, I began to realize that trying to stay near to God as I had thus far—motivated by a to-do list and the promise of a reward when I did something right (a transaction)—wasn't helping me feel closer to him.

A wise client once taught me that striving and desire are good, if built upon a foundation of acceptance and love, but can be counterproductive when built upon a foundation of fear, self-rejection, and shame. With time, I began to wake up to the emotional realities that most often motivated me, and I saw how much guilt drove—and spoiled—each potentially helpful thing I did. Ironically, my desire to do so many good things (and to do them perfectly) was actually taking me further from God. With these realizations, I felt that God was giving me permission to slow down and to be a little easier on myself.

As I practiced slowing down and extending myself grace, I began to notice how different it felt to have effort produced by love instead of by the fear of disappointing God. I experienced a shift—from thinking that God would love and bless me once I had proven myself to him through my own perfection, to knowing that he already loved and blessed me in all of my imperfection. I came to see that the pain of my experiences wasn't a manifestation of his displeasure towards me, but was actually the result of the realities of mortality that helped me carve out space in my heart for him. I used to see instances of darkness and doubt as interrupting my faith journey. I see now that they propelled it, deepened it, and helped it be more personal and relevant.

In the process of untangling my scrupulosity from God's character and relationship with me, I let go of a lot of what I had believed—and feared—about him before. This process was and continues to be deeply personal and difficult to describe. But in short, I've come to believe that God is a lot more like a hen than a wielder of deadly weapons—He's much more kind, gentle, and merciful than I had previously assumed. Coming to believe that God is a divine pair—a Heavenly Father and Mother—has been central to this transformation; integrating the feminine divine into my personal theology has brought balance to my view of God. I can more easily believe that I am not just acceptable but adored and totally loved. I can imagine how she feels about me as I hold my own daughter, put band-aids on her knees, and encourage her to keep practicing.

As I grew to better understand the character of my heavenly parents, as well as the purpose of being mortal, I began to realize that the guilt and fear that I felt so frequently were not what they wanted me to feel. They were not godly feelings deriving from some "super morality." They were pathological. This was revolutionary for me. I felt free, free to follow what was virtuous and lovely, and to use my agency in a way I hadn't before. My heavenly parents wanted me to use it! There was no way for me to become like them without using it and falling short sometimes. They provided a savior for me as I became wounded along the way. Their enveloping love provided a secure base that gave me the courage to explore my world and my questions even further. Tethered to their love and my covenants, I felt confident that my exploration would help me to become like them.

Thankfully, as I dove into searching for answers to my questions, my life overflowed with nurturing spaces to explore them. As I eased up on my self-judgment, I found a community with devout question-askers. My professors and mentors wept with me. My ecclesiastical leaders lovingly modeled that it was okay to not have all the answers. My friends didn't judge me. My family listened with compassion. My understanding boyfriend—who became my husband—was open to and respectful of my thoughts and feelings. There are many who haven't understood my questions and yearnings, and that's okay. As my mom says, "the church needs all kinds."

For many years I longed to find the answers to my questions in a book—in an archive, an essay, a lecture. I wanted the fiery pain in my heart to be quenched by some amazing insight or historical finding—something deeply wise that would satisfy my questions and ease my pain. And while I've found many amazing insights as I've studied, I've felt that the only thing that can go deep enough to reach the pain in my heart is God's unending compassion and love. I remain planted in the restored gospel of Jesus Christ not because I have complete certainty or because I've received all the answers that I've yearned for, but because I have experienced light and love here. Although it may at times go dim, I believe that that light will grow brighter until the perfect day (see Doctrine and Covenants 50:24). Like Moses, I affirm that "I will not cease to call upon God, [for] I have other things to inquire of him: for his glory has been upon me."[2]

My heart has made more room for Jesus. It feels good to have him there. And from this calming place of grace, I find

I can be clearer with myself about my faith and why I remain attached to the Church of Jesus Christ of Latter-day Saints. Here are a dozen reasons why:

> I stay because I believe in the plan of salvation, and in heavenly parents who want to give everything they have to their children.

> I stay because the Book of Mormon has taught me about Jesus and has spoken to my soul.

> I stay because I believe that I am good, inherently good, and not a result of a mistake or of an original sin.

> I stay because I've been nurtured in my questions.

> I stay because there is space in the body of Christ for all of God's children, and together I believe we can receive an ongoing restoration and build an expanding Zion.

> I stay because in the gospel I find balance, tensions of equal and opposing forces. I can feel at peace while not agreeing with every interpretation I encounter as our lives as a people unfold.

> I stay because of the faith of my foremothers and forefathers, by which I have been nourished.

> I stay because of the peace I have felt in the temple, in addition to the wrestle that the temple has been

for me. There is beauty, security, and relief in the covenants I have made.

I stay because following Christ and contributing to a community like the Church makes my life better; in the restored gospel of Jesus Christ I find light.

I stay because I like the feeling of mystery, of being reminded that I don't know everything and I don't need to.

I stay because I love how faith feels, and "I will declare what he hath done for my soul."[3]

I stay because of the promise of redemption. I need a Savior. I hunger for the growth and transformation he has promised—and I can't do it alone.

I'm lying now under a tree gazing at the golden sky. My hands are behind my head, my ankles crossed, and my cup is running over. I'm not there yet; I still have scrupulous thoughts and occasional panic attacks. Sometimes I squirm and fume and wonder. But I'm also filled with the love of my heavenly parents and a savior. They comfort me and I feel safe in their care. I now understand that the process of growing into whomever I need to be will necessarily involve a lot more mistakes and imperfections than I used to imagine. They know that I cannot be perfect in this world and it's guaranteed that I will need repentance many, many times. ⚘ This is not a failure; it is organic spiritual growth within God's tender embrace.

⚘ This idea was eloquently taught to me by a dear teenage client who has also struggled with scrupulosity and anxiety.

My Belief

RICHARD L. BUSHMAN

Reprinted from the 1986 collection,
A Thoughtful Faith: Essays on Belief by Mormon Scholars.

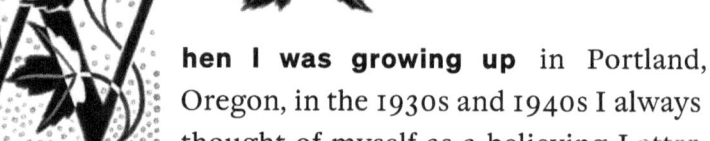

hen I was growing up in Portland, Oregon, in the 1930s and 1940s I always thought of myself as a believing Latter-day Saint. My parents were believers; even when they were not attending church regularly, they still believed. All of my relatives were Latter-day Saints, and so far as I could tell they accepted the gospel as a given of life, like food and drink. In Sunday School I tried to be good. I answered the teachers' questions and gave talks that brought compliments from the congregation. From the outside my behavior probably looked like the conventional compliance of a good boy. But it went deeper than mere appearance. I prayed faithfully every night, and whenever there was a crisis I immediately thought of God. I relied on my religion to redeem me. I often felt silly or weak, and it was through praying and religious meditation that I mustered my forces to keep on trying. In high school I was a thoroughgoing wallflower, at least as I remember it now, with no close friends. At lunchtime I often ate all by myself because no one noticed me, and I had no idea how to insinuate myself into a circle of people. At the end of my junior year, a Mormon friend in the class above me said it was my obligation, for the honor of the Church, to run for student body president. One thing I had learned in Church was to speak, and a good speech could win an election. I prayed that for the sake of the Church, God would help me get my speech together, and was elected. That made redemption very real.

Partly because of the responsibilities student government gave me I was admitted to Harvard, and left my family and Portland for Cambridge in the fall of 1949. I loved everything about Harvard—the people, the studies, the atmosphere. I was more myself there than I had ever been in my whole life.

Harvard helped redeem me too, but it also eroded my faith in God. I went to Church regularly and made good friends with Latter-day Saint graduate students, a faculty member or two, and the small circle of Mormon undergraduates. The undergraduates met Sunday afternoons to discuss the scriptures. We debated everything about religion, but we were all believers. I do not know why it was that by the end of my sophomore year my faith had drained away. Logical positivism was at high tide in those days, trying to persuade us that sensory evidence was the only trustworthy foundation for belief. At the end of my freshman year I wrote a paper comparing Freud and Nietzsche and confronted the assertion that Christian morality was the ideology of servile personalities who feared to express their own deepest urges. Until then I had prided myself on being a servant of God; was I also servile? These ideas, and perhaps the constant strain of being on the defensive for believing at all, must have eaten away at my belief. The issues in my mind never had anything to do with Latter-day Saint doctrine specifically. I was not bothered by the arguments against the institutional Church which so trouble people today, or by the problems of Mormon history, another current sore spot. I was not debating Mormonism versus some other religion; the only question for me was God. Did He exist in any form or not? I was not worried about evil in the world, as some agnostics are. I suppose Mormon theology had made the existence of evil perfectly plausible. I simply wondered if there was any reason to believe. Was all of religion a fantasy? Were we all fooling ourselves?

These doubts came on strongest in the spring of my sophomore year. During the preceding Christmas holiday I had been interviewed for a mission and received a call to New England, to serve under the mission president who attended the same Sacrament meeting as the students in Cambridge.

Did I have enough faith to go on a mission? I debated the question through the spring, wondering if I were a hypocrite and if fear of displeasing my parents was all that carried me along. And yet I never really considered not going. As I look back, I think that my agnosticism was perhaps a little bit of a pose, a touch of stylish undergraduate angst. It was true enough that my bosom did not burn with faith; on the other hand, I was quite willing to pledge two years to a mission. So I went.

The mission president was J. Howard Maughan, an agricultural professor from Utah State and a former stake president. In our opening interview in the mission home in Cambridge, he asked if I had a testimony of the gospel. I said I did not. He was not at all rattled. He asked if I would read a book, and said that if I found a better explanation for it than the book itself gave, he wanted me to report it to him. He handed me the Book of Mormon. The next day I left North Station in Boston for Halifax, Nova Scotia. For the next three months as I tried to learn the lessons and the usual missionary discipline, I wrestled with the book and wrote long entries in my journal. I thought a lot about the three witnesses: were they liars, had they been hypnotized, were they pressured? I believe it was at that time I read Hugh Nibley's *Lehi in the Desert*. I also read the Book of Mormon and prayed, sometimes in agnostic form: "if you are God . . . " After three months the mission president came up to Nova Scotia for a conference, and when it was my turn to speak I said with conviction that I knew the Book of Mormon was right. The reasons for belief that I had concocted were not what made the difference—though Nibley made a great impression; it was more the simple feeling that the book was right.

The mission left me with another impression. At Harvard in those days we talked a lot about the masses, envisioning a sea of workers' faces marching into a factory. In Halifax we missionaries met the masses every day as we tracted, and they did not exist. Instead there were a great number of individual persons, quite idiosyncratic, perverse, and interesting. They were no more a mass than the Harvard faculty or the United States Congress.

That realization planted a seed of doubt about formal conceptions. Did they conform to the reality of actual experience? After the mission, I never again felt that the issues debated in the academy were necessarily the issues of real life. This skepticism grew, especially after I entered graduate school in history and learned how formulations of the past had continually altered, as each generation of historians overturned the conceptions of its predecessors and made new ones for itself. Rational discourse came more and more to seem like a kind of play, always a little capricious and unreal, and in the end, compared to the experience of life itself, not serious. To confuse intellectual constructions with reality, or to govern one's life by philosophy or an abstract system, came to seem more and more foolhardy. My attitude as it developed was not precisely anti-intellectual. Ideas did not strike me as dangerous; they were too weak to be dangerous. I was depreciating intellectual activity rather than decrying it. But whatever the proper label for this attitude, it put distance between me and the intellectuals whom I so admired and whom, as it later turned out, I would aspire to emulate.

Paradoxically, in my own intellectual endeavors I have benefited from this skepticism engendered in the mission field, for it has led me to trust my own perceptions and experience over the convictions of my fellow historians, considered individually or *en masse*. I have always thought it possible that virtually anything taught and believed in the academy could be wrong. Repudiation of God by every intellectual in creation did not mean He was nonexistent. By the same token, any of the certainties of historical interpretation could be perfect errors. However fallible I might be myself, however much I was subject to influences and illusions, I had to trust my own perceptions above everything else.

After I returned from the mission field I no longer had doubts, but I did have questions. They were not specific questions about the meaning or validity of specific doctrines, wholesome questions that enlarge understanding. They were the questions of some unknown interlocutor who asked me to justify my faith. "Why do you believe?" the masked stranger asked. This was the old question of my sophomore year, asked now, however, of one who did believe, who had faith, and was being called upon to justify it. I suppose there was nothing complicated about the questioning. At Harvard I studied in the midst of people who made a business of defending their convictions. It was an unwritten rule that you must explain why you took a position or supported a proposition. "Why do you believe in God?" was a question that the trees in Harvard Yard whispered in one's ears without prompting from any skeptical inquisitors. In fact, when I returned to Harvard in 1953 the religious atmosphere was much more favorable to believers. The president, Nathan Pusey, was himself a believing person, and he had hired Paul Tillich as a University Professor and seen to the rejuvenation of the Divinity School. Even the agnostics listened respectfully to Tillich, and undergraduates talked more freely of their religious convictions. In my senior year I headed a committee sponsored by the student council on "Religion at Harvard," and our poll of undergraduates turned up a majority who said they had a religious orientation toward life. Even so, the mood did not quiet my faceless questioner. I still wanted to justify my convictions.

How those questionings came to an end is beyond my powers of explanation. For an undergraduate reader today, still fired by fierce doubts and desperate need to know for sure, one word may seem to explain all—complacency. But I myself do not feel that way. My questions have not simply grown dim over the years, nor have I answered them; instead I have come to understand questions and answers differently. Although I cannot say what truly made the difference, a series of specific experiences, small insights, revelations, new ideas, all addressing the same issue and coming over a period of thirty years, have caused me to change my views. I now have a new sense of what constitutes belief.

For a long time, twenty-five years or more, I kept trying to answer the questioner. I received little help from religious philosophers. The traditional proofs for God never made an impression on me. I did not find flaws in them; they simply seemed irrelevant. My empirical temperament and suspicion of grand systems worked against any enthusiasm for arguments about a prime mover. I never studied those arguments or made the slightest effort to make them my own. My chief line of reasoning was based on the Book of Mormon. It was concrete and real and seemed like a foundation for belief, not merely belief in Joseph Smith but in Christ and God. Joseph Smith and Mormonism, as I said before, were never the issues; it was primarily God. Although it was a lengthy chain from the historicity of the Book of Mormon, to Joseph's revelations, to the existence of God, it was a chain that held for me. I felt satisfied that if that book were true, my position was sound. Without it, I do not know where I would be. I have imagined I could be a religious agnostic were it not for the Book of Mormon. That is why Hugh Nibley's writings played a large part in my thinking. Although I recognized the eccentricities of his style and was never completely confident of his scholarship, there seemed to me to be enough there to make a case. First Nephi could not be dismissed as fraudulent; and, so far as I know, no one has refuted the argument he made in *Lehi in the Desert*. Nibley offered just the kind of evidence I was looking for in my pursuit of answers: evidence that was specific, empirical, historical.

Nibley's style was important enough that I made one attempt myself to prove the Book of Mormon in the Nibleyesque manner, and this effort came about in such a way as to confirm my belief. When I was asked to give some talks in Utah during the Bicentennial of the American Revolution, I decided to examine the political principles embodied in the Book of Mormon and make some applications to our nation's Revolution and Constitution. I thought this would be simple enough because of the switch from a monarchy to a republic during the reign of Mosiah. I was sure that somewhere in Mosiah's statements I would find ideas relevant to the modern world. With that in mind, I accepted the invitation to talk, but I did not get down to work until a few months before I was to appear. To my dismay, I could not find what I was looking for. Everything seemed just off the point, confused and baffling. I could not find the directions for a sound republic that I had expected. Gradually it dawned on me that the very absence of republican statements might in itself be interesting. Long ago I learned that it is better to flow with the evidence rather than to compel compliance with one's preformed ideas. So instead, I asked: What does the Book of Mormon say about politics? To my surprise I discovered it was quite an unrepublican book. Not only was Nephi a king, and monarchy presented as the ideal government in an ideal world, but the supposedly republican government instituted under Mosiah did not function that way at all. There was no elected legislature, and the chief judges usually inherited their office rather than being chosen to it. Eventually I came to see that here was my chance to emulate Nibley. If Joseph Smith was suffused with republican ideas, as I was confident he was, then the absence of such sentiments in Nephite society was peculiar, another evidence that he did not write the Book of Mormon. Eventually all of this came together in an article, "The Book of Mormon and the American Revolution," published in BYU *Studies* in 1976.

While circumstances and my predilection to justify belief influenced me up to that point and beyond, my commitment to this kind of endeavor gradually weakened. Perhaps most influential was a gradual merger of personality and belief. By 1976 I had been a branch president and bishop, and was then president of the Boston Stake. Those offices required me to give blessings in the name of God and to seek solutions to difficult problems nearly every day. I usually felt entirely inadequate to the demands placed upon me and could not function at all without some measure of inspiration. What I did, the way I acted, my inner thoughts, were all intermingled with this effort to speak and act righteously for God. I could no longer entertain the possibility that God did not exist because I felt His power working through me. Sometimes I toyed with the notion that there could be other ways of describing what happened when I felt inspired, but the only language that actually worked, the only ideas that brought inspiration and did justice to the experience when it came, were the words in the scripture. Only when I thought of God as a person interested in me and asked for help as a member of Christ's kingdom did idea and reality fit properly. Only that language properly honored the experiences I had day after day in my callings.

More than anything else, church work probably quieted my old questions; but there were certain moments when these cumulative experiences precipitated new ideas. Once in the early sixties, while I held a post-doctoral fellowship at Brown University and was visiting Cambridge, I happened into a young adult discussion led by Terry Warner (I believe). He had the group read the Grand Inquisitor passage in *The Brothers Karamazov*. The sentences that stuck with me that time through were the ones having to do with looking for reasons to believe that would convince the whole world and compel everyone to believe. That was the wish of the Inquisitor, a wish implicitly repudiated by Christ. The obvious fact that there is no convincing everyone that a religious idea is true came home strongly at that moment. It is impossible and arrogant, and yet that was exactly what I was attempting. When I sought to justify my belief, I was looking for answers that would persuade all reasonable people. That was why I liked Nibley: because he put his readers over a barrel. I wanted something that no one could deny. In that moment in Cambridge, I realized the futility of the quest.

I was moved still further in this direction by a lecture which Neal Maxwell invited me to give at Brigham Young University in 1974 as part of the Commissioner's Lecture Series. I cannot for the life of me recall why I turned to the topic of "Joseph Smith and Skepticism," but that was the subject. In that lecture I sketched in the massive effort to demonstrate reasonably the authenticity of the Christian revelation. The effort began in the early eighteenth century, when Deism first took hold in earnest, and continued through the nineteenth century. The Christian rationalists assembled all the evidence they could muster to prove that biblical miracles, such as the parting of the Red Sea, were authentic and therefore evidence of God's endorsement of Israel. In the course of the nineteenth century, as agnosticism waxed strong among intellectuals, the volumes on Christian evidences proliferated. I can still remember sitting on the floor in the basement of the Harvard Divinity School library, flipping through these books, each one almost exactly like the others. I realized then that the tradition of seeking proof was very strong in the nineteenth century, and that Mormons had been influenced by it. More than any other Latter-day Saint, B. H. Roberts, a man troubled by questions as I had been, borrowed these methods. His *New Witness for God* was a replica of the books in the Harvard Divinity School basement, except with Mormon examples and conclusions. Hugh Nibley dropped the nineteenth-century format for works of Christian evidences, but his mode of reasoning was basically the same.

Awareness of the affinity of Nibley with these Protestant works did not dilute my own interest in evidences. The study of Book of Mormon republicanism, my own contribution to the genre, came along two years later. But the contradictions were taking shape in my mind and readied me, I suppose, for a personal paradigm shift. It occurred in the early 1980s at the University of Indiana. Stephen Stein of the religion department had some Lilly Endowment money to assemble scholars and religious leaders from various denominations to discuss their beliefs. With Jan Shipps' help he brought together a handful of Mormon historians, some historians of American religion, a local stake president and regional representative, and a seminary teacher. The topic was Joseph Smith. The historians among us made some opening comments about the Prophet, and then over a day and a half we discussed the issues that emerged. It was a revelatory assemblage from my point of view because it brought together in one room representatives of the various groups involved in my religious life—Church leaders, non-Mormon scholars, and Mormon scholars. Although all of these people had been represented in my mind symbolically before, they had never been together in person before my face, talking about Joseph Smith.

Their presence brought together notions that previously had been floating about separately in my head. Sometime in the middle of the conversations it came to me in a flash that I did not want to prove the authenticity of Joseph Smith's calling to anyone. I did not want to wrestle Stephen Stein to the mat and make him cry "uncle." It was a false position, at least for me, and one that I doubted would have any long-range good results. I recognized then that the pursuit of Christian evidences was not a Mormon tradition; it was a borrowing from Protestantism—and not at a moment when Protestantism was at one of its high points. At any rate, it was not my tradition and I did not want to participate in it. There was no proving religion to anyone; belief came by other means, by hearing testimonies or by individual pursuit or by the grace of God, but not by hammering.

By the time of the conference I had completed the manuscript of *Joseph Smith and the Beginnings of Mormonism*. The Book of Mormon chapter in that book hammered at readers. My urge was to show that the common secular explanations of the Book of Mormon were in error and to imply, if not to insist, that only a divine explanation would do. In the revision, I tried to moderate the tone without complete success. I did not wish to dissipate the basic argument, which is that the counter-explanations did not adequately explain the complexity of the book, but I sincerely did not want to push readers into a corner and force them to come out fighting. The desire to compel belief, the wish of the Grand Inquisitor, was exactly what I had abandoned.

At the present moment, the question of why I believe no longer has meaning for me. I do not ask it of myself or attempt to give my reasons to others. The fact is that I do believe. That is a given of my nature, and whatever reasons I might give would be insufficient and inaccurate. More relevant to my current condition is a related question: how do others come to believe? I would like to know if there is anything I can do that will draw people to faith in Christ and in the priesthood. My answer to this question is, of course, related to my personal experiences. I no longer think that people can be compelled to believe by any form of reasoning, whether from the scripture or from historical evidence. They will believe if it is in their natures to believe. All I can do is to attempt to bring forward the believing nature, smothered as it is in most people by the other natures that culture forms in us. The first responsibility is to tell the story, to say very simply what happened, so that knowledge of those events can do its work. But that is the easy part, the part that could be done by books or television. The hard part is to create an atmosphere where the spiritual nature, the deep-down goodness in the person, can react to the story honestly and directly. Some people can create that atmosphere quite easily by the very strength of their own spiritual personalities. It is hard for me. There are too many other natures in me: the vain aspirer formed in childhood, the intellectual fostered at Harvard, the would-be dominant male created by who knows what. But I do believe that when I am none of these, and instead am a humble follower of Christ who without pretense tells the story to a friend whom I love and respect, then they will believe if they want to, and conversion is possible. Questions may be answered and reasons given, but these are peripheral and essentially irrelevant. What is essential is for a person to listen carefully and openly in an attitude of trust. If belief is to be formed in the human mind, it will, I think, be formed that way.

Absence, History, and the Burning Bush

J. SPENCER FLUHMAN

t **eight years old** I looked for angels in vain. I might have seen one, but my mother's response hardly hid her skepticism. Even back then I realized that I had probably been looking too hard. Truth is, I was bitterly disappointed and worried that my failure to glimpse beyond the veil revealed something lacking in me.

My angel search took place during the 9:00 a.m. session of the Jordan River Temple dedication on November 16, 1981. It was a big deal that I was there and I knew it. I had turned eight less than a month before, the minimum age for attendance, and realized that compared to my younger sister and most of my friends, I was lucky to be so old. It is no overstatement to say that my anticipation for the event had been building for years.

One of my earliest memories came three and a half years earlier. On April 16, 1978, not yet five years old, I had been brought to a Bountiful, Utah, pulpit by our Latter-day Saint stake president and presented with a dollar. He asked what I would buy with it and I reportedly responded, "eggs." He asked for the dollar back and announced that I had just made the stake's first donation to the construction of the Jordan River Temple. I vaguely remember the loss of the dollar but, more, my pride at being the first to help build the sacred place. Three years later, I attended the temple's cornerstone ceremony in late summer. Two months after that I toured the new temple at the open house preceding its dedication on my eighth birthday.

In the weeks and months before the dedication itself, my family had talked of temples and dedications and I was ushered into a sacred narrative stretching back from me to the 1830s Ohio Saints. I could not forget the angels said to have attended the temple dedication there. And I was determined to see one. The first cautions came from Mom. *Appearances of angels are rare. Something so sacred doesn't happen every day.* Even with the stakes thus raised, I readied myself for visions, undeterred. When I wondered afterwards if the guy who seemed momentarily out of place at the beginning of the service had been an angel, Mom lovingly professed agnosticism. (The stories, the cautions, and the tender skepticism all came from Mom. I didn't remember my father having been at the dedicatory session at all until I checked his journal. Always, scripture and doctrine came from Dad, narrative and charismata from Mom.)

In a way, this was my own childhood version of the "Great Disappointment," the shock that forerunners to the early Adventists experienced when Jesus did not return as predicted in 1844. Still, I pushed the letdown from my mind and instead remembered the experience as a treasured time with Mom that provided a profound sense of belonging—a placeholder in the space where angels might have been. I eventually brushed off later absences, too. Where was God when this terrible thing happened or when that critical question remained unanswered? If God knows sparrows and numbers hairs, where was he during holocausts or genocides? Like my fruitless childhood angel quest, I suspected for many years that the absences in experience or gaps in explanation were my fault. For a few years in adolescence, I wondered if they pointed to a more shattering lacuna—perhaps there were neither angels nor a God to encounter at all. Even after finding faith again in my late teens, the questions remained, in modified forms, but eventually I acclimated to the apparent gaps.

In other words, that childhood experience has played out time and again throughout a Latter-day Saint lifetime. God and angels have remained stubbornly absent, especially at times when I think I need them most, but skepticism, adulthood, and modernity have not fully stamped out my primal Latter-day Saint yearnings, either. I still long to keep company with angels and touch the face of God. I'm told that, as a young child, I got a neighbor friend to help me reenact the scene of Moses before God's fiery presence from Cecil B. DeMille's film, *The Ten Commandments*. Mom found us kneeling in the yard, shoeless, and I explained we were on holy ground. I think I will always crave the burning bush. More than four decades later, I find myself still magically drawn beyond the immanent, secular framing of reality even as I have acclimated to its rhythms, priorities, and habits of mind.

My story is embedded in a much more extended set of stories. The entire history of modern Christianity can be seen to pivot on the axis between notions and experiences of divine presence and absence, between the "religious" and the (secular) "modern." I recognize that the terms "modern" and "religious" were themselves constituted in a single, complicated historical process, and acknowledge that they combine to form the water I swim in. Many scholars maintain that the "secular" and the "religious" are more like sides of the same coin than definitional opposites. From this perspective, we're all swimming together, culturally, at least in the modern West. But understanding the complicated processes that made our modern world does not spare me from their effects in my own life or in my own thinking. So, even as "modernity" insists that the gods survive primarily as "symbols, signs, metaphors, functions, and abstractions," they have refused to remain so safely contained. The founding narrative of the Church of Jesus Christ of Latter-day Saints seems to mightily strain against that cultural stream in its insistence on rather spectacular divine interruptions into the ordinary. That fact excited my earliest imagination and fueled my yearning for the holy, and it does so still. That said, I was left with a sobering problem: those dramatic divine obtrusions seemed to elude me. It turns out that both my religion's vibrant rejection of the world's "disenchantment" and my thoughtful distance from its extraordinary founding convulsions are both in their own ways emblematic of the American sojourn over the past century.[1]

That being said, I have always belonged among the Latter-day Saints. Life in a ward, time as a missionary, and my undergraduate years at Brigham Young University provided the warm, embodied, and communal contexts for my earliest religious experiences, comparatively undramatic though they were. Those environments cultivated a keen sense of at least proximity to the holy, which has long felt mostly good enough in lieu of direct heavenly presence.

Yet while I experienced foundational, formative spiritual sparks in those nurturing spaces, none of them made much sense of divine absence for me. Why didn't divine realms make themselves more obvious to us? Nor did these spiritual beginnings meaningfully address the vast challenges we encounter in life, including paradox, complexity, irony, failure, and change. My youthful religious sensibilities primarily had been occupied with certainty, absolutes, and "eternalities." Back then, religion was the agent that smoothed rough edges and made stories simple, linear, and triumphant. But those reassuring traits also made religion brittle for a stretch during those teenage years, when it seemed ill-equipped to handle the big existential questions (*Whence evil? What is universal truth? What is enduring amid the changes of history?*). As a missionary, though, those same sensibilities proved to be powerful glue for diverse people striving together in fledgling wards and deep motivation in the face of rejection or drudgery. Emerging from that missionary experience, I had grown accustomed to pretending that the absences or complexities did not exist or did not matter.

This changed, permanently, when in 1998 I arrived at the University of Wisconsin to begin a doctoral program in American history. As the first rigors of graduate study seemed to threaten the fraught détente of compartmentalization I had brokered between the intellectual and religious worlds swirling within me, it was Richard Bushman who helped make the absences and paradoxes count. By that, I mean that he gently refused to ignore them, and asked me and an eager band of young researchers to live more wholly, more candidly, and more simultaneously in the worlds of mind and faith. I had been hired along with seven other Latter-day Saint graduate students to work in an intensive summer seminar. We would work on our own all morning and then meet in a group seminar with Professor Bushman each afternoon. Those three weeks were transformative. Bushman's approach to the vexing questions was a masterstroke. He refused to steer around problems. He put us to work, together. He extended charity for all involved, living and dead.

I was inspired by Bushman's method and tone. His brand of truth-telling, courageous and pastoral in turns, has helped spawn a "golden age" for Latter-day Saint intellectual life in the years since he penned the 1986 essay reprinted in this volume.[2] His patterns of mind and spirit have been expertly described by others of his academic protégés, and he has sometimes described his own way through the world. Most insightfully, a non-Latter-day Saint mentee described Bushman's manner as a coherent "hermeneutic of generosity": unless faced with intractable evidence to the contrary, he habitually gives everyone the benefit of the doubt.[3] His mentoring, according to another grateful apprentice, amounts to a refined practice of deep listening.[4] In his own words, the "strain" of living faith in a secular public world that increasingly seems alien to it is "a stimulus and a prod." It is the seedbed of creativity itself.[5] These ways of being and working have surely formed me and my generation of Latter-day Saint scholars, teaching us how to tether deep faith to an informed intellect.

In this mode, academic history became less of a threat. Instead it became essential to the way I navigated the absences, contradictions, and paradoxes of human life. It also became a way I live faith. History became a means to see people (all of them) and hear people (even the ones who have passed on and cannot speak to us), and a model for doing so in the present. It became a way I attempt to offer generosity and compassion to friends and strangers alike. It is a way I stretch my mind to lead souls to salvation (mine, most often), as Joseph Smith taught:

> Thy mind O Man, if thou wilt lead a soul unto salvation must stretch as high as the utmost heavens, and search into and contemplate the lowest considerations of the darkest abyss.[6]

History invariably forces me into the dark human abysses. The story of life on this planet is only punctuated with success, harmony, and joy. The broader strokes are frighteningly consistent in their violence and suffering. Those themes are inescapable, but their net effect on this historian has been to a large extent theological. That is, I have felt inexorably drawn to questions of meaning and divine intention. *What kind of God is implicated in such stories as these? And what does redemption look like in such a world? What is love, here?* I have thus experienced modernity less as an acid on my discipleship than as a complementary pole—or even a prod—to it. The space between my "modern" and "religious" sides, now hardly a chasm at all, forms the necessary void in which a thousand sparks of faith can flash.

I am not so naïve as to think that academic work always has this effect. I cannot fully explain why it has worked this way in me. On the one hand, history's intellectual work has tamed and contained the scandals of my tradition that have vexed so many. Plural wives? Seer stones? Theocracies? Race bans? There is nothing new under the sun. I quit "clutching my pearls" less than two years into my graduate-school huddle in the Wisconsin Historical Society's library stacks. Embarrassment at historical facts begins to give way as one learns where all the bodies are buried. And then, as one realizes what a staggering number of bodies there are, in any history, a certain calm sets in. A few historical anomalies can set off alarms, but as they proliferated in my mind through study, I began to recognize the play of human nature common to us all, in all societies. Our Latter-day Saint particularities look different at a wide angle. I began to savor the humanness implicated in all the striving, complexity, and even failure.

But history does other work, too. Forced as a historian into lives that remain ghosts always beyond my full perception, I'm nevertheless repeatedly faced with the miracle of the human person, not to mention the evident (to me) fact of the human soul. Even as contexts, layered stories, and shifting frameworks have readied me for the muddle of human, or American, or Latter-day Saint stories, my moral sensibilities have sharpened apace. I have found it impossible not to care about race or class or gender or sexuality or violence or addiction or poverty or environmental matters or any number of human conundrums. What did that in me? Was it intellectual life or those primal Latter-day Saint yearnings for justice, love, meaning, and divine encounter?

Far from being in corrosive tension, the academic study of religion and my own Christian discipleship have conspicuously converged. And I have found fellow-travelers across the spectrum of faith. Ham-fisted approaches to religion persist in the academy, but the best work expresses a kind of humility before the diversity, power, and mystery of religious experience. Not every scholar thinks they're exposing a bumbling charlatan behind a curtain. My favorite writers on religious history—Anthea Butler, Jon Butler, Kathryn Lofton, Laurie Maffly-Kipp, Mark Noll, Robert Orsi, Leigh Schmidt, Grant Wacker—each in their own way convey a kind of wonder before what I take to be the profundity of religious life. My Latter-day Saint life never feels diminished as I wrestle with the stories they tell. Rather, it seems to take on added integrity and enhanced vibrancy as I let their ideas splash over my practice of faith. I find myself reading as a scholar and as a Latter-day Saint, almost simultaneously. I can't reliably disentangle the two modes anymore; both are routinely enriched through engagement with my academic field's best work.

We used to use the term "bracketing" to describe the impulse towards this kind of openness, respect, and avoidance of value judgment. A scholar could "bracket" out questions about a particular tradition's truth claims in order to secure a "neutral," respectful space to comprehend and explain it. The bracketing ideal has unsurprisingly generated debate. In graduate school, for instance, some bracketing felt like condescension to me, as if it was merely the scholarly habit of trying not to tell Latter-day Saints or Pentecostals or Roman Catholics that our religious lives are ridiculous. But the folks listed above don't really "bracket." They apply the scholarly tools at hand with skill but seem quite clearheaded about what those tools can and cannot wring from the archives' documents. At mid-career, I have found a satisfying and sustaining community among scholars of various stripes who do not condescend to their religious subjects. Truth is, I have found belonging in academic life, just as I have in religious life. I'm not the first Latter-day Saint to experience this kind of scholarly belonging, and I won't be the last, but I did not expect it. I am certainly a better Saint for it.

These days, my scholarly and disciple sides converge in a kind of parallel surrender. My submission to the mystery of God's work in the world converges with that scholarly capitulation, enacted by our best practitioners, before that which our tools cannot explain. The two surrenders feel similar to me and meet in humility. I have found convergence, too, in what I regard as a collective set of shared motivations among some of my academic colleagues. One example is emblematic of this shared pursuit. Through an extended correspondence, I have become good enough friends with a colleague—one who does not practice any religion—to be deeply inspired, in the religious sense, by her scholarly motivations and production. More than a decade ago, I gently suggested that we shared more than we had acknowledged. I wrote in an email, "for all your theory, brilliance, and achievement, you are possessed by a rather fierce love. . . . in your own way, you soothe, you scold, you redeem. Not *quite* religious, but . . . " This was extraordinarily personal; I immediately regretted sending it. Luckily, she declined to take offense. She responded by needling me

---

Accordingly, I find Tom Simpson's account of the first generation of LDS scholars' discoveries of "belonging" in American universities familiar and moving.[7]

with what she had learned from me about a Latter-day Saint bishop's life: "stop seeing me so clearly! it's scary. now i know, a little, what all your little 'ward-lets' must feel as you sit across the table and ask your church-appointed inquiries. he sees, he sees, he sees."[8] As scholars of religion, non-religious and Latter-day Saint respectively, we were drawn together in a mostly-unspoken search for meaning, community, beauty, and truth . . . even as we continue to debate just about everything. And I have found that our collective academic yearning to understand the voiceless, forgotten, and tyrannized fully resonates with my disciple-side. I have not found that magic with all colleagues who do not share my religious commitments, but with a surprising number I feel rather at home in my faith. They find it odd, no doubt, that I speak about angels and seem to mean what I say, but they stopped clutching their pearls long ago, too. There is nothing new under the sun.

Complexity, nuance, and academic rigor are not a religion, though, so I have not ceased seeking the burning bush. I remain struck by a line I have heard quoted more than once from an Evangelical theologian-friend: "I do not give a fig for the simplicity that is prior to complexity; but I would give my right arm for the simplicity that lies *beyond* complexity."[9] The Church of Jesus Christ of Latter-day Saints has proven a congenial setting for that search, and then some. Heavenly angels still avoid me but earthly ones come with stunning regularity. If I haven't yet stood before visible divine fire, I've at least seen its reflected glow over the hill. I've felt its warmth, too, sometimes subtly but once in a while hot, holy. In this search, I could not do without the life of the mind. Sometimes, modernity checks my religious extravagances. Often, faith checks my modern ones. Typically, I am left dizzy in the spin between the two critiques, not sure what I want or need or think. I have become content to let scripture, or the temple liturgy, or the faith stories of fellow-travelers, or the volcanic religious experiences within me, remain wild, disorienting, and disruptive of the "knowing" that could possess a modern mind so given as mine to books, so eager to understand and categorize and contain. Robert Orsi, one of the more skilled narrators of the titanic shifts in the modern thought-world, wisely reminds us that divine "presence is a fearsome thing."[10] One wonders if angels avoid me or if I stand a half-step away, unwilling to abide their company. Either way, I can't quite stop looking for them.

Through a Glass Darkly

BEN SCHILATY

"For now we see through a glass, darkly; but then
face to face:
now I know in part; but then shall I know even as
also I am known."
(1 Corinthians 13:12)

t has not been easy to continually choose to move forward as an active member of The Church of Jesus Christ of Latter-day Saints. In many ways a path outside of the Church would seem logical given my life circumstances, which include being an openly gay, active, striving church member. And yet the few times I have considered stepping away, I have felt a divine pull to stay. My faith isn't about ease, logic, or reason—it's about fruits. My faith is grounded in the experiences that I have had. Pondering the scriptures and feeling my mind and heart expand. Attending the temple and walking out of those sacred buildings feeling spiritual strength and power. Praying for a miracle and feeling God's love. Seeing my life improve as I follow inspired prophetic counsel. Connecting with fellow saints who enrich my life. But the fruit that most grounds my faith comes from my experiences with the Atonement of Jesus Christ, experiences that have often been facilitated through the Church. The restored gospel has taught me how to access God's redeeming love, and I stay not only because I yearn for more of those experiences, but because I'm confident I still have so much to learn.

My belief in the teachings of Jesus Christ requires that I do some pretty tough things. Chief among those is forgiving those who reject me, misunderstand me, and cause me pain.

I have had lots of practice with this aspect of the gospel. As a gay man, I embody a paradox that is sometimes beyond people's ability to comprehend. Consequently, I have spent much of my adult life explaining my existence to individuals on all sides of the spiritual, political, and cultural spectrum. I often find myself asking, why am I always required to be the bigger person? Why is it my responsibility to demonstrate to those who reject me that I actually belong? Why do I have to respond to hostility with kindness?

In May 2021 I received a message from a woman named Jen. She explained that her husband Brent was planning their stake youth trek and they wondered if I'd be willing to be one of five speakers to address the youth. I don't love camping and the thought of using vacation days to spend a weekend in the woods with a bunch of strangers wasn't terribly appealing. I also thought that the stake would never approve having a gay man talk to the youth about being gay. However, a few weeks later Brent called to confirm the invitation. Two months later I was on a plane to California.

I was surprised that local leaders had approved my visit. I'm regularly asked to give firesides and a fair portion of them get canceled. If they don't get canceled, there is almost always some kind of hefty pushback. It is not uncommon for parents and leaders to complain, and sometimes General Authorities are called in an attempt to shut down such events. It doesn't matter that I was a BYU administrator. It doesn't matter that I have a current temple recommend. It doesn't matter that I am a high priest, serving faithfully in the church. It doesn't matter that I have a book published through Deseret Book on the topic of same-sex attraction. None of that matters because I am going to talk about my experiences as a gay man in the Church of Jesus Christ of Latter-day Saints. That's a reality that many church members do not feel comfortable talking about.

When I arrived in California I learned that while the stake presidency was excited to host me, some parents were upset. Several families said that they would no longer be sending their kids on the trek if I was going. One youth cried, saying she didn't want to go on a "gay trek." One adult expressed concerns that I would encourage the youth to be gay. They were afraid of me and how I would negatively impact the kids.

As part of their preparation, the stake president and other stake leaders spent hours listening to the concerns of worried parents. They encouraged skeptical members to get a copy of my book to familiarize themselves with my story and message. Because of all the hubbub about my coming, tons of people from the stake had read my book by the time I arrived, and many began to see me not as some caricature of a gay man but as a real person with strengths and weaknesses, continually evolving into something better. Essentially, they began to see me as I see myself. They got to know me through my own words. And that changed hearts. Almost all of the initially concerned families ended up sending their kids on the trek because the leaders had listened respectfully to their objections but also invited them to see my heart.

The morning we gathered at the staging area, I hadn't yet learned of the campaign to diffuse the tension surrounding my participation. I was wondering which of the people loading belongings into handcarts didn't want me there. I worried that I would have to spend the next three days working hard to win everyone over, but the leaders had already done that work for me, and people seemed genuinely happy that I was there. The sack lunch that Jen made me for that first day contained a note: "Thank you for being willing to come—even if we did end up being weirdos." One young woman walked up to me and said, "My parents had me read your book. I loved it. You're really cool. Wanna eat lunch with us?" Many of the youth started calling me Uncle Ben.

Throughout the three days of the trek I spent time walking with almost all the youth, getting to know them and what mattered to them. I went out of my way to spend time with the LGBTQ youth since I imagined they hadn't spent much time with an LGBTQ adult in the Church. I wanted them to know they were not alone. The first night I sat next to a stream and wrote the following in my journal: "C.S. Lewis said that we'll never look in the eyes of someone that God doesn't love. I got to meet so many people that God loves today."

On the second day we gathered in a mountain meadow and I spoke to the youth about personal revelation and the Atonement of Jesus Christ. I talked about the Jaredites and how they were led "into that quarter where there never had man been" (Ether 2:5). I testified that God will guide us as we walk paths no one has ever been on before. After my message I received so many handshakes, hugs, and sincere expressions of gratitude.

The Sunday after the trek I gave a fireside for the entire stake. Hundreds of people came to hear me. My efforts to learn people's names on trek had paid off, and I knew the names of at least 50 people there. As we sang the opening song and I looked out over the packed chapel, I started to get emotional. How was I so lucky? How did events unfold in such a way that I had been loved and embraced by these strangers who had so quickly become my family? I had experienced a slice of Zion in California.

After the fireside youth dragged their parents up to the front so they could introduce them to me. A mom handed me a pin that said, "Keep up the good work! You're doing great!" She said, "Please don't get discouraged. We needed you here this weekend." The truth is I had been discouraged. It's tough to know that my reality makes people feel uncomfortable. It's tough to know that some parents initially didn't want me around their kids. But that weekend I had felt seen, understood, and loved. When I got on a plane that evening I was looking forward to the day that I could come back to see these people I had come to love.

The apostle Paul taught that in our current state "we see through a glass, darkly" (1 Cor 13:12, KJV). The lens through which we view the world, ourselves, and others is opaque because we see with mortal eyes. The more widely used New International Version (NIV) translates Paul's imagery a little differently: "For now we see only a reflection in a mirror. . . ." Modern mirrors are made from glass that is coated in a thin layer of silver or aluminum. So when I look into a mirror, I am seeing through a glass and into a dark metal. And what do I see when I peer into this dark glass? I see myself. I am in the foreground and everything and everyone else is in the background. By definition a mirror is focused on me. But if I were to remove the dark layer of metal my focus could shift, and a window would open to a whole world, a new view of places and people and all kinds of beautiful things. As we begin to see in this way, we learn to see as our Heavenly Parents see and know us.

When I first learned that there were many members of the stake planning to keep their kids home because I would be on trek, I saw these people through a glass darkly. Seeing myself as the protagonist of this story, I didn't see any of them clearly. The words *homophobic* and *ignorant* swirled in my head as I considered these people who were afraid of me, my words, and my reality. And if not afraid, at least uncomfortable. I felt unseen by these Latter-day Saints who had never even met me, and in return I judged them and failed to see them. None of us saw clearly until we got to know one another. For the parents, taking that initial uncomfortable step into my life story was essential for them to really see me. In turn, I needed to give them space and time to grow without dismissing them out of hand. As Sister Sharon Eubank taught: "We may not yet be where we want to be, and we are not now where we will be. I believe the change we seek in ourselves and in the groups we belong to will come . . . by actively trying every day to understand one another. Why? Because we are building Zion—a people 'of one heart and one mind.'"[1]

Defined in this way, Zion is a work in progress. This construction zone has been a place where I have experienced acceptance and healing on the one hand, rejection and pain on the other. When I moved to Provo, Utah in 2017 I told my new bishop I was gay in our "get to know you" meeting. He responded with so much love and kindness that I was immediately grateful I had disclosed my orientation and looked to him for spiritual guidance. In a beautiful demonstration of humility he asked, "What do I need to know and understand so I can serve you better?" With that question, I immediately felt that he wanted to see me through a glass clearly. The foremost thought in his mind was how to minister to me. I knew I had landed in the right ward. As I walked to my car the Spirit told me I had found a place where I would belong.

Months later during an elders quorum lesson I mentioned my orientation as part of a broader remark. I had already come out to the ward in a talk and had been well received, and I didn't think this would cause any waves. After class a fellow quorum member told me rather forcefully that I shouldn't talk about my "perversions" at church. I was shocked. I was angry. I was hurt. I was seen through a glass darkly. I walked down the long hallway wondering if I could return next week. As I pushed open the doors to leave I felt a clear impression: "Forgive him, he doesn't know what he's doing." In the moment when I was ready to write off this fellow saint forever, the Holy Ghost helped me see him just a little more clearly. He wasn't coming from a place of hate or malice, just discomfort and a lack of experience. So I returned the next week, but for the next six months I didn't mention being gay at church because I feared further hurtful comments. This ward that had been so kind and welcoming had also left me wounded. I stayed silent until I felt a familiar prompting to be more open as I was teaching elders quorum, the same location where I had previously been called out for mentioning being gay. As I opened up once again I felt a blanket of spiritual warmth envelop me. I experienced God seeing me clearly. After class a few quorum members stayed to chat with me and express their gratitude for my vulnerability. This time no one called me a pervert. This time I felt seen.

My ward—this bit of Zion-in-the-making—was at once my spiritual home and a place of periodic rejection and pain. In his "glass darkly" passage Paul was looking forward to a future time when Zion will be fully healthy and completely kind: Jesus Christ sees us clearly and compassionately. He understands our motives, histories, and decisions. The *Guide to the Scriptures* on churchofjesuschrist.org explains that *compassion* means "to suffer with." Christ has suffered with us and because of His experiences with us He sees us completely clearly. Perhaps for me to see others like He does I will need to spend more time suffering with them and joining with them in their experiences.

Unfortunately, when imperfect humans come together, even in holy settings, inevitably things will happen that should never happen. As Elder Holland taught, "Except in the case of His only perfect Begotten Son, imperfect people are all God has ever had to work with. That must be terribly frustrating to Him, but He deals with it. So should we."² In the church—this aspiring Zion—I have experienced nearly universal good intentions, but good intentions can still lead to painful impacts. Many painful experiences occur because a fellow Latter-day Saint is placing themself in the foreground by seeing through a glass darkly. How different would my experience have been if instead of telling me not to talk about being gay, this quorum member had tried to see me clearly by asking me about my experiences as a gay Latter-day Saint? And what if instead of immediately dismissing him as ignorant, I tried to see him more and understand his discomfort?

The man who referred to my orientation as a perversion later moved away. After more than a year he stopped by the ward one Sunday when he was visiting town. He was kind and friendly as he caught me up on his life. Then he asked what was new with me. A lot was new, actually. Since we had last spoken I had published a book and had started a podcast, both dealing with the experience of being a gay Latter-day Saint. I briefly considered not mentioning these projects, not because I was embarrassed, but because I was afraid of how he would respond. But I realized that if I wanted him to see me clearly, I needed to allow myself to be seen. So I told him about my book and he looked quite surprised, especially when I mentioned that it was published by Deseret Book. I told him where he could buy the book and then changed the subject. I wanted to give him the opportunity to see me more clearly, but I also wasn't anxious to field more hurtful comments.

Frankly, being often and deeply misunderstood by fellow Latter-day Saints is pretty exhausting. It is draining to be vulnerable and then to feel misunderstood or even attacked. It makes me tired when people try to cancel my firesides. It wears me out to know that my existence makes people uncomfortable. And when I'm exhausted, tired, and worn out, my natural reaction is either to flee or to attack. But neither of those is helpful. I need to try to see them as the Savior does, so that they will want to see me, too. And maybe as I see them more clearly, they'll look back and see the parts of me I wish they would see. But that requires a lot of grace: from the Lord, from others, and from me.

The Book of Mormon shows how kindness can be so astonishing that it changes hearts and minds. King Lamoni's father was incredulous when he found out his son was galavanting around with Ammon the Nephite. He reminded his son that Nephites "are sons of a liar" who "robbed our fathers" and now "come amongst us that they may, by their cunning and their lying, deceive us, that they may again rob us of our property" (Alma 20:13). Talk about seeing through a glass darkly! He then tells Lamoni to kill Ammon. When Lamoni refuses, the king himself tries to kill Ammon. Ammon overpowers the king, who offers to give him half of his kingdom to spare his life. What the king doesn't know is that Ammon has already refused to be a king over the Nephites, and has no desire for political power or personal gain. He doesn't understand Ammon's history, motives, or values. Ammon refuses the king's offer and instead only asks that his brethren be freed and Lamoni retain his kingdom. Ammon's request is so unexpected, so outside of the king's understanding of what a Nephite represents, that the king "was astonished exceedingly" (Alma 20:27).

A few chapters later Ammon's example is still etched in the king's mind. When Ammon's brother Aaron arrives to preach to him he says: " . . . I have been somewhat troubled in mind because of the generosity and the greatness of the words of thy brother Ammon . . . " (Alma 22:3). Aaron, a Nephite, now has the opportunity to preach to the king. After hearing Aaron's words the king famously kneels down in prayer and tells God, " . . . I will give away all my sins to know thee . . . " (Alma 22:18).

Not only does the king change his view of the Nephites, but that change opens the way for him to become converted to God. And the catalyst that started this chain of events was a former prince who was hated and attacked and responded to his hateful attacker with unearned kindness. Ammon's generosity shattered the dark, opaque parts of the king's glass, and he was astonished when he began to see this Nephite clearly. Could I possibly offer this same kindness and generosity to those who feared, disliked, or attacked me, too?

An article I wrote titled "Lessons in Listening" was published in the Summer 2021 issue of Brigham Young University's *Y Magazine*. A few weeks after the article was published a lengthy letter arrived in my BYU mailbox, saying awful things about me and the sinful behavior that I was promoting as an openly gay BYU administrator. My heart sank as I read, and I was filled with fear. I told my colleagues about the letter's contents and laughed about how ridiculous his fears and conclusions were. But I still couldn't dismiss it. His words continued to sting.

The letter sat on my desk haunting me for weeks. Eventually I picked it up and reread it. When first I read it I dismissed the man's accusations as silly and baseless. As I read through his words again I saw a man who was scared. I noticed at the bottom of the letter he had written: "BYU class of '73." Since that time his beloved university, and much of the world, had changed. He was afraid that homosexuals like me were infiltrating it and changing it for the worse. I saw that he was experiencing discomfort and fear that was manifesting as an attack on me and LGBTQ folks. I pondered his discomfort and realized that in his worldview homosexuals are perverted and dangerous. Could he ever see me as a friend, a brother, and a positive contributor to the community? I decided that instead of blaming him for the world he lived in, maybe I could metaphorically take his hand and help him experience the discomfort in a less threatening way. Maybe he'd see something he hadn't seen before.

I grabbed a copy of my book *A Walk in My Shoes: Questions I'm Often Asked as a Gay Latter-day Saint* and wrote a note to him on the inside cover. I thanked him for taking the time to read my article and send his letter. I told him I could tell that he cared deeply about BYU just as I did. And I invited him to read my story and walk in my shoes. I stuffed the signed copy of my book into a padded envelope and before mailing it I held the package to my chest, praying that the Spirit would teach him as he read.

Two weeks later I got a letter back from him. He had read my book! In another long letter he shared some personal experiences he had had with LGBTQ folks, most of which had made him wary of the community. There were still some highly problematic things in what he was saying, but he had entered into the discomfort and had grown because of it. And then at the end of the letter he said he would be sharing my book with his friends.

I don't understand why I, representing the minority, need to offer grace and kindness to the uncomfortable majority. It doesn't feel fair that I have to constantly be the bigger person who extends grace and patience to those who hate and attack me. It feels out of balance. But when I extend grace, hearts change—including mine. It feels good to try to see someone more clearly and to be seen the way I am. But it takes forgiveness, vulnerability, humility, and patience—attributes that I don't always have on hand.

The difficulties I face as a gay Latter-day Saint are not rare, but they pale in comparison to some of the truly horrific events that happen in this world. The 1994 Rwandan genocide stands as one of the most tragic events in my lifetime.

In the space of 100 days, over one million people were killed, and the killing was done by former neighbors and friends. After the genocide in Rwanda, the country had to find a way forward. Rwandan leaders came to the difficult conclusion that forgiveness was the only path to healing. Instead of imprisoning all the perpetrators, as they were vehemently urged to do, they worked to rehabilitate and educate them. The survivors were asked to forgive them and move on. An astonished, offended survivor of the genocide asked the president: "Why are you asking us to forgive? Haven't we suffered enough? We were not the cause of the problem. Why must we find the solution?" President Kagame replied, "I am very sorry. I am asking too much of you. But I don't know what to ask of the perpetrators. Only forgiveness can heal this nation. The burden rests with the survivors because they are the only ones with something to give."[3]

In my own context, am I the only one who has something to give? Do those ignorant of our experience have nothing to contribute to heal the pain in the Latter-day Saint LGBTQ community? My belief in the restored gospel requires me to believe in the divine potential of every soul that I interact with and their capacity for growth, expansion, and progress. It requires that I strive to see them as God sees them, especially when they are unable to fully see me. And perhaps as I work to see them, they will be able to see me a little more clearly. In many instances they already have. Maybe some don't have much to give at present, but others ask what they can do. They can give a listening ear and a heart that is ready to learn. They can give the gift of seeking to know others as we are known. And what we can give each other is the often painful gift of forgiveness and grace. It's the gift that the Savior offers me, and if I want to be like Him I need to offer it, too.

If people were to see me, all of me, as the Savior does, they would see that parts of me need some serious work. I have too much weakness, ignorance, and malice in me. The Savior sees all of that clearly, but this is not what He focuses on. He chastises me when necessary, but mostly He praises me and inspires me to be the man He knows I can become. What if I saw others the way that Jesus does? What if I could see each individual through His eyes and find ways to praise and inspire them? I believe that seeing them clearly would compel me to offer them exactly what the Savior offers me: grace and love. "For now we see through a glass, darkly; but then face to face: now I know in part; but then shall I know even as also I am known."

The youth from the California trek sent me a thank-you gift along with a card signed by dozens of them. On the front of the card were the words: "Thank you for walking with us." I could just as easily have sent a card thanking them for walking with me. I can imagine the Savior watching us all during the weeks leading up to trek when discomfort and fear were at their highest and then pleading with us to take a step out of the darkness of our own weakness and into His light, His love. I picture Him smiling as strangers knitted their hearts together in love. So why do I have to be the one to give? Because that is what He did, and that is what He will always do. Our Heavenly Parents believe in each of us and give us a multitude of chances to grow. If I want to be like Them, I need to believe in their children, too. My choice to follow the Gospel of Christ means I choose to walk with God's children and I can choose to walk with them no matter their understanding or comfort level. As we walk this road together, we come out of the darkness into astonishing clarity. We see one another as sisters and brothers, siblings in the divine family.

The Landing

EMMA LOU THAYNE

Reprinted from the 1986 collection,
A Thoughtful Faith: Essays on Belief by Mormon Scholars.

It was the 24th of July, hot and blue just as it should be in Utah. On the program for sacrament meeting in the Third Ward were a scout, a Merrie Miss, a fifteen-year-old teacher, a seventy-eight-year-old high priest, and an eighty-nine-year-old matriarch, all telling stories about their pioneer forebears. They were prepared, personal, touching. Each brought warmth, faith, information, even humor to the pulpit as the congregation radiated acceptance like hummingbirds at a feeder.

The bishop beamed; the song leader had us singing "Utah We Love Thee" and "Come, Come Ye Saints" at the top of our collectives; the sacrament had come and gone like a good dream in spite of one prayer's having to be repeated twice because the newly ordained nerves of the priest kept mixing partake and sanctify. Sitting in that red-carpeted chapel among the twenty-five-years-familiar dear faces and constantly changing backs of heads, I belonged as surely as my pioneers belonged to their wagon circles on the prairie or conferences on folding chairs in the half-finished Tabernacle on Temple Square. My head spun with being at home, and my spirit went shimmering off like the sun on Great Salt Lake to meet my mother and father, grandmas and grandpas who I knew were singing along with me on a blue sky 24th. It was my church, my culture, an intimate province that held and fed me among my people then and now. I absolutely loved it. And through it, the gospel.

But then the contradictions.

In the week since, a friend has been inconsiderately released from a responsible administrative position she occupied with candor and courage, not knowing of the change until her perhaps milder successor was announced. While a brother I know has escaped a coronary bypass through prayer, a young friend who talked in profound confidence to her home teacher about an indiscretion has been excommunicated. In the past several weeks I've seen the Church mobilize generosity and stem a flood to win the amazement of the world, and at the same time be editorially petty about what an under-researched newspaper article in a neighboring state said about a "Zion curtain." I've listened to a lesson on compassionate service, but I've also heard of lessons on what not to read, seen the expulsion of a questing paper from the BYU campus and the investigation of writers for sister publications to the Exponent, and heard of machinations for positions that I in younger days might have expected to be filled by inspiration.

I've seen one missionary go out and come home under a mission president who built him, helped him master his diffidence, who gave him faith in himself and his relationship to Jesus Christ; I've seen another come home from another mission and another mission president, her self-worth bludgeoned by guilt and debasement for failing to find converts in a mission now closed for want of success.

Perhaps most unnerving of all, I see people afraid of the Church that I grew up regarding as refuge and sustenance, purveyor of truth and love. Who has not observed the historian afraid to write history, the young mother afraid to turn down a call, the parents panicked, expectations smashed for a son who doesn't want a mission. And all the time believers afraid to confront unbelief even as they search for believing.

Everywhere, every week, I see the good and the far from good influences and eventualities of life in the Church, my church. There have to be ways to come to grips with the contradictions, to have enough belief in the good to counteract distress at the bad. Maybe my willingness and ableness to handle the contradictions could be seen as a lot like the fear and faith I take to the big swing at our cabin.

The swing is up a gully and then up a steep dusty mountainside. You get on the single thick rope from a platform hammered to a rough pine, grab a knot straight out from your arms, see that the seat—a shiny skinned three-inch round of mountain mahogany—is pulled tight between your legs, shove up on your toes, and take off.

No matter if it's your first or two-hundredth time, your heart will tattoo your ribs and your mouth go dry as you drop and then swoop up over forty feet to look back—if you dare open your eyes—to the platform somewhere over there on the mountain you just left between two ancient spruces aching and swaying to hold your flight. It's a "beaut" of a swing, one we built as kids more than forty years ago.

The swing was always central to our parties from the time we were twelve until we had our own children daring their friends to try it. And still I get up there and take off with an assurance of terror that makes even my past half-a-hundred-year-old lungs need to "wa-hoo" on that first plunge, as my legs kick me out and about for a heady landing three swings later on the bank grown steep and treacherous under the canyon boots of three generations of thrill seekers. I know I'll make it. I've never failed. Oh, sometimes I've missed my footing as I've tried to land and had to hang and dangle out and back for another try, sometimes even to have somebody grab and hold till I could get off. But I've always made it. It's something I can count on.

In like fashion in the Church, I've often gone off swinging onto new skies, examining, cheering, chafing, opposing, espousing, hoping for change, loving sometimes unequivocally a status quo. Most of all wanting urgently to continue—nay, grow—in my believing. I've found plenty to believe in—like the inspiration behind that program Sunday. But I go less often now up that gully and onto the swing. It seems OK simply to know it's there, that others are whooping on it, and that anytime I want to, I can go for it and be sure of both flying and finding a landing. I've learned that maturity can help positively only what I have control over, and more and more I gravitate to what little I can control—mostly in private spheres.

Maybe that's what's happened with other enterprises that used to compel and challenge me. Like getting up on one water ski. Or thinking it was possible to rewrite lesson manuals for the Beehives, MIA Maids, and Laurels with a General Board committee who thought with me that we could make them last even through Correlation for at least a decade. Or trying either to make sense of our changes in traditions that suppose credibility in the Church only for the playing of established roles, or the signing of class rolls, or the delivery of hot rolls around the block. I just quit needing to do all of it, maybe because I already knew I could and needed to move on. Or, more likely, because the ground for landing after even the most expectant foray can so often slide and break if not my spirit, very often my heart. Too often I sense a closing down of options of where to land, a suspicion of diversity and more often than not a landing in Leviticus rules and brimstone where John might offer spirit and hope.

Sometimes I find myself with a new gnawing fear of what power or insistence on conformity can unleash—and it's a far cry from the "wahoo" of taking off on the swing, the challenge of a new idea or way of going. So I simply choose not to swing so much anymore.

This is a good time of life. Mostly I am on solid but private ground, ground cut out and smoothed and made comfortable by my own landings or the landings of others willing to share their space with me. It is a place of believing, of letting in, and of being grounded in solid essentials. All intimately mine, all supplied by years of selecting and becoming comfortable with where I have come to flourish.

The arrival? When is there such a thing as arrival in believing? Nothing was ever more dynamic. But where I am now feels good. Full of believing—in the gospel of Jesus Christ and, if not in busyness in the Church, then in the support and camaraderie of those I love and in being about our Father's business as well as our own.

Of course I have often over the years pleaded, "I believe. Help thou mine unbelief!" But the unbelief has given way to—or been discarded in—the gradual and not always easy comings of belief. Time and inclination finally preclude my dealing with supposition or speculation—or even caring about what I don't know and have yet to encounter. There is little enough time for dealing with what is here and now, for trying to find out how to be human before I worry about how to be divine. But time is short. I'm about to turn the age my father was when he died—fifty-nine. It feels young, but now I'm the matriarch propounding by my life as he did for his following.

My mother and father talked little in a formal sense about what they believed. I never remember either bearing a traditional testimony. Their lives were their message: They were fair and kind and full of humor. And never condemning. More, what they chose seemed to make them happy and replete with possibilities—as they expected their children to be. They never set us up for rebellion by removing our options. Swings were there to be conceived, built, and swung on. Each of the four of us remembers going with their sanction to our own ways in the Church, attending and not attending and staying together as we came back to the same landings—non-conformists in our conformity.

I'd like very much for it to work in such a fashion for our five daughters, each of them as different as her coloring, as "active" as her convictions and sense of well-being.

Now in the Sabbath of my days, I claim more than ever the right to selective recall, endurance, ecstasy, expectation. "My" church is actually mine—a combination of "Abide With Me," " . . . that His Spirit may be with you . . . ," and hugging in the foyer. I love teaching an institute class and learning more from my co-instructor and students than I ever teach. I watch "the word" in action up and down my block and among good people everywhere, LDS and not, all living what more and more makes ultimate sense in this passage from the Book of Mormon:

> And because of your diligence and your faith and your patience with the word in nourishing it, that it may take root in you, behold by and by ye shall pluck the fruit thereof, which is sweet above all that is sweet, and which is white above all that is white, yea, and pure above all that is pure; and ye shall feast upon this fruit even until ye are filled, that ye hunger not, neither shall ye thirst. (Alma 32:42)

What has been there for me to pluck seems most precious. But my feasting and not hungering or thirsting has taken different shapes over the years. It's been a long time since I've signed a roll or read a manual for the classes I attend or felt uneasy about missing Sunday School to visit my friend Margaret, 89, or to be home for house calls from my brothers, one at a time, between their comings and goings. Like one of my mentors of years ago, I'm reading less and thinking more. I'm loving my children as adults, finding from them and their husbands new ways to see. My husband and I with our different approaches have broadened each other and learned together that to praise one thing is not to condemn another. In our now almost empty nest, we're realizing that constructive togetherness can mean sometimes prickly, often comfortable accommodation to difference.

In that accommodation I'm getting as addicted to solitude as I am to gatherings of kindred spirits, related or un-, the dozens gradually giving away to the one-to-ones.

If I like swinging over the kingdom of God in that gully and gasping at the thrill and the beauty of a green world, I also like inordinately having landed on the dark brown earth to watch the flights of others, knowing at least for now where I've come from, pretty much where I am, and not really a whole lot concerned about where I'm going. Only that it's bound to be full of wonder. And that the land under me and the people around me and the tetherings inside me all seem to make a lot of sense and connect me surely to what I know with the faith of my childhood—that someone way beyond me is there to make sure that the kingdom greens or sheds in the season thereof, with predictable unpredictability.

If I have come to live more easily with some of my own frailties—and they don't become fewer with age!—surely I can allow the same for the Church that I love and am so often dismayed at. It has given me far more than I it—and continues to. I have to play fair with it collectively as I would hope to individually. Its people, its practices, its truths have grounded and blessed me. I must grant it at least a modicum of the understanding I have come to expect from the Lord Himself for my struggles and failings. I must remind myself to be uncondemning as I pray for the patience and forbearance I hope just might be reciprocal.

With as many kinds of goodness to respond to as there are ways of looking at a sunset, I can be happy with my church only if I have neither the time nor the inclination to be unstrung by what might seem to me mismanagement, striving, discrimination, even witch hunts and paranoia. My landing and my being sure of my swinging, or of helping anyone else's, derive from that private kingdom that is within me telling me that only I can know when to go from the platform, how many times out before I lift myself from the seat and try for another landing, how long before there will be no swinging at all. And how to look for the serenity of having held onto the landings so I can love what the 24th of July is all about enough to counter depletions of what it isn't.

So far, what there is to love helps make manageable any perspective on the plunge. I trust it always will.

I'm a Pilgrim, I'm a Stranger

MICHELLE GRAABEK-WALLACE

When You Are in the Wide World

Hans Christian Andersen is a famous Danish writer of beloved fairy tales, such as the ugly duckling and the princess and the pea. As a native of Denmark, I grew up with his fairy tales and poetry as a staple of my cultural and literary diet. It was while I was in Italy studying toward my PhD that I came across one of his poems that resonated deeply with me, titled "Er du I Verden vide" ("When you are in the wide World"). Andersen wrote this poem when walking alone in the mountains near Setubal in Portugal in 1866. The first stanza reads,

"Er du I Verden vide"

Er Du I Verden vide,
Du er dog Hjemmet nær,
Gud aander ved din Side
I Luft og Blomst og Træer;
Du høre kan hans Stemme
I Dig og rundtenom,
Og føle du er hjemme
Hvor Du i Verden kom![1]

"When You Are in the Wide World"

When you are in the wide world,
You are yet close to home,
God breathes by your side
In Air and Flower and Tree;
You can hear his voice
In you and all around,
And feel that you are home
Where in the world you've come!

In many ways this poem encapsulates some of the key tenets of my belief in God. Regardless of where in the world I might find myself and the state-lines that humankind has drawn on its maps, this beautiful world was created for us as our home during this mortal journey. And wherever I may be both physically and spiritually on this journey, God breathes by my side and I hear his voice.

I grew up feeling that I was indeed in the wide world. From the age of one I was an immigrant, moving from Denmark to England to Ireland, back to Denmark and then back to England again. While living in Denmark as a teenager, I had the dubious honour of attending a school that Hans Christian Andersen himself had attended, which he apparently hated. I was often not fond of it myself, as it was here I was made to feel that because I had lived elsewhere, suddenly I wasn't Danish enough. I found myself constantly having to justify my own heritage. It pained me to feel that something so core to most people's identity as their nationality was in some sense taken from me.

Something my father said eventually changed the way I viewed my cultural identity. Perhaps because his own mother was a German emigrant and he too had grown up juggling his Danish and German heritage, he concluded over time that, while he thought of himself as a Dane and more broadly as a European, the most important identity to him was that he was a Latter-day Saint. This made me reflect on how I myself rooted my identity in my relationship to my religion and my God. It would also lead to my studying history, in particular where migration, religion, and gender overlap.

As I started university in England, I grew interested in how migrants historically constructed, enacted, and negotiated their cultural identity. I began to be more aware of the role that culture plays in our daily lives. I discerned that many truths or norms we hold as essential are instead rooted in our cultural upbringing. For example, as a child in Denmark I had a teacher tell me that eating rye bread was the only way I'd grow up healthy and strong. Not until much later did I see that, while there may be health benefits to rye bread, this commitment was rooted not in some eternal, universal principle, but in a Scandinavian dietary habit. Few of the children I grew up with in England ever ate rye bread; despite that, I'm confident most of them grew up quite healthy. Similarly, in Denmark the norm is to cycle to work, to school, to the beach, to most everywhere. My mother still tells me it gives her a sense of satisfaction every time she sends us off somewhere on a bicycle. However, in England when my brother cycled to school as a child, complete strangers called the school to complain about it, as a child cycling to school on his own was construed as parental negligence. In England walking is the cultural staple. People love to walk, and ancient footpaths that people have trod for centuries are protected so one may walk across them freely, even if they happen to cut straight across a farmer's field. The more I saw these contrasts in different places I lived, the more I began to question most practices and beliefs, curious to know which were a universal part of the human experience and which were embedded in mere cultural norms.

Naturally, I later began to apply this orientation to my religion. Some things seemed obvious. In Europe, drinking root beer is the Mormon thing to do. (Here I use the term "Mormon" purposefully in a cultural sense separate from the teachings and religious life of the Church of Jesus Christ). However, root beer isn't commonly sold in Europe. We could get imported root beer only at one of the few Latter-day Saint bookstores that existed in Europe. Even today one only finds root beer in specialty international food stores. Not until I was an adult did I realize that, to Americans, root beer was just another kind of soda. It wasn't anything especially 'Mormon.' But to me growing up in Europe it had been a special treat, the "Mormon Beer." It is part of a European Mormon culture, influenced by its American roots.

But there are other things in our religion that are less obviously cultural rather than universal eternal truths. Just as root beer became associated with Mormon culture, many other practices and ideas also cling to the faith because the history of the gospel's restoration took place in North America, and church headquarters is in Utah. This affects, for example, what we deem appropriate clothes to wear to church on the Sabbath. I have known Bishops who insisted only those wearing a white shirt and tie could bless the sacrament, thereby excluding African immigrant members who came in their own beautiful ethnic costumes. While I believe in keeping the Sabbath day holy, and in reverence for the Sacrament, this exclusion is rooted in Western culture of what"Sunday best" looks like. Another example is the way in which the United States Constitution is held in reverence in the church. I understand that this is rooted in a passage in the Doctrine and Covenants and diverse comments by General Authorities of the Church, and I won't dispute that the writers of the Constitution were at times inspired by God. However, I will assert that this is not equally true of many of the constitutions of other nations. For example, the Danish Constitution in June 1849 granted Danes religious freedom, only months before Latter-day Saint missionaries arrived in Denmark in 1850. One of these early missionaries, Erastus Snow, wrote in his journal, "Thus we saw that the Lord had been preparing the way before us in a manner that we knew not of."[2] I believe that the Danish Constitution was inspired by God, but it was only ever the inspired U.S. constitution of which I was taught in seminary and Sunday school lessons growing up. These often unintentional "Americanisms" can leave those of us who reside outside the United States feeling alienated. That can present a bigger problem for some than for others, but given that an increasing majority of members live outside the U.S., it is a problem for the church as a whole.

Gender is another area in which we often confuse culture and doctrine. While I believe that our teachings on the value of marriage and eternal families is doctrine, the female virtues I was taught in the Young Women's organization growing up felt stuck in 1950s America and were often difficult to reconcile with 2000s Europe. From experience I can say I am not a very good knitter. Sometimes these cultural gulfs are not just geographical but generational, especially internationally because translation and distribution of church materials takes time. Both in Denmark and in Italy I and others have experienced confusion about correct church procedure because of the delay of translation of church handbooks.

These experiences have in no way caused me to conclude that the church isn't true. But they have required me to develop the skill of differentiating between culture and doctrine. Given the Church's U.S. center, believers outside of the U.S. are prompted more pressingly and more often to navigate these tensions.

The need for such navigation is not unique to our time. The Book of Acts records how Peter in vision was told to preach the gospel to the gentiles. In doing so, arguments arose among the Saints, and even their leaders, about whether circumcision was required of them. To the Jews circumcision was symbolic of the covenant God had made with Abraham. It was no small matter. But after discussion so protracted that it nearly split the church, the practice was abandoned as a requirement for gentiles. The ancient apostles too had to learn to differentiate between culture and doctrine. The atonement of Christ is doctrine. The truth that we are all children of God is doctrine. Although more important in its time and place, circumcision, like root beer or wearing a white shirt and tie to church, was cultural and tribal rather than eternal.

God Breathes by Your Side

Slagelse, Denmark is where I grew up as a teenager, and where Hans Christian Andersen went to school. It is also where Hans Henry Petersen was born on Christmas day in 1835. Petersen heard the Latter-day Saint missionaries together with his parents when he was sixteen and was baptised on 19 June 1853. He trained as a weaver, though at the time of his baptism he was working as a farmhand. It was as a member of the church that he joined the Copenhagen Latter-day Saint choir and discovered a love for music. In Copenhagen he embarked on a self-study program of musical education and invested in private lessons from music professors. His motto in life, which he applied to his study of music, was "whatsoever is worth knowing at all is worth knowing well."[3] He emigrated to Utah in 1862, where he organised the first Scandinavian choir in Salt Lake City in 1863. He composed music and wrote several hymns, two of which are still in the Latter-day Saint hymn book.

One of these is the beautiful hymn, *Secret Prayer*. The other is perhaps less familiar and less often sung, *I'm a Pilgrim, I'm a Stranger*. "I'm a pilgrim, I'm a stranger cast upon the rocky shore of a land where deathly danger surges with a sullen roar, oft despairing, oft despairing, lest I reach my home no more ... O my Father, I entreat thee, let me see thy beck'ning hand; and when straying may I meet thee ere I join the silent band. Guide me, Father, guide me, Father, safely to the promised land."[4] Petersen's hymn means a lot to me because he and

I share a common root and share the experience of finding ourselves pilgrims and strangers, and yet at home in foreign lands. Like Hans Christian Andersen, these are the words of a man finding himself far from home, who there finds a closer relationship with his God.

Sometimes we find ourselves on symbolic rocky shores. These are the moments when I particularly struggle to differentiate between Church culture and doctrine as it is currently taught, and I find myself wrestling with spiritual questions. I see others, people I respect and admire, who fail to navigate the rocky shores, who crash and break against them or retreat and decide this isn't a place for them. People sometimes come to me with their rocky questions. Many such questions are rooted in history. It has been said that "the past is a foreign country" and here too I am a pilgrim and a stranger trying to find my way. One example is polygamy. In Europe, this is often the one thing people consistently know (or think they know) about the Latter-day Saints. It is easy to tell our non-member friends and co-workers that Latter-day Saints haven't practised polygamy since 1890. And that we never did so in Europe. We distance ourselves from the practice, in both time and space. And yet it haunts us. I remember an elder on my mission saying, with the confidence only young men seem to have, that all Latter-day Saint women would have to live the law of polygamy to enter the Celestial Kingdom. He wasn't impressed when the sisters objected. Polygamy is consistently a rocky shore that women of my acquaintance have asked me to help them navigate. Sadly, I don't have a map. Perhaps the best analogy is that in my historical research I found a rock on which I am precariously balanced, but in a slightly better position to see more of the surroundings, which I can describe to others.

Yet I also wonder how useful it is if all I can say from on top of that rock is, there is no clear path, it's foggy in that direction. There can be no doubt that polygamy was agonizing, controversial, and messy for many women, for men and families as well, and for the church as a whole. Nonetheless, I believe it is too easy to proclaim from the twenty-first century that the men who instituted polygamy in a very different context two centuries previous weren't that inspired by God after all. From my perch, reviewing accounts of personal revelation written by Latter-day Saint women in the 19th century, I do see evidence that the practice of plural marriage was troubling. However, I also respect the right of women to their own stories, which in some instances make clear they felt the practice was something their God was asking them to live.

For example, Anne Katrina Hedvig Rasmusdatter and her husband Hans Christian Hansen joined the Church of Jesus Christ in Denmark in 1851 and emigrated to Utah the following year. Hans Christian Hansen had no intention of entering into a polygamous relationship, but while in Salt Lake City in 1860 on his way to serve a mission in Denmark, he met Marie Sophie Jensen and had a strong feeling he should marry her. Marie herself had had a dream the night before that she was to go to a friend's house where she would meet her future husband. Anne Katrina Hedvig Rasmusdatter meanwhile also had a dream where she saw Hans and Marie, and the following morning left her children with her mother-in-law saying "I am going to Salt Lake City today. Hans wants me. He is going to take another wife. I have seen her."[5] She arrived that evening, embraced Marie as a sister and gave her blessing. Who am I to say such women were uninspired or out of tune with the Holy Ghost?

When we find ourselves on strange shores, either physically, historically, or theologically, it can be all too easy to feel lost and alone as we try to navigate. Does God walk among such sharp and fog-shrouded rocks? Sometimes we are discouraged from walking here and asking our rocky questions because others see it as bringing us out of range of the Holy Ghost. When I was a young woman we were told "the Holy Ghost goes to bed at midnight." It is the kind of pithy line you tell young people, so they don't stay out late. But it never sat well with me. I believe that the Holy Ghost has no bedtime, needs no passport, and is not afraid of the dark. I know apostles and prophets throughout history have felt God by their side in prisons, wildernesses, and stormy seas. Yes, I believe we should strive to "stand in holy places." But to stand still is never what God intended for us. Wilderness narratives are the refining fires of every book of scripture we call canon. Certainly, in these wildernesses we make mistakes. The Israelites built a Golden calf. Lehi murmured alongside his family when food was scarce. Discontent reigned in Zion's Camp. Sometimes as we explore the depths of our questions, we forget that the most reliable traveling companion we can invite along is the Holy Ghost. I remind myself to ask as Henry H. Petersen did, "O my Father, I entreat thee, let me see thy beck'ning hand," and that when I do, in the words of Hans Christian Andersen, "God breathes by your side." Like these two Danes abroad, I choose to allow strange shores to be exactly the place in which I find God. When I say, "God breathes by my side," I do not mean he [always?] gives me the answer. When God breathes by my side, it means that he and I are traveling along this shore together. I trust that God is always within my reach, wherever I may find myself. In the hymn *Secret Prayer*, Hans H. Petersen wrote, "When sailing on life's stormy sea, mid billows of despair, 'tis solace to my soul to know God hears my secret prayer."[6] These are the prayers in which I more often draw closer to God.

Sometimes that means that all I can do is quote Nephi and say, "I know that he loveth his children; nevertheless, I do not know the meaning of all things."[7] This may look to others like blind faith. But to me it is trust in a God who sees a much bigger picture than I do. C. S. Lewis wrote, "Complete trust is an ingredient in that relation—such trust as could have no room to grow except where there is also room for doubt. To love involves trusting the beloved beyond the evidence, even against much evidence. No man is our friend who believes in our good intentions only when they are proved. No man is our friend who will not be very slow to accept evidence against them. Such confidence, between one man and another, is in fact almost universally praised as a moral beauty, not blamed as a logical error."[8] So when I face strange rocky shores, for which I find my map patchy and lacking, I trust in God. I trust in a God whom I firmly believe loves all his children. I trust that when God says that all shall be made right through the atonement of Christ, that implies there are paths here that I do not yet see. And sometimes that has to be enough for a season.

As I have lived in different places, I have been struck by the geographical variety of this world. In Denmark I love the sea more than anything. In England I relax as I drive through narrow country roads lined by green trees and hedgerows. I have fond memories of exploring lakes and rivers in Ireland. In Italy I look forward to olives being harvested in the olive orchards around my home. In Utah I stand in awe of mountains. The world is beautiful in all its variety. Sometimes this variety also makes things difficult. Being a stranger isn't easy. I may struggle with understanding the language or the culture. I always find navigating a challenge. Driving on one side of the road or the other, trying to figure out the differences in how public transport works, or trying to interpret signs. Luckily, Young Women's camp taught me how to read a map, and the map on my phone is pretty sophisticated these days. And yet sometimes they fail me, and I get lost, take a wrong turn, and get disoriented. We are all pilgrims and strangers in this world, both physically and spiritually. Being a pilgrim and a stranger in life means to explore, to learn, and, yes, sometimes to feel a little lost. As I journey throughout this life, I remind myself that God breathes by my side, and that I feel sufficiently at home, wherever in this world I've come and whatever strange shores I explore. I don't lose faith during the seasons when I feel lost, frustrated, and surrounded by strangers. Instead, I trust in the moments when the clouds clear and on a beautiful clear night on the shore, God reaches out a hand and connects the bright stars of a constellation, by which I can navigate in the darkness.

God, Atheism, and the Perils of Love

SAMUEL MORRIS BROWN

Introduction:
Kate Rebukes Me

We were driving home from Pilates in a frigid April rain, too late in the spring to be so cold. My fingertips ached a little as they curved over the steering wheel toward the windshield. The heater in my car wasn't working because thieves ("meth heads" in the bitter story I told myself) had tried to steal my car stereo, and the local garage didn't replace the instrument panel correctly. I hadn't joined my wife, Kate, at Pilates this week because I'd just lost a cracked second molar to an oral surgeon. I was biting down, a little too hard, on salt-wet gauze, trying to persuade the socket where the molar once stood to stop oozing blood. It wasn't my finest moment as Kate's companion and occasional chauffeur.

I'd been listening to the 2016 Gifford Lectures in Natural Theology during the prior week's commute. The lecturer was an atheist cosmologist, Sean Carroll, a politer alternative to the more famous Richard Dawkins. After a lively introduction to particle physics and quantum field theory, Carroll was making his way through the philosophical problems that come *after* the theories of physics. He's a confident and polished speaker. He was entertaining if a bit smug, and his early lectures flowed well. Then came the hard problems that have always been the Achilles heel for atheism: how do we explain consciousness, morality, and meaning? After much fanfare, foreshadowing, and throat clearing, Carroll's solution to the big issues was to sidestep them. "Meh," he seemed to say. They're illusions. Get over it. Go be true to yourselves, whatever that might mean in a giant ball of quantum fields, and enjoy what time you have left with your illusions of love and consciousness.

I'd been hoping he would have something to say about the big problems of existence. I like to learn and was looking forward to new arguments. I found myself disappointed, even irritated. I meant him no harm, but I wanted to yell at my smartphone that there was nothing new in his pontifications. He had no more defended atheist naturalism as an overarching philosophy than he had bent a spoon with his mind. His account of empirical observations about particle physics seemed valid, but his defenses of his life's moral compass were sophomoric.

As my wife and I chatted our way home, I complained about how stupid Carroll had been and how frustrated I was with the quality of his intellectual engagement with God and religion. Maybe, I suggested to her, I should write something about how dumb modern atheism is, using these obtuse lectures as the outline. The piss and vinegar in my brain leaked into my words.

"Maybe you should pray to love him," Kate said.

My tooth socket buzzed with its loss and my embarrassment. I closed my mouth and drove into the rain, cursing under my breath. Sometimes I hate it when she's right.

The Call of Atheism

I stare, sympathetically, at atheism from time to time. Maybe it's because atheism is cool right now. That's as may be. But I also remember its charms for me as a boy. I recall some of the emotional pleasure it brought, especially the sense of power that comes with incredulity. I enjoyed defying tradition. I liked how tidy atheism felt, like a bedtime story in a board book of bright reds and deep blues. *Goodnight, Moon. God is dead. Don't be naïve.*

Atheism has been on my mind again of late. I suspect I'm thinking about it more these days because some people I love tell me that they are, more or less, atheists now. Whereas I'm religious and have been for thirty years. Why are they doing the same thing that I got so wrong as a child? I tell myself that the main thing that irritates me about atheism is that it is so obviously wrong. But I'm being simplistic. There's more to it than that.

I wonder sometimes whether modern atheism affects me the way it does because I'm not naturally good at a life of faith. Belief is not my equilibrium—unbelief is where entropy pushes me. For a long time, I cherished being an unbeliever. Atheism is in my nature. Like many another feral impulse or appetite, this one happens to be misplaced, but that doesn't change the basic reality. I know that for me life in God takes work, commitment, and resistance.

My affection for atheism is an emotional attachment. I know intuitively that what's marketed as atheism isn't rational in any non-circular sense. I get that it requires a kind of willful blindness. But I know how tempting it is anyway. So sometimes I suspect that when I hold atheism in my hands again, I'm like a sober alcoholic remembering the touch of single malt whisky on my throat as I pass by a liquor store. Or the adulterous man who can't stop ogling a distant celebrity. I know the beauty and power of life in God but can never shake entirely the giddy stupor of my teenaged atheism.

There's also an aspect of not wanting to feel embarrassed. I worry that religion makes us seem stupid or antiquated. I

watch the responses to modernism from within fundamentalist Christianity and often cringe. I'm arrogant. I don't want
to look like a hillbilly. There's enough of that in my socio-
economic background. I've spent adulthood fleeing from the
painful humility of being too poor to fit in. I'm weary of a
nagging sense of shame about religious belief.

Maybe that's why I'm spoiling for a fight. I feel like the
atheist entertainers like Dawkins and Carroll are peddling
delusions in the hopes of persuading people to abandon the
communities and modes of being that matter most—those
grounded in the love of God. In place of God they sell a smug
and stuporous modernism. And I know how persuasive those
false stories can sound to people like me. I know how easy it
is to become embarrassed by religious belief. It's this beautiful thing, and people are throwing rocks at it because they
pretend it is ugly. So maybe I also feel like I'm witnessing an
injustice—to borrow the convoluted metaphor of postmodern
argument, the atheist entertainers are "gaslighting" people,
some of them my close friends.

The Rhetorical Problem: I Love to Fight

So why do I keep fighting in my head with the atheist entertainers? Why is there hatred rather than love in my heart? I like
to argue. The fight has been in my heart since the beginning.
The main thing I did in high school besides skipping classes
and antagonizing authority figures was debate, the flavor we
called "policy" or "cross-ex." By the end of my senior year,
half of my classes were directly supervised by our ever-indul-
gent debate coach. (I'd persuaded other teachers that it was
in their best interest to not require me to stay physically in
their classes.) I loved debate, and I was good at it. We spoke
fast, twisted our words, and bush-whacked through logical

arguments. At one point in my debating career, I wondered whether I should be a trial lawyer.

When I was an adolescent atheist, my love of argument aimed its sights on religious folk. I knew and loved the anti-Mormon and anti-Christian arguments. I felt strong and wise.

I still cherish a good argument. That much will never change. I think I feel about arguments the way culinary sophisticates feel about wine. I love them viscerally, delight in their strange *terroir* and the pleasant buzz that comes after.

But there's something else going on. It doesn't feel like a fair fight right now because the format of current debates about theism creates a handicap for people of faith. The atheist entertainers get to use the crass caricatures, the breezy dismissals, the crude jokes, and the curse words. Their polemical writings are often exuberantly fun. This bombast is part of their charm. And we religious folk are supposed to be quietly respectful, to avoid vulgarity and cruel indifference. We're supposed to model true piety, to turn our cheeks to the mugger.

But I'm not good at being polite and respectful. I want to fight fire with fire. I've been planning a diatribe against modern atheism for years. I'd fill it with curse words, rude jokes, and caricatures. I'd make atheism laughable. I would, in a word, turn the invective back on religion's critics. It would be awesome.

Until Kate rebuked me in the car, I think I'd believed that we religious intellectuals have given too much ground to our critics through polite restraint. We're too prim for the real contests. There are exceptions—some religious thinkers do love to shout. But by and large we have been uncomfortable descending into the Colosseum in all its naked gore. Why shouldn't a religious scholar use words that rhyme with spit and duck in a full-throated counter-assault in the war of words? Seriously.

Why not? For years it seemed to me that such restraint was mere Victorian prudery.

But it has come to me after Kate's correction that what we religious have to offer is not a simplistic argument or petulant turn of phrase. The reason the life of faith matters is not some high school debate trophy. God is about life, presence, and experience. Divine love is what's at stake. And that love is inaccessible by way of rage or hatred. I've had to come to terms with that fact: however addicted I am to debate, the life of God does not come through animosity. It's like trying to grow tomatoes in a beaker of sulfuric acid instead of a pot of soil.

In case it needs to be said explicitly at this point: God and religion aren't contrary to logic. Life in God is not sullen and solemn. Not at all. The life of faith is deeply rational if one allows it to be, and it is full of laughter and surprises. Crucially, though, clownish debates are distractions from the real goals of life and consciousness. Loving someone is harder and more important than besting them in argument. Making fun is easier than creating. Our goal as thinkers of faith is not to assert our dominance or to look cool. Our calling is to introduce people to God and the possibility of ultimate fulness. That's the mission. So we must take the higher road. That road is unpaved; boulders choke it, and rainstorms have eroded the soil into deep channels with sharp edges. The path requires our hearts and minds and all our energy. What cannot survive the journey is our hate. Jesus (and Kate!) was clear about that.

God's Thinking & Love

When I was in college, one of the associate deans decided that I was supposed to go for a Rhodes Scholarship my senior year. I had no particular interest, but I was ambitious enough that if you put a prize in front of me I would compete for it. I was like one of those rats in the laboratory cages who keeps pushing its nose against the lever to dispense cocaine pellets. Somehow I made it to the final stage of the contest.

The ultimate interview was a snooty hazing ritual, where powerful old men pepper you with questions to evaluate your knowledge, but mostly to test your mettle. No genius was required to see that I was religious—one of my claims to fame was that I had translated a Russian biography of Jesus, and I hadn't hidden the fact of my LDS mission to Louisiana. The interviewers pushed me to explain my belief in rationalist terms. Matching pretense for pretense, I said that if Descartes could ground his philosophy with *cogito ergo sum* (I think therefore I am) then I could get launched with *cogitat ergo est* (he thinks therefore he is). I had experienced God's mind as surely as I had experienced my own. They didn't like the answer, and they didn't especially like me, so I headed back to my senior year of college without the scholarship. But that witticism stuck with me—there was something about the encounter with the mind of God that had shaped me.

I met Kate in Boston when I would have been heading to the UK if I had won a Rhodes, and our relationship felt like the true prize. Over the years she taught me better and better what it was I meant when I tried to deflect the Rhodes committee's dismissive questions. During my first real religious experience at the age of 18, the one that drove me to finally abandon atheism, I felt God thinking inside me. That's the best I can do to explain it. And what God was thinking was "love." It made me consider that maybe Paul's sermon about love in 1 Corinthians 13 was a sideways reflection on what happened on his road to Damascus. Maybe he too had felt God's mind, the world-making *Logos*, saying love in his heart.

The Anglican professor-priest Tom Wright writes about an epistemology of love as a Christian counterpoint to detached rationalism. I think he's onto something. Love isn't just nice; it's a way of seeing and understanding the world. Wright sees love as a soulful engagement of another person or of the physical world or of God and the divine realm. Love is interested in who they are, what worries them, what special gifts they bring to bear. Love is not antagonistic to the workings of mind, but it does guide such cogitations. This Christian epistemology is wide open. It's open to the range of the world in compassionate fascination. Such a truth quest isn't worried about seeming weak or stupid, even as it is concerned with being true. "True" here means faithful, in the sense of speaking to the beauty and grace at the center of the world and making that grace real throughout the world.

I find myself convinced. The best and most important and truest things I've learned have come through love in this expanded sense. There is no truth in hate, there is only the hate itself. This was the lesson Kate was teaching me that cold April afternoon.

But of course if love is more than a platitude, then it will bear terrible risks.

The Risks of Love

The fact that Christ has to command us to love suggests that there's something difficult about loving, especially when it comes to those who bring us no discernible benefit and may even wish us harm. Loving can be perilous; this real love is more than casual affection or the flash in the pan of infatuation. We can be deeply wounded when we love. We can be duped or misled.

Part of the modern atheist account is a dismissal of certain axiomatic understandings. They and others hope that love is just a network of chemical reactions or buzzing of neural tissue, a flow of energy in various entropic states that helps to perpetuate specific collections of genetic material over millions of years. Whatever else it is, this physicalist campaign is an effort to sap love of its power. This brand of atheism seems to manifest a desperate fear of the possibility that love will actually lay claim to us. That's why love gets deconstructed, genealogized, defanged, and explained away. In other words, the etiologic fairy tales of evolutionary psychology—people experience the chemical burst they call "love" because it got their genes reproduced on the African savannah 50,000 years ago—serve a *protective* rather than just an *explanatory* role. It's like putting eclipse glasses on to look toward the sun as the moon moves across it. These attempts to explain away love strive to limit its claims upon us.

We know the risks at a statistical and societal level. The most robust communities, those based in reciprocating love and respect, are the most vulnerable to what lawyers call affinity fraud. Bernie Madoff exploited his Jewish community because its members trusted each other. Affinity fraudsters in Utah are a dime a dozen; billions of dollars have been stolen. Many of the Saints have been swindled by health remedies and investment schemes that came to them from a trusted member of their community. In less grandiose terms, we have all been mistreated at some point by someone we trusted. It may have been a romantic relationship that broke or a situation at work that didn't resolve in our favor or squabbles at church over who got what calling. We have all felt disappointed by intimacy. That is unavoidable when we love as mortals.

We are not the only ones disappointed by love. However we ultimately sort out the meanings and mechanisms of atonement, Christ loved us and we betrayed his trust. We treated him cruelly, but he loved us anyway. He saw his love of us as the real and true meaning of his entire life. Special son of

God, the anointed king of Israel, the mightiest being born of woman on our earth, and his life goal was to be betrayed in love and then forgive that betrayal. That fact ought to give us pause. If we live as Christ, we will necessarily love our way into disappointment.

Then there's the risk we don't acknowledge as readily but which is substantial. It's the chance that we will be changed—even transformed. Here I think we need to be willing to dwell in atonement. The more deeply we love, the more our identities overlap. We do not lose ourselves entirely in the beloved. Nor do they disappear into us. But functionally this melding is what happens in love. I see my wife in me and I in her, and I welcome that process and reality. I'm not the same person I was when I began to love her. This sense of opening oneself to the influence of another sits in the soul as a mark of the nature of love. And that can be frightening.

Love the Enemy

Jesus declared his uncomfortable peace in the Sermon on the Mount. In the spare phrases of that sermon, he reconceived righteousness. He drew focus away from outward acts and toward the shape of souls. His is a higher and harder law that guts the natural person. Contrary to reasonable expectations, this love is the way of true peace.

Honestly, I struggle with all of the Sermon on the Mount. It has always been easier for me to work hard than to be good. In Matthew, Christ works to set up the difference between traditional scripture and his transforming Gospel. He's already distinguished several old traditions from the new life in him before he says, "Ye have heard that it hath been said, Thou shalt love thy neighbour, and hate thine enemy." (He's apparently referring to distorted readings of Leviticus 19:18 among his peers and kin.) Jesus realizes how upset Israel has been about its political subjugation by Gentile overlords. He seems to know that his people are hoping that, as the Anointed One, he will end foreign domination and annihilate the Roman occupiers. Instead of the desired promise of spilt blood, though, Jesus says, "Love your enemies, bless them that curse you, do good to them that hate you, and pray for them which despitefully use you, and persecute you; That ye may be the children of your Father which is in heaven: for he maketh his sun to rise on the evil and on the good, and sendeth rain on the just and on the unjust" (Matthew 5:44–45). In other words, you want to hate the Romans and see them dead. That is not what God wants. Jesus couldn't have been more disappointing to his listeners' political aspirations.

After this hard saying, Christ contrasts his Christian disciples to the publicans. The latter are a class of men widely reviled because they have sided with the occupiers. The publicans extract tribute from fellow Jews on behalf of the Romans: they are turncoats and traitors, enemies to Israel. Christ's painful rhetorical question reads like this in King James: "if ye love them which love you, what reward have ye? do not even the publicans the same? And if ye salute your brethren only, what do ye more than others? do not even the publicans so?" On first read-through, the text may feel a bit murky. But I think Christ is saying, if you can only love your friends, then you're as bad as your enemies. If you cannot love your enemies, in other words, then *you are what you imagine them to be*.

I will happily admit that according to some Bible scholars this is an uncertain text. We do not have an audio recording of Jesus's sermon. We're always having to do a certain amount of guesswork about ancient scripture. But maybe what Christ is talking about is this ironic fact: if you despise someone because you disagree with them, then you are the one worthy of spite. This can sound a bit cruel—Jesus is apparently criticizing the oppressed for hating their oppressors. As a society we've become more aware of the plight of the oppressed in recent decades, which is a good thing. I think Christ means this in a more descriptive sense, and it seems to gesture toward solutions to oppression that transform the terms of a difficult relationship. It's not that you are consigned to your enemies' fate by an external tribunal if you despise your enemies. It's that you become what you despise through the power of spite. It's like a moral law of nature. Christ identifies a path out of oppression that is other than hatred. He seems to be saying that there is strength in love, a strength that can overwhelm oppression and cruelty.

There's a story told about one patron saint of modern atheism, the German linguist, poet, and philosopher Friedrich Nietzsche. Some students of Nietzsche protest that it's hard to categorize his complex, often obscure, and inconsistent writings, but many readers have seen him as criticizing Christianity for creating a "slave mentality" that needed to be resisted. According to this interpretation, Nietzsche hated what he saw as the weakness of turning the other cheek and loving the enemy. I don't hate Nietzsche, and I feel sad that he died slowly and miserably of a dementing illness. But the traditional Nietzschean concern about the risks of love exemplifies the poison that Christ was trying to extract from our world.

What I think this philosophy is unable to fathom is the immense and transformative power that comes from loving in Christ. This is not the force of bombs, guns, or the will to power. It is not the rhetorical strength of public denunciation. It is not the dominion of state violence. The love of Christ is something else entirely. It is a love capable of transforming those who love and those who are loved.

If we were to try to translate Christ's instructions to love the enemy for this modern era, we might say that Christ taught that love was about more than utility and concerned with something other than power. Loving your friends only is the path of utilitarian Darwinism. You feel good when you're with them; they look out for you, through most of human history they have shared genetic material with you. It makes good practical and evolutionary sense to love the people who have your back and protect your genetic material. Loving your enemies, however, breaks the rules of naturalism. It's not about success or glory or personal satisfaction. It's about lifting those around you. It's about the shedding forth of Christ's grace in and through the world, about the transformation of the world, about the marriage of heaven and earth. It's about the forging of Zion.

Christ's commandment to love enemies is immediately followed by another injunction. It's one of the most popular lines from the sermon, and it's the last verse in the chapter: "be ye therefore perfect, even as your father is perfect." There's a lot of debate about what that phrase means, but I find myself persuaded by the context here. A perfect being is one that can love the good and the bad, the friend and the enemy. That's a wholeness of love to which we can and should aspire. It's the wholeness of heaven and earth together.

I'm aware that professional Bible scholars have taken to arguing on the basis of their typical sensibilities that the last verse in Matthew 5 probably doesn't belong there. The injunction to be perfect may not even belong to the Sermon on the Mount at all, they say. This school of scholarship—some good, some bad—tries to break down the Bible we have now into different bits and pieces, shattering the apparent unity many readers find in it. This approach, as useful as it is at times, seems offended by the notion that the Bible could speak in a coherent voice. But this often frivolously reductionist view of scripture misses the possibility that God could work on large time scales and that access to eternal meaning can arise in the twists and turns of mortal life. Scripture, in other words, doesn't need to be written all at once by one person to be true. At a personal level, I find myself moved and educated by the scriptures as we have them through the Church. Trusting the integrity of scripture in the company of the Saints is one of the great gifts of the Restoration. So it matters to me as a Latter-day Saint that this summary statement calling us to divine perfection follows immediately after the injunction to love our enemies as well as our friends. Want to be "perfect" or whole like God? You better love your enemies.

What Shall We Do?

So then how do I speak love to atheism? Or is my mandate instead to love atheists (much easier because the vast majority are quite lovable) and love the world atheism has debased with its talk about mere mortality? I suspect it's a combination of all three. This quest is framed in the eternal echoes of the God who turned the "welter and waste" (*tohu wa bohu*) of unformed chaos into the Goodness (*tov*) that God announced on the eve of the world's first sabbath. ⚘ Why do we love those who denounce us as credulous believers? Because God loved us all into this mortal existence.

The old-new Epicurean canard about meaningless clusters of atoms careening around an indifferent universe just doesn't cut it as an answer. This ideology is a parody of existence. In response to parody, we can bring only love. And to

---

⚘ This is Robert Alter's elegant rendition of the *tohu wa bohu* that the King James Translation renders as "without form and void."

fight fire with fire is to give in to the parody rather than to real and abiding love.

What is it we think we want when we consider the goals of missionary work? The reason we want people to be religious is so that they can bask in the love of God and shed it forth into the world. Why would we do the opposite in pursuit of that goal? We are not obligated to keep our mouths shut when horrible and cruel things are said. But when our mouths open, our hearts must be open too.

I still think most modern atheism is a fairy tale recited as a dirty limerick. I'm glad I abandoned it when I became an adult. But what I'm realizing is how little that fact matters. Yes, I think modern atheism is a morally bankrupt and intellectually incoherent position. But most people who understand themselves as atheists are drawn to that affiliation not by mere reason, but also by their hearts. And what the heart feels is important. Much to our shame as believers, many are driven to atheism in response to a palpable hatred flowing from Christian fonts. We who believe have repenting to do. In Christ, we are up to the task.

What matters most, for all of us, is the extent to which the spirit of God fills the world, and that spirit does not live in hate. The light of Christ lives in love. That is where, and how, we must dwell.

From Seminary Teacher to Scientist to Institute Director: Learning by Study and Also by Faith

UGO A. PEREGO

orking late one evening as a doctoral student at the University of Pavia in Italy, I was in the middle of preparing several plates containing DNA samples from individuals carrying maternally-inherited genetic profiles specific to Native American ancestry. During that time, I was well aware that no one had at their disposal as much data and DNA samples as I had to address questions pertaining to the origins, dispersal, and expansion routes of indigenous groups of America's double continent. These samples resulted from several collaborative efforts with institutions and universities in diverse parts of Central and South America, and from volunteer submissions from the general population of the United States and Canada. As often happened in those days, I was the only one in the lab at that late hour, alone with my thoughts. Although my research objectives as part of Professor Antonio Torroni's scientific team had nothing to do with religious matters, I could not help but reflect about the genetic origins of these people and the controversy surrounding the narrative found in the Book of Mormon. Because of the nature of my doctoral work, my employment with the Sorenson Molecular Genealogy Foundation, and my membership in The Church of Jesus Christ of Latter-day Saints, I had been approached several times with questions and high expectations that such research could shed some light on whether "Lamanite DNA" could be detected, settling once and for all the question of an Israelite origin of the people of the Book of Mormon. For some reason, although I was interested in providing some science-based answers to such queries, I was not troubled by them. My understanding of the principles governing population studies based on genetic evidence had deepened and expanded, and it was clear in my mind that the answers to Book of Mormon people's origin questions were not to be found in the DNA samples in my hands.

That experience was one of many that helped me sort through a number of issues pertaining to the apparent conflict between faith and science-based matters. Things that I have learned, studied, and researched, and things that I do not have an answer for, including occasional personal struggles, doubts, or confusion, have gradually and steadily faded into the background in the face of my relationship with the Divine. Yes, I, like many others, have experienced faith challenges and times of loneliness and loss. During those moments, I learned to stop what I was doing, sit back, and ponder whether my heart and mind were set on what really mattered, and whether my faith was rooted where it was supposed to be. Years later, I found great similarity between how I occasionally felt and the words of Elder Lawrence E. Corbridge given at a 2019 BYU devotional. Elder Corbridge taught the importance of focusing on a set of "fundamental questions" rather than running in circles over the "marginal questions."[1] From personal experience, I can attest that this pattern has worked for me. Elder Corbridge summarizes the primary questions as follows:

1. Is there a God and is He our Father in Heaven?

2. Is Jesus Christ the Son of God and the Savior of the world?

3. Was Joseph Smith a prophet?

4. Is The Church of Jesus Christ of Latter-day
Saints the kingdom of God on the earth? ⚜

Working on the most important questions first requires diligence, humility, faith, and patience. In a recent conversation
with a friend from another faith, I felt impressed to share my
sense that sometimes a lack of knowledge on a specific matter,
including the nature of the Godhead, is an act of mercy from a
loving Father in Heaven so that we can be accountable for our
actions based on our knowledge. "To want more from Him
means to do more for Him and in doing more for Him, we
become more like Him," were my words to my good friend. I
am therefore persuaded that an open and willing heart and
mind will eventually be filled with God's light. I also believe
that what we currently acquire as knowledge in this mortal
journey is very, very little when compared to the wealth of
divine knowledge He is waiting to share with us. Coming to
an understanding that everything in life has a purpose and
that our Heavenly Parents really care about us and want the
very best for us is the most important element to a peaceful
and meaningful experience on this earth.

In my adult life, as I have continually worked on becoming a better scientist and a more committed disciple of the
Gospel of Jesus Christ, I have had a number of experiences
that required a recentering on the fundamental questions,
as outlined by Elder Corbridge. One of them happened in
2002, when I was a young and inexperienced researcher at
the Sorenson Molecular Genealogy Foundation in Salt Lake
City, Utah. Under the mentorship of molecular biologist
Scott R. Woodward, I began working on the reconstruction
of Joseph Smith Jr.'s genetic profile. That project was an

⚜ These questions are quite similar to those posed by Leonard Arrington in his
essay in the original edition of A Thoughtful Faith.

early experiment, or template, for what was quickly becoming a worldwide interest in combining family history with DNA information. During that process, I was contacted by a descendant of early apostle Parley P. Pratt, asking if I could use the knowledge on the Smith family's DNA to address questions related to Joseph Smith's polygamy and alleged children born to women other than Joseph's first wife, Emma. I was somewhat familiar with the practice of plural marriage in early church history, but I had never spent much time learning about it. The man who reached out to me explained that there were records in his family history supporting the possibility that one of Parley's sons, Moroni Pratt, was actually the biological son of Joseph Smith.

In order to build a proper case study, I began investigating more about Joseph Smith's gradual introduction and practice of plural marriage during the Kirtland and Nauvoo era of church history. I learned that most writings on the subject were laced with sensationalism and authors' biases. It became difficult to know what was historically correct and what was speculation. In a few instances I was quite disturbed by the way that certain authors decided to frame the alleged actions of the prophet. I felt like I was drinking mud from an old boot. I remember pushing my chair away from the desk as if I could distance myself from the feelings by distancing myself from the text. I took a deep breath.

Amidst this distaste for what I was encountering, I had the clear impression that I needed to do something else before continuing to work on that project: I had to re-assess my primary questions. I had to re-evaluate where I was standing with my personal testimony of the restoration. I spent the next few days reading scriptures, pondering, and pouring out my soul to the Lord, specifically asking about the reality of the First Vision. The answer came, and it was clear and personal. I felt at peace. I could continue to work on a project that became a significant area of my research and put me in contact with wonderful people from the Smith family over the course of the following two decades. Additionally, I began studying church history more diligently from that time onward, including the rich material surrounding the multiple accounts of the First Vision.

Five years previous to this experience I had the life-changing opportunity to attend the BYU Summer study abroad program in Jerusalem. I returned from the Holy Land with a clear desire to become a full-time seminary teacher, and enrolled in the seminary teaching pre-service course. I also had a new bishop in my student ward: the same Scott Woodward, who later invited me to join him in the molecular genealogy journey I described above.

Interviewing me in his office in the old Widtsoe building on BYU's campus, Dr. Woodward went over the usual questions regarding personal worthiness and commitment to the restored gospel. When the interview was over, we continued to chat for a while. At one point he asked a question that had a tremendous academic impact on my mind. He was curious to know how I was going to answer when a seminary student inquired about the theory of organic evolution. Although I cannot remember what I said (as I don't think I had ever thought about it before then), it was the initial spark that ignited my curiosity about the relationship between science and religion. From that time onward, I took as many opportunities as I could to learn more about the Church teachings regarding specific scientific topics. Thanks to that intriguing question from Bishop/Doctor Woodward, I made the decision that day to embark on a fascinating journey.

Brigham Young University is one of the best places in the world to ponder the mysteries of the universe and at the same time learn how to look for the hand of God in all things. During my undergraduate and graduate years there, I probably spent an equal amount of time in buildings named for the scientists John Widstoe and Henry Eyring as in the building named for the prophet Joseph Smith. Religious education was just as fascinating to me as attending a lecture on evolution. My bachelor's and master's degrees in scientific fields were accompanied by twice as many religion courses as were required for graduation, and in addition I acquired a graduate minor in ancient scriptures. My trajectory did not change substantially after graduating, as I worked for more than a decade as a researcher for Dr. Woodward at the Sorenson Molecular Genealogy Foundation, collecting and analyzing genealogical and genetic data to study the recent and ancient history of individuals and populations, while at the same time volunteering as an instructor at the Salt Lake Community College's institute of religion. I found equal joy and satisfaction, spiritually and intellectually, in studying and sharing both scientific and religious notions. I learned that if I left my mind and heart open to be taught and if I surrounded myself with people who knew a lot more than I did, both my mind and my spirit were continually expanded. How true is the saying that the more you know, the more you know how little you know!

Those were also the years in which I was given the opportunity to work on my doctoral degree. My colleagues and I at the Sorenson Molecular Genealogy Foundation collaborated with several world-renowned scientists. One of them was Professor Antonio Torroni from the University of Pavia, who suggested that I come to Italy to do graduate work using the data produced by Sorenson as part of my dissertation. It was a dream opportunity for me to be involved in a prestigious collaboration and to study in the field of population genetics with one of the top international experts in my discipline. Curiously, when I submitted my graduate research proposal on autosomal DNA as a tool to trace family histories,[2] Professor Torroni suggested that I instead take up a project he had worked on as a post-doctoral researcher at Emory University. This work would expand the current knowledge of Native American origins and migrations through the analysis of complete mitochondrial DNA genomes. For more than a decade, very little on that subject had been researched and he felt that the time was right to employ new advances in technology and the large dataset from Sorenson to reassess ancient migration routes to and within the Americas.

At first under his mentorship, and later with Professor Alessandro Achilli from the same department, I was given the opportunity to experiment with different genetic markers and populations which resulted in several peer-reviewed scientific publications in journals of influence. My doctoral research and continued employment with the Sorenson group resulted in numerous trips around the globe, attending conferences, collecting DNA samples, and learning about diverse cultures and histories. My training included work in population migrations, anthropological genetics, and evolutionary biology. We studied everything from Neanderthals and Denisovans and their likely admixture with anatomically modern humans, to the different expansion routes followed by our ancient ancestors thousands of years ago as they left the African continent to "colonize" the entire planet, to the biological relationships shared by individuals living in the recent past and today.

Amidst all this work, my fellow Latter-day Saints kept directing questions to me. How did I reconcile ancient human events that science showed happened tens or hundreds of thousands of years ago with the biblical account of the creation that seemed to imply that humans have been walking on the earth for no more than six millennia? Additionally, my scholarly work in the field of DNA and the origin of Native Americans placed me in the middle of the debate about whether there was any genetic evidence to support the historical identity of the people whose stories are narrated in the Book of Mormon.

There is an overwhelming body of scientific evidence brought forth by many different disciplines that support the existence of hominids dating from a time much earlier than the biblical Adam and Eve. The theory of evolution is not a mere guess about human origins. It is a well-supported explanation about the biological origins of our species. The genetic hierarchy that results in the nicely organized "world tree of all living organisms" is just the last of a mountain of scientific evidence showing a likely evolutionary path for our physical body.[3] So how do we reconcile assumptions about what scriptural accounts seem to be saying about the creation, together with the views of past prophets, and the theory of evolution? Having studied the matter from a scientific viewpoint as well as from the teachings of the restoration, my personal understanding is that The Church of Jesus Christ of Latter-day Saints preaches an historical Adam and Eve as the first two modern humans to enter in a covenant relationship with the Divine, and that their spirits, along with all the spirits of every person who ever lived on this earth since their time, is a spirit child of Heavenly Parents. However, regarding the creation of their physical bodies and whether others lived before them, the Church has not taken an official position,[4] leaving the matter entirely to science and to some future time when the Lord will explain how biological life was organized on this planet (D&C 101:32–34). In other words, modern revelation has not spoken on the matter of organic evolution. What we

learn about the creation of man and woman from the scriptures does not provide the complete story. With such an information gap and with what science has brought to the table so
far, there is no inevitable conflict between science and religion, particularly since each field has its emphasis in addressing related questions: science is concerned with how we came
to be, while the gospel provides answers about why we are
here. Science and religion may be construed as complementary. On the matter of Book of Mormon "genetics": a few years
ago I wrote a comprehensive essay explaining that using
DNA testing to attempt to identify biological descendants of
Lehi, Ishmael, Mulek, and other personages mentioned in
the Nephites' record is unlikely to succeed.[5] Eventually, that
article was reviewed, edited, and shortened by both scientists
and a special Church committee to be included as one of the
Gospel Topics essays available on the Church website.[6] Based
on nearly two decades working directly with ancient and
modern DNA samples from several international populations,
including those from the Americas, I continue to affirm what
I wrote then. The answer to the question of the genetic origin
of Book of Mormon people is not in the data that have been
gathered by research groups I have been associated with or
in data gathered by others. To understand why the data will
not yield the sought-after answer, we need to examine the
assumptions underlying the use of genetic evidence to answer
the question of historicity of Book of Mormon people. Simply
stated, the DNA of a single family of about thirty individuals
coming 2600 years ago to an already populated region of the
American continent would be swallowed in the indigenous
gene pool, leaving no genetic legacy detectable in the generations to follow. In contrast to various claims and assumptions
made by certain authors, DNA is not a viable tool to prove or
disprove an ancient origin of The Book of Mormon. My own

experience confirms that of others before me, that certain tools work well for certain questions, and matching the tool to the proper question is both wise and productive, while applying a tool to a question it is not designed to address brings confusion and dissatisfaction.

For the past decade I have continued my dedication to both genetic research and religious education from our home in Italy, where I directed the Rome Institute of Religion, and continued a scholarly collaboration with colleagues at the University of Pavia and other prominent institutions. Both my scientific and religious endeavors provide me with new opportunities to engage in the probings and debate of science and religion, especially in guiding the younger generation. As I did nearly a quarter of a century ago, they are navigating through questions dealing with the interplay between secular and spiritual matters.

I will summarize my final thoughts using the words of colleagues I've never met from BYU-Idaho, whose words also beautifully reflect my own convictions regarding the relationship between science and the Divine: "Revealed truth provides instructions for salvation, moral standards, and knowledge of God's will, but rarely provides knowledge about how things work, including how the physical world works. While God could choose to reveal anything, He rarely reveals what we can discover on our own." As I have worked to maintain intellectual humility, accepting my own personal limitations when it comes to understanding all that surrounds me, together with a sense of gratitude for all the people and experiences that have enriched my life, I am convinced that I have been rewarded with knowing more than what the natural world has to offer. I long for a time when our intellect will have fewer boundaries, our bodies will not be imprisoned in this dimension, and our divine potential may finally be reached. Until then, I will continue to search and embrace truths, wherever they might be and by whatever means they may persuade me, as scripture invites us to do (D&C 88:118).

A Sacred Yes: Hope in the Gospel of Jesus Christ

ASTRID S. TUMINEZ

A Foundation

God and ghosts inhabited my childhood. The ghosts came first, running rampant across my parents' villages in the Philippines. I was born in my father's village of Tigbauan, where spirits seen and unseen inhabited our fields and homes. Three men dressed in white once followed my father as he walked across rice paddies in the middle of the night. Then the shadow of a big mango tree tracked his steps as he walked home after a temporary shift as a policeman in town. My oldest sister, atop a *serisa* tree in our cousin's yard, picking tiny, sweet berries, suddenly felt an ice-cold hand wrap itself around her wrist. We took for granted the reality of things we didn't understand—hairy growling creatures coming down from the hills and sticking coconut frond spines up the slats of my aunt's bamboo floor, my uncle running away from a witch disguised as a cat that incessantly bounced up through his grass roof and down through his bamboo floor and back up again, and an angry wild boar jumping on my Chinese uncle-in-law's breakfast table (after he had killed some animals while hunting), staring him down with a curse, and causing him to die the next day.

When I was two my family left the rice fields for the city, where my life took a decidedly different turn. We built a hut on stilts in the slums on a beach that looked across to my mother's hulking home island called Guimaras. Along the beach a short distance from our hut stood the walls of a beautiful Catholic school founded in the late 1800s and run by the Daughters of Charity. Every year, young nuns visited the slums, bringing clothes, canned goods, and catechism to poor families like mine. That's how Sister Elvira Correa, a cherubic-faced nun with a heart to match, came to knock on my hut. After speaking with my mother and older sisters, she determined that we were smart enough to be invited to attend school for free. The nuns ran one of the most exclusive and expensive schools in the city, but had started a "free department" for poor girls, whose studies would be subsidized by the tuition-paying children in the main building across the street. I was five years old.

On the first day of Catholic school, I asked my aunt to accompany me to the registrar's office. The officer behind the glass window asked me to write my name on a form. My aunt and I looked at each other, realizing we didn't know how to spell my name. "Astrid" was a Scandinavian name, picked by my mom from a stray magazine that featured Queen Marie-Astrid of Belgium, and gifted to me. We wrote down "A-S-T-R-E-D."

I soon learned to spell my name correctly. The school— Colegio del Sagrado Corazon de Jesus (College of the Sacred Heart of Jesus)—was my equivalent of the wardrobe that led C.S. Lewis's kids into Narnia. I entered a magical—if daunting—new world of numbers and letters, classrooms with electric lighting, nail inspections on Monday mornings, uniforms, book-borrowing privileges, and weekly mass and confession. I also learned more about God (less about ghosts) in one of the strictest settings for that kind of learning.

We called our school Sagrado for short. Religion (later renamed as "Christian Living") was permanently part of the curriculum. A senior nun, known as Mother Superior, ran the institution. Other nuns served alongside lay employees as teachers and administrators. I looked to the nuns as authorized and authoritative servants of God. They floated ethereally along the Spanish-tiled corridors in their perfectly pressed white habits, blue wimples, and black rosary beads dangling on the front of their floor-length skirts. In class, they showed glossy colored pictures that made me stare in endless awe: heaven and hell, the devil with his pitchfork, angels behind a fair-skinned lady listening in rapt attention to a church sermon, a suffering Jesus (with a crown of thorns wrapped around his flaming heart), and an all-powerful, stern God sitting on a throne in heaven. This early religion made me fear God and think of him as a punisher. But the narrative had a mitigating figure: the Blessed Virgin Mary. She was everywhere—in the chapel, in books, on medallions, in calendars, and in all the churches and cathedrals of the city. We prayed to her more than to God the Father. In the rosary, we recited "Our Father" only once for every ten "Hail Marys." Mary interceded with love and mercy between me and the Father, and between me and Christ. She was understanding and kind. We sang the beautiful "Magnificat," which told of the angel Gabriel's appearance to Mary, the revelation that she would become the mother of God, and, because I loved her, that she was my mother, too. My own mother had left my family at that point, her relationship with my father having become too hard to endure. As a result, the phrase in the song that "Mary is my mother, too" meant the world to me.

As a child, I wanted to know good from evil. I wanted to please God and repent of my sins. Every week at mass and in the confessional box, I acknowledged my stumbling and failures, and humbly accepted penance. I prayed many times a day. I obeyed. I wanted to do well on the checklist of faith that the nuns taught me.

One day, I had a brief but life-changing conversation with Sister Susana Palces, the bright, young nun who taught my

Christian Living class. We were doing a reflection—just a small group of girls who were 9 or 10 years old—and she looked at me and said, "You know, Astrid, to follow Christ means you need to see God in every person." That phrase struck my very soul. Up to that point, I had thought of religion as a points system with rewards and punishment. I did things for points, in return for which the punitive God wouldn't punish me and I would not have to burn in hell. I had also judged others as hapless souls who were doing more poorly than I in the points system. Sister Susana's counsel made me pause and reflect. Perhaps religion was something else. Perhaps it was less about points for going to mass or confession or saying *novenas* (long, special prayers) or rosaries or engaging in self-flagellation (which many Filipinos literally enacted each year on Good Friday). Perhaps it was more about whether, in my thoughts, words, and actions, I could truly see God in others and treat them with kindness, respect, and reverence. It seemed like slow, hard, lifetime work.

Sister Susana's counsel led me to begin trying to see others truly as divine beings. I continued to believe fervently in God. Prayer buoyed and comforted me. When I was remorseful, I felt forgiven. In my poor, perilous, and sometimes frightening neighborhood, I felt angels nearby, witnessing the efforts and suffering of many souls. I turned for solace and kindness to Mary as my mother. My childhood belief in the world of spirits made it easy for me to have faith, the "evidence of things not seen." But I had evidence, too.

I was walking to school one day and about to cross an intersection when I distinctly heard a voice, "Unbuckle your shoe." Sagrado required black shoes and white socks as part of our uniform. I bent down to unbuckle my shoe. At the precise moment I crossed the street—perhaps due to my or the driver's inattention—a jeepney (one of those elongated jeep contraptions that ferry people everywhere in the Philippines) ran over half my right foot. Because the shoe was unbuckled, I managed to yank my foot out just in time. I arrived in second grade class that day with my heart pounding but my mind calm, knowing that God somehow saw me and wanted me to know it.

Absolute Certainty

I was baptized into The Church of Jesus Christ of Latter-day Saints when I was ten. Missionaries from Utah and Arizona found my family in the slums. They taught me and an older sister, who were laggards in the conversion process. My two oldest sisters in their late teens were first to join the church. They then referred my mom and a sister in Manila to the missionaries, and they, too, got baptized. My older brother was next. I hesitated to listen to "the Mormons" because I still felt loyal to my Catholic faith, the nuns, and my weekly rituals of mass and confession. I also liked to drink beer with my father. Several sets of missionaries came and went. The kindness of one of them led me to listen. This elder was gentle, listening, and playful. He and his companion took my questions seriously. As they taught me about the Plan of Salvation, I had the distinct impression that it was a better and truer story for my life and the lives of all children of God.

My journals from the age of eleven voice an absolute certainty and great happiness and hope in finding "the only true church." I embraced the doctrines, culture, and activities of my new church. I accepted a blueprint for my life, one that would take care of me from earth to eternity. It felt great! I felt like I was one of the luckiest people on earth. How, in a sea of billions, was I chosen to be among the very few to have the only light and truth that would take me from this difficult, unpredictable, and often miserable mortal existence into a realm of endless glory and progression? The nuns at school felt hurt by my family's change of religion. Sadly, I did not have the compassion to think of their feelings at the time or to have the confidence to explain to them why I had chosen another church. I was focused on having found the "pearl of great price" and reconfiguring my life to comply with my new religion.

My family still lived in the slums, but celebrated our new identity. We developed high levels of discipline, setting and achieving goals that reflected faith in our divine and unlimited potential. We spent practically the whole of every Sunday in our little branch meetinghouse, singing, teaching, worshiping, planning, filling out reports, and leading others. Two of my siblings served missions despite our need for them to begin working to support the family. I knew they had made the right choice. I tried to convert everyone I knew. I taught Primary and Sunday School even though I was only twelve or thirteen because our little branch needed all the help it could get, and I knew English well enough to read all the manuals without difficulty. I also filed many attendance reports (since my brother was the branch clerk), gave a million talks and testimonies, and became a weekly seminary teacher at fifteen. I learned about Utah, where the prophet and all the apostles lived. It was my promised land. I heard about Brigham Young University (BYU) and decided that I would study there.

Brokenness & Wholeness

It took three tries, a lot of tears, days of fasting, and the intervention of LDS Mexican-American friends in Manila before the U.S. embassy finally gave me a visa so I could attend BYU. I had already had over a year of college at the University of the Philippines, where I was attending on a full government scholarship, but my dream remained to go to Utah. At eighteen years old, I arrived in Provo. I majored in Russian language and literature and International Relations, worked as much as I legally could as a foreign student, and found outstanding mentors. My church membership and activity continued to be as important to me as ever, although I did begin having questions about my future as a woman. The culture at BYU and Utah in general seemed to emphasize marriage so much that I began to wonder if something was inherently wrong with me because I had myriad aspirations that had nothing to do with marriage. I was a good student, wanted to go to graduate school, and aimed to see the world.

After BYU, I got my master's degree in Soviet Studies at Harvard, received a fellowship at the Harvard Kennedy School of Government, and entered the Ph.D. program in political science at MIT. My faith journey continued to evolve. As I think about this period in my life, I think about a dear friend, the son of my late Ph.D. adviser at MIT, who is an Episcopalian minister in New Hampshire. A former full-time leader in conservation and an agnostic who had never read the Bible, he repeatedly heard the voice of God calling him to become a priest. It was a call so powerful that, despite his stubborn resistance, he did eventually drop his work and, in mid-life, pursued divinity studies and committed himself to serving God by "transforming people" and "renewing earth." When the COVID-19 pandemic hit, my friend moved to the woods or what he calls the *poustinia*, the Russian word for wilderness. He is the pastor of Kairos Earth or Church in the Woods. He and his flock worship in 106 acres of woods and wetlands. They break bread and drink wine in the forest. The sacred earth is their "church."

My friend writes a newsletter as he observes life and death, perfection and imperfection, despair and hope in the wilderness. He sees all these daily in the rocks, woods, trees, flowers, mushrooms, animals, birds, insects, and seasons. Nothing in this wild, natural world is ever entirely tidy. Everything is change. Everything is beautiful and worth experiencing and observing. Everything breaks and dies and rises again. Everything is the body of Christ.

As I read my friend's posts, I think about my initial years in Utah, which indeed proved to be the promised land, overflowing with literal and metaphorical "milk and honey." I had a life of abundance for the first time, with food, running water and electricity. Many of my religious certainties were confirmed. I had joy in my faith and my community. But, like in my friend's *poustinia*, I also discovered that everything was change. Life and faith proved to be less tidy than I thought. At BYU and in the decades following, I have experienced discomfort, doubt, and discouragement. I have felt the ebb of faith, the waning of hope, and the rise of despair. I have felt waves of serious absurdity. The same religion that gave me wholeness has also left me feeling broken.

What caused my pain and distress? In the age of the Internet and the deluge of confessional postings on doubt, separation, abuse suffered, and departure from church among Latter-day Saints, little about my personal faith crisis feels particularly new or remarkable. I became disturbed by aspects of church history, including the denial of priesthood to black people prior to 1978. I was ashamed of polygamy. I was angry about my naïve assumptions regarding "eternal marriage," the overly prescriptive roles assigned to men and women, and the injustices that these gender roles sometimes caused. I remember once in Relief Society telling my beloved sisters that, as an LDS woman, I felt that my size 7 feet were being made to fit in size 6 shoes. It was unendurable. The idealized portrayals of Joseph Smith did not seem to withstand historical scrutiny.

I began to question dogma and the uninformed certainty of others' declarations. I observed gaps between the marketing of my faith and the actual reality of church members' lives. As I got older, I wondered whether there was more judgment and shame—instead of Christlike love and kindness—in my religion.

As an LDS woman, was I supposed to suppress my energy and aspirations, and find absolute and pure fulfillment *exclusively* within the domain of domestic life? Should I suppress the joy I felt in exploring the world, becoming a leader and decision-maker, and pursuing goals that made me feel relevant and alive? How was it that no single church leader ever encouraged me or validated my aspirations? After twenty-seven hours of labor, why couldn't I hold my first child during her blessing in the chapel? Why did my church exclude me in this and other ways? I once heard the poet, Carol Lynn Pearson, talk in a podcast about her experiences and feelings as a person of "second-class spiritual citizenship" by virtue of being a woman. I understood that the church did not intend that effect. But that's how it felt for me, too, and the feeling hurt and continued hurting. Finally, as life and work taught me a deeper appreciation of the rich spiritual lives of other people not of my faith, I became more uncomfortable insisting that there was one and only one valid way to return to God. In a world of seven billion people with only a few Latter-day Saints, and perhaps only a handful of those Latter-day Saints attaining truly Christ-like character, the numbers did not seem to me to add up. Where is my God who loves and sees *all* of his children and provides them diverse paths to wholeness and a return to their heavenly home? Haunted by such questions, my "dark night of the soul" lasted nearly a decade. Nonetheless, I kept going to church because I believed that faith required persistence and endurance.

The *coup de grace* in my faith crisis came from a conversation with a bishop while I was living in New York City. He had asked to meet. I was then juggling a husband, two children, and a very demanding job. The bishop asked about my work. I felt a sudden hope, thinking that my ecclesiastical leader finally saw me as I was and wanted to listen to my successes and struggles as a human being. Instead, he began telling me that I was *not* a good mother. He said that my having a nanny proved that I was not raising my children. I wasn't worthy. His words crushed me. Guilt and shame, fear and sadness, exhaustion and doubt, and anger and resentment engulfed me all at once. I felt that I was destined to fail as a mother. I felt that my church had little to offer me at that point in my life. I wept bitterly. In the days following, I knew that I faced a fork in the road. Was I to abandon this faith that had been so real and sustaining to me?

The answer to that question—part answer, part decision—came over several months. The answer was *No*. The roots of my faith were deep. Everything I had become as an adult seemed in one way or another linked to my years of commitment to my religion. I also realized that I had to ask better questions: Was I in the church to get approval from certain circles, or to become more Christ-like? How should I exercise my faith independently of the approbation of men? How do I face God daily with a clear conscience instead of a manufactured or officially approved appearance of goodness? How do I set boundaries between my *self* and the pervasive, even overwhelming culture of my religion? As a woman and a child of God, I decided that I would no longer let the unkind or uninformed judgments of men in the church, or in any realm, define me. In coming to this hybrid decision, I felt great clarity and peace.

Reverend Stephen Blackmer, my friend from Church in the Woods, once pointed out that the Bible is all about broken people finding their way back to wholeness. Christianity is imperfect, but it offers a way back. It is exercised by "fallible human beings." I am one of those fallibles, trying to find my way back over and over again, and for as long as is necessary. I came to see that the Church of Jesus Christ helps me do that. I remain a Latter-day Saint because I think I have found a way to explore, through my faith, community, and religion, what the philosopher Friedrich Nietzsche calls a "sacred Yes."

A Sacred Yes

I am not a Nietzsche expert and, unlike this esteemed philosopher, I retain a devotion to the Divine. But a Nietzschean metaphor I value is that of the Camel, Lion, and Child, used to describe the three phases of potential human evolution towards our highest and best selves. The Camel is simply a beast of burden, unconscious of her own will and a stranger to wisdom. She is the product of her inherited environs—many things she could not help—such as my childhood world of ghosts, spirits, dogma, and absolute certainty. In contrast, the Lion asserts freedom, innovates, and rejects illusions, but remains reactive to other people and external motivations. She says "no" to many things and rejects what she used to accept so easily, reminding me of my decade of struggle with my religion. Finally, the Child sees things with new eyes. "The child is innocence and forgetting, a new beginning, a game, a self-rolling wheel, a first movement, a sacred Yes," according to Nietzsche.[1] The Child's Yes is sacred because she is willing to embrace true freedom, creativity, and responsibility; unburden herself of the past; discover or re-discover her beliefs as if for the first time; and create new meanings and commitment.

To me, the Child exhibits what Buddhists call a beginner's mind. Zen teacher Shunryu Suzuki says, "In the beginner's mind there are many possibilities, in the expert's mind there are few."[2] In the Bible, Christ notes that ". . . Except [we] be converted, and become as little children, [we] shall not enter into the kingdom of Heaven" (Matthew 18:3). In Book of Mormon language, the Child is ". . .submissive, meek, humble, patient, full of love, willing to submit to all things which the Lord seeth fit to inflict upon him, even as a child doth submit to his father" (Mosiah 3:19).

Becoming the Child is neither passive submission nor uncritical, comfortable absolutism. It is, instead, an active exploration founded on humility, curiosity, love, and awe. Humility—because God is greater than I am and through his perfect grace wants to teach me (Isaiah 55:8). Curiosity—because God's glory is "intelligence" (D&C 93:36) and curiosity is native to intelligence. Love—because that is the ultimate antidote to fear and shame (see 1 John 4:18 and 2 Timothy 1:7). And Awe—because there remains so much spiritual truth and so many spiritual gifts to discover and experience. The Child looks at everything with wonder and new eyes, sincerely asks questions, and, in faith and patience, says Yes to a creative and worthy (if sometimes slow) path forward, while embracing complexity, paradox, ambiguity, duality, doubt, and loose ends.

The greatest trial of my faith had to do with real feelings of "second class spiritual citizenship" as a woman. In the mode of the aspiring Nietzschean Child, I have acknowledged these feelings while yet finding joy and affirmation in my ongoing "Yes" to gospel teachings and the best elements of Latter-day Saint values linked to womanhood: my divine worth (a principle I was taught by both the Catholic nuns and Latter-day Saint missionaries); hard work and striving toward worthy goals; charity and service; family and fidelity; strength, courage, and leadership; divine love and forgiveness; and eternal relationships. Like mother Mary, who asked Gabriel a question before accepting her calling ("How shall this be, seeing I know not a man?" Luke 1:34), I, too, can ask questions. And, even if the answers are not tidy, I can celebrate the questions and thought process as a gift from God. As a believing woman, I also embrace my choice to be a mother, as imperfect as I am in that role. I love my children and husband deeply, and rejoice in my belief that our links and affections transcend this life.

My sacred Yes is also rooted in my testimony of the "Prodigal God." "The Prodigal God" is a book title by Timothy Keller, a Presbyterian pastor in New York. Keller reinterprets the parable of the prodigal son, focusing on "prodigal" not as "wayward" or wasteful, but as "recklessly extravagant, having spent everything."[3] Both brothers in the parable are lost—one having wasted his father's inheritance, the other being so self-righteous and moralistic that he does not join his father's forgiveness and welcome of his lost sibling. More strikingly, Keller observes that the father, symbolic of God, is also prodigal—extravagant and reckless—in his forgiveness, love, and grace for both sons. As a woman, willing to "magnify the Lord," I have experienced the love and grace of the prodigal God. I am supported in my moments of doubt, suffering and frailty. I am seen for everything am, and loved beyond measure. Because of the prodigal God, I can be the Child with the sacred Yes, willing to leap into the miracle of the atonement and saying Yes to becoming an instrument of God's will and His peace.

During my dark struggle with faith, I remember one morning riding the express bus from New York's Upper East side to Wall Street. I was reflecting on my suffering and loss of certainty when, suddenly, the noise of the city stopped. A deep silence filled my mind and I heard a voice say, "You are loved." That day completely changed me. I felt and knew God. My proper course was to surrender to this God. I thought about the "kernel of wheat" in Christ's parable recorded in John 12:24, in which the Lord implies that death is necessary for life and growth. Amidst this personal revelation on love and my meditation on the link between death and life, I realized that my old ideas, my pride and prejudices, my clinging to absolute certainty, and my judgment, shame, and anger had to die. Instead, I had to hold out my hand, open my ear, allow my heart to break open, and let the magnificent prodigal God ignite the divine seed already in me and in others, to make all of us alive and fruitful over and over again.

Finally, what we used to call "Mormonism" keeps me open to the paradox of mystery and trust. Christ, ironically like Nietzsche, instructs that we must become as little children (Matthew 18:1–11). If the Child is "willing to submit to all things," then I must be willing to submit to mystery, especially the mystery of knowledge and revelation. I can trust that my understanding will expand both in this life and the hereafter, even as I am baffled by many things. I can continue to discover light and truth through conversation, observation, experience, prayer, study, meditation, broad and deep reading, and compassionate living in my community among the Saints and in the larger world. I can trust the reality of things I don't understand fully, but have experienced as divine. I have not arrived at a destination, but am on a sacred journey. I no longer need the dogmatic certainty of my childhood. Quoting William James, "I am no lover of disorder and doubt as such. Rather I fear to lose truth by the pretension to possess it already wholly."[4] The metaphorical Child can thrive in a realm of imperfection, discomfort, questions, and exploration, while touching truth and the divine on a daily basis. I need not—I ought not—limit myself and the ways that God can influence me and my life.

I am willing to embrace a wide-eyed approach to possibility, to hear the voice of God as I am prepared to listen and understand. I am back sometimes to the child I was, revisiting that open experience of spirits and the mystical in my parents' villages. I relish the language of scripture and the process of "likening" it to myself, my circumstances, and my religious community. I am humbled to hear the voice of God. That can happen at church, in the woods, in my office, during prayer, while running, or as I sit waiting at a traffic light. As my friend, the Reverend Blackmer, sums it up from his wilderness in New Hampshire: "I am not good at prayer, am constantly distracted by events in the world . . . . None of what I am doing makes rational sense. I cannot explain it using the categories that the world knows . . . This is none of that. God is in charge. I am following, trying to listen, trying to be obedient. I don't really understand, but I don't need to. I trust. I am staying put."[5]

Discipleship, Persons, and Institutions

TERRYL GIVENS

Of all the moral virtues, courage holds pride of place in my own pantheon of revered qualities. Having read the historical accounts of Christianity's first martyrs, I am most moved by the words of the aged Polycarp. Led to execution by immolation, he had merely to renounce his faith in Christ to escape the flames. Eyewitnesses recorded his response: "Eighty-six years have I served him, and he has done me no wrong. How can I blaspheme my King and my Savior?" And so he perished, as did hundreds of others of his era who did not merely profess belief, but enacted their faith at horrific cost. The key to understanding such courage may be reflected in the words of the scholar of early Christianity Marcellino D'Ambrosio: these martyrs, he wrote, "died for a person, not an ideology."[1]

The young Polycarp had known the aged John the Apostle, but he was born almost four decades after the death of Jesus. It is the more remarkable, therefore—assuming as I do that D'Ambrosio is correct—that one's connection to Christ, one's feeling of love and loyalty, could attain to such a pitch of personal intensity, catalyzing such absolute courage and sacrifice. The same may be true of many martyrs throughout history, and of many among our own community of Saints. I would hope the same is true of myself, but I have not been called upon for such acts of raw bravery and cannot know.

However, in our religious lives as Latter-day Saints, the presence of that institution through which we learn of Christ, and through which we worship Christ, continually threatens to loom larger than Christ himself in our hierarchy of loyalties. Far larger, in any case, than was true in the small, tightly knit associations of Christians of Polycarp's era, who met in house churches and were presided over only by local pastors within their own orbit. Our relationship to Christ, in other words, is much more profoundly mediated, conditioned, shaped, formed, and contextualized than was the case for Christians of the first few generations. And we need—or at least I need—to constantly consider that institutional presence, and what it means for my discipleship.

I take it as a given that the church is "true and living." More importantly, it is, ideally, steeped in truth and "life-giving," in the words of the second-century church father Irenaeus. Yet, it is beyond dispute that its leaders are not infallible, and its members can individually and collectively, in the words of a Book of Mormon prophet, be "a great stumbling block" (Alma 4:10). Still, this particular incarnation of the body of Christ was formed under divine guidance. Through its inspired prophet, the "great story" of humankind's eternal saga was restored; as were the true (plural and passible) nature of God, the origin and destiny of the human soul, and the durability of what we most cherish: human love, relationships, "sociability."

In what precise sense, then, is the church *living* or *life-giving*, and how to proceed when those epithets no longer ring true in our personal life? My devotion, like Polycarp's, is to the Christ, "the light which is in all things, which giveth life to all things" (D&C 88:13). My personal faith is in the felt actuality, the literal truth behind those words. And my fidelity to the church resides in my trust that the institution has most fully revealed him, provided me the practical resources to learn to emulate him, and stewards the holy powers that empower me to be eternally "at one" with him—and with those I love. If those three propositions are true, then the negative dimensions of the institution, as of any institution filled by human servants, are in the end beside the point. That does not entirely ameliorate the frustrations, the pain, and the personal costs those temporal realities bring in their turbulent wake.

Orson Pratt was, to my mind, the most heroic instance of a disciple who could experience the crushing disappointment of watching good men building a stumbling block, and still remain unmoved in his commitment to Christ and to truth. ⸙

In the more contemporary era, and much more abundantly documented, we have the case of Eugene England as a Saint who wrestled with the conflicts he felt between personal conviction and institutional loyalty. I offer his story not for its moral exemplariness or for the solutions it offers, but for what it might teach us about the perseverance in our church culture of the original dilemma of Eden: how do we face with fortitude and resolution those conflicts we inevitably encounter between competing Goods? And as we Saints continue to work through our own "late to the party" version of a modernist crisis, his prescience about the insistent demands of a historical consciousness in treating our own historical past and institutional formation are especially timely.

England's adult life was a perpetual series of conflicts with both local and general authorities. Many of his injuries were self-inflicted, and many were aggravated by his propensity for provocation. Beginning in the 1970s, a common theme emerged: England, who had worked for a time as a researcher and writer in the historical department of the church, felt growing alarm about official founding narratives and institutional histories that were ultimately untenable and indefensible. Even though his questions never led him to doubt the essential core of Latter-day Saint teachings, he correctly

---

⸙ At one point in his apostleship, he was summoned to a quorum meeting and chastised jointly for being the lone holdout against Brigham Young's Adam-God teachings. His brothers in the quorum rebuked him, among other pejoratives, for stubbornness, opposition to truth, selfishness, hardness of heart, and spiritual darkness.[2] Pratt humbly maintained his convictions, conceding "as far as my conscience would allow me." In 1902 and more emphatically in 1976, the leadership repudiated the Adam-God doctrine.[3]

perceived that thriving in a more complex and contested religious environment would require serious adjustments to those definitions and paradigms that were widespread among his fellow Saints. His remedy was to attempt to place the many contraries he saw into constructive dialogue.

His most famous foray into a kind of preventative apologetics was to engage the competing conceptions of God the Father (patriologies) taught by Joseph and Hyrum Smith. Joseph expressly taught of a God who had once been man and achieved his divine status through an educative process of theosis. He further taught that in some sense, God continues to grow in dominion as he brings his posterity to an exalted position like his own. Joseph Fielding Smith interpreted his grandfather Hyrum to espouse a more conventionally absolutist God, who was always omnipotent and omniscient. And so, two parallel traditions persisted within the church, little observed by modern members but lurking beneath the surface of Latter-day Saint consciousness. In England's 1979 prescription, "These Church leaders were using two different, but complementary, ways of talking about God based on two different aspects of the Mormon understanding of God, both of which . . . are essential to our theology and must be maintained."[4] Attempting to reconcile the two ways of talking about God, England incurred the wrath of Elder Bruce R. McConkie, and was not only publicly censured (twice) but directed to cease speaking and writing on the subject.

Other provocations had already erupted. In 1973 England had defended the church's controversial priesthood ban even as he decried the racism that he argued was responsible for the policy—a racism he laid at the feet not of the ban's instigators, but rather the membership. The spiritual immaturity of the church, he argued, made such a tragic ban necessary for the establishment and early growth of the church. In the case of the priesthood ban, the threatening contradictions that would increasingly vex the reflective faithful were both historical and scriptural. Joseph had ordained Blacks to the priesthood, and the Book of Mormon expressly taught that "He denieth none that come unto him, black and white" (2 Nephi 26:33). Yet blacks *were* denied—priesthood, temple ordinances, and the means of exaltation.

Theology rather than history was at the root of another dissonance England detected and protested: The Church's unofficial but frequently expressed support for the Vietnam War. "Renounce war and proclaim peace," reads D&C 98:16. Nevertheless, England's public expressions of opposition to the war aroused the ire of the Brethren and his colleagues alike. In a fourth instance of dissonance that England wanted to transmute into dialogue, he worked to reconcile his feminist commitment to full gender equality with the divinely mandated practice of polygyny. Even while affirming the practice's inspired origins, he wrote that "the Church . . . developed a semi-official sexist theology to support it."[5] The critique was unusually brazen for a faithful member, but his greater sin in official eyes was to deny the eternal status of the principle: "it was for mortal purposes and not to be practiced in heaven."[6] He was called in to church headquarters and told to publish no more "speculative theology."

Faith Crisis 2.0

It is tempting to see the current convulsions of the early twenty-first century, marked by widespread disaffection, alienation, and exodus, as unprecedented. (And not solely—or principally—in terms of scope; anyone familiar with church history knows the Kirtland exodus was proportionally more massive). It may appear to some that efforts to respond to the crisis by teaching prophetic fallibility, a larger human factor in the Restoration saga, and broader conceptions of "translation," are desperate innovations born of necessity. In reality, these are not concessions to progressivism or liberalism but are steps in the direction of neo-orthodoxy. This is one of the most underappreciated legacies of England's provocations: he was not a progressive trying to move the church into harmony with emerging moral norms (though in some cases that would have been the effect). He was, in fact, an utterly orthodox Saint, who was working to rehabilitate the original vision of Joseph Smith across a spectrum of issues.

The genuine aberration in Latter-day Saint historical development was the anti-intellectualism and strident fundamentalism of the mid 1930s-1990s (which continues in some quarters even today), unfolding in disregard for Joseph Smith's foundational principles and to the personal cost of England's career. A thorough intellectual/cultural history of that era is not possible in these few pages. I will instead make that case by sketching a number of illustrative moments in that narrative. My thesis is that the recent crisis may yet prove therapeutic, in precisely the way England himself anticipated: "The increase in questioning, even in skepticism, since the Enlightenment, . . . some see as evidence of Satan's battle against the Restoration. But, on balance, I believe that such skepticism has been positive: it has certainly undermined false religion and bad faith . . . If skepticism is properly understood and used it can reinforce the need for both religion and faith . . . Skepticism, in the perspective I am searching for here, the questing, questioning approach of heart and mind, leads directly back toward the balance of humility and fearlessness we find only in true *faith*."[7]

England was referring to the larger historical catalyst of the Enlightenment as a salutary force that undermined the kind of faith alluded to by Milton: "A man may be a heretic in the truth, and if he believe things only because his pastor says so, or the assembly so determines, without knowing other reason, though his belief be true, yet the very truth he holds becomes his heresy."[8] One happy consequencc of Enlightenment norms concerning justice, moral agency, and rationality, for instance, was that it precipitated a steep decline of belief in the sovereign, capricious, vengeful God of Calvinist influence.

In analogous fashion, the long-range impact of the internet, social media, and (among the Saints) a late-blooming historical consciousness of the ways Saints construct their faith paradigms could turn out to be deeply beneficial. The most untenable and historically oblivious features of LDS gospel understanding are overdue for consignment to the theological ash heaps of history. A few examples from early church history provide lessons that Saints unfamiliar with the past are having to learn, painfully, a second time.

Joseph Smith & Prophetic Fallibility

In 1830, Joseph produced a revelation that suggested four elders should go to Canada where they could sell the copyright to the Book of Mormon and garner desperately needed funds. "Ye shall go to Kingston seeking me continually through mine only Begotten & if ye do this ye shall have my spirit to go with you & ye shall have an addition of all things which is expedient in me & I grant unto my servent a privelige that he may sell <a copyright>."[9] The venture was a dismal failure and David Whitmer later pointed to it as a prime instance of Joseph's prophetic failings.

"We asked Joseph how it was that he had received a revelation from the Lord for some brethren to go to Toronto and sell the copyright, and the brethren had utterly failed in their undertaking. Joseph did not know how it was, so he enquired of the Lord about it, and behold the following revelation came through the stone: 'Some revelations are of God: some revelations are of men: and some revelations are of the devil.'"[10] Even admitting overstatement on the part of a disgruntled Whitmer (and the prophecy about selling the copyright could be read as conditional, with its caveat, "if the People harden not their hearts against the enticeings of my spirit"), Joseph's response does not sound entirely out of character. He was openly frank about his own flaws and fallibility. "If you will not accuse me, I will not accuse you. If you will throw a cloak of charity over my sins, I will over yours—for 'charity covereth a multitude of sins,'" he said on another occasion.[11] He professed himself one of the "weak things of the earth" (D&C 141:1), pronounced that it would take "patience and faith" to sustain him (D&C 21:5), and frankly confessed, "I don't want you to think I am very righteous, for I am not very righteous."[12]

In one of his most revealing statements about his self-understanding, Joseph complained that "he did not enjoy the right vouchsafed to every American citizen—that of free speech. He said that when he ventured to give his private opinion" about various subjects, they ended up "being given out as the word of the Lord because they came from him."[13] When not speaking with prophetic authority, in other words, he claimed no authority at all—which is why his pronouncements on subjects from the location of Lehi's New World landfall to the prospects of the Kirtland Bank were as liable to error as other men's.

The Church as Divinely Led

The source of the most egregious errors in Protestantism (and the creeds God condemned as abominations) is the concept of divine sovereignty. In claiming that God is the "source of all that is," Calvin, for example, stipulates that God ordains all events, historical and personal, tragic and horrific, that unfold in human history. Calvin's God does not merely foresee and permit all that transpires; as Sovereign, He personally planned and orchestrated the entirety of history. In this view, all events are in God's blueprint, including "the fall of the first man and in him the ruin of his posterity," which God "at His own pleasure arranged." In Luther's language, "nothing takes place but as [God] wills it."[14] God "foresees, purposes, and does all things according to His immutable, eternal, and infallible will. By this thunderbolt, 'Free-will' is thrown prostrate and utterly dashed to pieces."[15]

Most Latter-day Saints would be surprised to be told how deeply their own assumptions about a divinely led church incorporate Calvinist preconceptions about an all-powerful deity. The ubiquitous laments, "why didn't God x," or "couldn't God have z," in reference to tragedies like the long-delayed priesthood ban reversal, or the church's so-late-in-coming recognition of a genetic component to sexual orientation—presuppose a God whose desires for his people are always unambiguously communicated and perfectly executed by those directing the church. In no other case were such expectations more utterly overthrown than in Wilford Woodruff's 1894 announcement to what must have been a stunned congregation. At the time, temple sealings united individuals to prophetic lines, not ancestors, in a practice known as dynastic sealing. Increasingly troubled by the lack of congruence between that practice and the words of Malachi linking "fathers" and "children" (4:6), President Woodruff told the Saints that for some time he had felt that the practice of disrupting the natural family order felt "wrong." So, after a

half century of such dynastic sealings, he "sought more revelation concerning sealing under the law of adoption" and was
answered by the Spirit of God, who told him, "let every man
be adopted to his father."[16]

Today's Saints have often shown little spiritual tolerance
for developments that do not follow a divinely mandated
and divinely supervised script. Nineteenth-century Saints
typically had a different conception of *our—and our leaders'—*
limited capacity to perfectly register and enact God's will. One
listener to the 1894 course correction wrote his uncle, "Why
does the Lord permit things to go on in a wrong or loose way,
where the dearest rights and tenderest feelings of the human
heart are involved?" He then answered his own question: We
have to "gain knowledge and wisdom by repeated trials and
mistakes, He has left us in a measure free to act and see what
we would do."[17] His uncle, the avid journalist Warren Foote,
responded with total equanimity: "The revelation of the Lord
through President Woodruff on the subject of sealing children to parents, brought a great relief to my mind. I never
could understand the practice of adopting persons of one
family into another, thereby robbing parents of their children.
Elijah was to turn the hearts of the fathers to their children,
and the children to their fathers, not to some other person's
father. The word of the Lord through Prest. Woodruff agrees
precisely with the mission of Elijah, the way I have always
thought it should be."[18]

In a similar, all too-human way, nineteenth-century leaders
had acknowledged some missteps in implementing plural
marriage through various phases and forms, as apostle Amasa
Lyman did from the Tabernacle: "We obeyed the best we knew
how, and, no doubt, made many crooked paths in our ignorance. We were only children."[19] When baptism for the dead
was revealed, Saints initiated the practice without order or

record-keeping and had to retreat and restart. Wilford asked the congregation rhetorically, "Why did we [act precipitously]? Because of the feeling of joy that we had," he explained.[20]

A few years later, another prophet reminded the church of a Restoration still in progress, with leaders as well as members liable to err and stumble and grow: "Seventy years ago this Church was organized with six members. We commenced, so to speak, as an infant. We had our prejudices to combat. Our ignorance troubled us in regard to what the Lord intended to do and what He wanted us to do. . . . We advanced to boyhood, and still we undoubtedly made some mistakes, which . . . generally arise from a . . . lack of experience. . . . When we examine ourselves, however, we discover that we are still not doing exactly as we ought to do, notwithstanding all our experience."[21]

By the late twentieth century, however, the dominant narrative in the church was one that closely approached infallibility on the part of prophets, flawless linearity in the church's history, and near-perfect harmony in the manifold doctrinal pronouncements of the leadership through time. And so Saints are re-learning the previously understood fact that the Restoration is a process, not an event, and it is still incomplete. We know this for scriptural as well as historical reasons. The Book of Mormon itself refers to that Nephite record as intended to recapture "much of my gospel" (1 Ne. 13:34). Doctrinal restoration is progressive. And the role of human weakness and human agency is incompatible with a sovereign God who orchestrates the unfolding of his plan like a master puppeteer. The fact that Latter-day Saints worship a God who weeps should be sufficient evidence of a world and a church that do not always act in perfect compliance with his desires.

The Nature of Translation

Similar to these misunderstandings regarding the role of fallibility and agency, we see the development of dangerous misconceptions—of recent origin—concerning the nature of revelation and translation. Joseph never considered himself a stenographer of the divine mind (though others then and now have), else he would not have recruited half a dozen associates to help him edit the revelations prior to publication, as abundantly attested in the manuscripts. ✤

First presidency member George Q. Cannon spoke plainly of the human element in revelation, using language that is almost entirely foreign to contemporary Latter-day Saint assumptions: "The revelation we may get, imperfect at times because of our fallen condition and because of our failure to comprehend the nature of it, comes from God. . . . Man is but the medium, but the instrument, is but the conduit through which it flows. . . . This is the position occupied by the Latter-day Saints. We believe in revelation. It may come dim; it may come indistinct, it may come sometimes with a degree of vagueness which we do not like. Why? Because of our imperfection; because we are not prepared to receive it as it comes in its purity; in its fulness from God. He is not to blame for this."[23]

The most prominent case in point concerns the translation of the Book of Abraham. According to some surveys, a high proportion of those disaffected from the church trace their motivation to questions concerning the validity of the Book of Abraham translation. Critics point to overwhelming evidence that Joseph was an imposter, since his translations do

---

✤ The Joseph Smith Papers volume, *Revelations and Translations: Manuscript Revelation Books*, is a facsimile edition that conspicuously highlights the various editorial hands at work, using various colored inks.[22]

not correspond to the purported original fragments. Die-hard orthodox defenders of the faith insist he accurately translated, verbatim, an ancient text authored by Abraham. However, over a century ago, church leaders and scholars alike acknowledged a good bit of uncertainty regarding the exact nature of Joseph's "translation" efforts. Prominent educator and writer John Evans wrote that "It does not matter, so far as philosophical or practical purposes are concerned, where or how he got them. The only questions we may properly ask about them, are they true? Are they consistent with one another? Do they produce good results in the lives of those who accept them?"[24]

Book of Mormon scholar J. M. Sjodahl noted that, unlike that scripture, transmitted by "the gift and power of God," the Book of Abraham "was given by the power of the Spirit of God but [also] through the usual channels of research." Therefore, "if a mistake should be proved in the translation of the Egyptian documents, . . . such a mistake might be due to the channel through which the inspiration flowed."[25] B. H. Roberts also acknowledged that Smith's efforts as a translator were not always a claim to scholarly authority: "in the translations Joseph Smith has given to the world—confessedly not by scholarship but by inspiration, by his own spirit being quickened by contact with God's spirit—that in those translations are truths that are part of a mighty system of truth, the like of which is not found elsewhere among men."[26] And finally, Junius Wells (founder of *The Contributor* and first Young Men's president of the church) spoke with a liberality far from the panicky entrenchment of many modern Saints: "We have not been lax, nor afraid to learn from whatever light the wisdom of the world might throw upon the illustrations of the Book of Abraham and their translation by the Prophet

Joseph." ⟶ In other words, we find several examples here of letting the facts rather than assumptions drive the understanding. And an altered understanding, not utter skepticism about the prophetic mode, is the result. Today, by contrast, ingrained assumptions about how translation and revelation should transpire often take precedence over a frank humility in the face of divine processes and bewildering spiritual phenomena of the type that left even a visionary like Paul perplexed about his own experience: "Whether in the body, or out of the body, I cannot tell" (2 Cor. 12:3).

Prescience & Pressing Forward

When England was pressured to resign from Brigham Young University in 1998, the tragedy was not just the personal alienation and public humiliation of a devout disciple whose labors had kept many in the church: the tragedy was also in the punished prescience that was implicitly recognized only after his death. England, in spite of his flaws, was perfectly accurate in his diagnosis of a principal cause of the looming upheavals among the faith-tried, and in his prescription for its amelioration. As England was being exiled from the institution he had so loved and tried to improve, he made a tragic prediction: "I think we are going to have a situation where these people ['bright and experienced and more liberal in their views'] are just going to leave."[28] Two decades later, a leading Latter-day Saint scholar could retrospectively confirm the prognosis:

⟶ Compare with the fragile, unyielding—and historically unjustified—dogmatism of an entrenched literalist: "by opening the semantic range of "translation," John Thompson maintains, "The miraculous claims of Joseph Smith must continue to be watered-down and explained away."[27]

Speaking of the "twenty-year chill between the church's administrative and intellectual leaders" that began circa 1980, Philip Barlow writes, "The earlier permafrost . . . exacted an ongoing toll on a new generation whose native tongue was the internet. . . . This medium's cacophonic choir introduced a widening public to versions of the historical and social problems that [Leonard] Arrington and his colleagues"—foremost among them being Eugene England— "had earlier attempted to address, with erudition, in the context of faith. The result of the marginalizing of Arrington and England among an unprepared populace was frequent dismay, even panic, and a sense of betrayal. 'Why weren't we told these things while growing up in the church?' The dismay proved contagious among a widening minority, contributing to the Mormon inflection of a growing societal disenchantment with organized religion."[29]

Many aspects of England's non-conformity that incurred censure from church leaders have over time become mainstreamed. He wrote about the impediments to female equality that were institutionalized in the church's culture and practices; today, the church is in the midst of numerous adjustments that bring women into many (not all) of its governing councils, eliminate sexist language from temple ceremonies, and more equally apportion resources to the young women of the church. He exuded compassion for the gay community and spoke at some of their early gatherings—at a time when church rhetoric condemned not only the practice but the very condition of same-sex attraction. His position that elicited criticism for pushing boundaries at the time would now be considered, in most quarters, relatively tame.

While the racism he decried may never be thoroughly expunged from all those who call themselves Saints, he would be pleased to see such developments as the churchwide commemoration of the priesthood ban's cessation in 2018, the

NAACP's invitation to president Russell Nelson to address their annual convention in 2019, and President Nelson's calls for member repentance for lingering racism in 2020. Although McConkie's *Mormon Doctrine* with its unredacted racist entries continued to be a perennial best seller for a few more years, the church publishing house ceased its publication in 2010. A Society for Mormon Philosophy and Theology was organized in 2003 and publishes its own journal, *Element*. At the same time, scholars who engage in "speculative theology," even if making no authoritative claims, can still meet with censure and sanctions. *Dialogue* continues to thrive as a journal, although the venue can continue to be problematic for scholars seeking employment or advancement at BYU.

Institutionally, the Latter-day Saint church has in many cases responded in precisely those ways England advocated, and for which he was often censured, decades ago. He aroused consternation when he gave firesides in which he confronted unflinchingly the Mountain Meadows Massacre, orchestrated in 1857 by local church leaders, and the Willie and Martin handcart company, an apostle-blessed enterprise that ended with catastrophic loss of life.[30] Such honesty is now part of Latter-day Saint institutional culture: in 2011 the church sponsored an unflinchingly honest account of the atrocity;[31] the Joseph Smith Papers project encompasses a comprehensive, unexpurgated record of all Joseph Smith's writings, sermons, and correspondence, and a new multi-volume church history is in process, acknowledging with unprecedented frankness Smith's polygyny and polyandry, and the church's follies and foibles as well as its much broader faith-building accomplishments.[32] In the most dramatic and substantive paradigm shift, the Church Educational System has a new apostolic mantra, admitting the insufficiencies of its past pedagogies and insisting on a more open, historically informed, and liberal approach. Elder M. Russell Ballard in a world-wide address noted that "It was only a generation ago that our young people's access to information about our history, doctrine, and practices was basically limited to materials printed by the Church. Few students came in contact with alternative interpretations. Mostly, our young people lived a sheltered life. Our curriculum at that time, though well-meaning, did not prepare students for today—a day when students have instant access to virtually everything about the Church from every possible point of view."

Elder Ballard continued, "Gone are the days when a student asked an honest question and a teacher responded, 'Don't worry about it!' Gone are the days when a student raised a sincere concern and a teacher bore his or her testimony as a response intended to avoid the issue." Then, directly countering the anti-intellectual attacks and controversy-avoidance of the 1980s, he recast brutally honest scholars—of the type England was—as assets rather than challengers of the faith. "If necessary, we should ask those with appropriate academic training, experience, and expertise for help. . . . Inoculate your students by providing faithful, thoughtful, and accurate interpretation of gospel doctrine, the scriptures, our history, and those topics that are sometimes misunderstood. To name a few such topics that are less known or controversial, I'm talking about polygamy, seer stones, different accounts of the First Vision, the process of translation of the Book of Mormon or the Book of Abraham, gender issues, race and the priesthood, or a Heavenly Mother." "Gospel transparency," and "spiritual inoculation" are the "best antidote," he summarized, encouraging teachers to "study. . . the best LDS scholarship available," describing almost precisely the very strategy that had cost England the good will of the leadership. He would have rejoiced to hear the frank correctives to Latter-day Saint mythologies pronounced by D. Todd Christofferson of the Quorum of the Twelve: "Not every statement made by a Church leader, past or present, necessarily constitutes doctrine,"[33] and the unavoidable truth that, in Elder Dieter Uchtdorf's words, "leaders in the Church have simply made mistakes."[34]

If one lesson stands out from the life and legacy of Eugene England, and their relevance to the faith challenges of the twenty-first century, it is this: A life of genuine discipleship is fraught with danger.[35] In reference to England's life, the Russian scholar and church patriarch Gary Browning called it "holy danger." The holiness was in his commitment to the centrality of Christ in all he said and taught. The danger was in his courageous confrontation with "any issue that faith might raise, no matter how troubling, no matter how vexing the questions it provoked."[36] The truth is robust and the truth is resilient, and I share England's trust that ultimately its pursuit will align us with Christ. Ultimately, if not immediately.

On Finding Truth and God: From Hope to Knowledge to Skepticism to Faith

EUGENE ENGLAND

Reprinted from the 1986 collection,
A Thoughtful Faith: Essays on Belief by Mormon Scholars.[1]

A student once came to me for counsel. I had taught him at the Institute of Religion and had served as a member of his bishopric while I was doing graduate work at Stanford. He told me that he had tried on his mission—and with particular intensity during the year since he had returned—to get a spiritual witness of the Book of Mormon. He had read and reread the promise of Moroni and had tried to fulfill the conditions—reading the book, pondering, praying, yearning. But, he told me in tears, he simply had not experienced any response—any knowledge or even spiritual comfort. How, he begged, could I explain this "failure"—or better, how could I help him find success?

I don't think I was very helpful. I didn't know then—and don't now—how to "explain" and thus control the *gift* of grace or the meanderings of the Spirit, which "bloweth where it listeth." The operative word in Moroni 10:5 is "may": "And by the power of the Holy Ghost ye *may* know the truth of all things." And that is the word used by Alma in his great chapter (Alma 32) on epistemology, on the process of finding (creating) truth in this lone and dreary world: "Now, if ye give place, that a seed may be planted in your heart, behold, if it be a true seed . . . , if ye do not cast it out by your unbelief, that ye will resist the Spirit of the Lord, behold it will begin to swell within your breasts" (Alma 32:28). The processes of knowing and the role of our individual agency are so subtle and intertwined yet so important that neither pride nor despair behooves any of us engaged in this pilgrimage. And I can only be thankful that I did not further burden my young friend with allegations that he had not *really* fulfilled Moroni's conditions—or that he must be sinful or at least delinquent in obedience to the gospel if the promise wasn't being fulfilled. But the years since then have brought experience and perhaps a little wisdom.

My essay's title contains both my subject and my conclusions: I am convinced, both in theory and from experience, that it is possible to find a truth that matters and a God who is personal, ravishing, and an accessible guide and model. I believe the quest must start in *hope*—an active desire that this universe is a meaningful and potent one. Such hope includes a yearning for meaningful, individual life after death—and also some willingness to accept the responsibilities that such potential life implies, such as eternal marriage, continual repentance, and preparation to meet God. I've learned that knowledge comes in abundance from such questing. However, if the quest is honest, skepticism also comes. All the faith that is possible in this vale of tears lies on the other side of skepticism and is made possible in part by our being energetic and persistent in that skepticism. Alexander Pope's *Essay on Man* reminds us that "[a] little learning is a dangerous thing"—but so also is a little skepticism. Finally, I believe that there is precious little faith possible for many "intellectuals"—that is, for those who are blessed (and cursed) with the "gift of knowledge." But faith *is* precious—above all that is sweet and precious—and it is sufficient for our needs.

It may seem strange that an essay on faith and hope should depend so much on such seemingly weak reeds as skepticism and what I later on shall call "the null hypothesis." But we shall see that such weak things of human experience can be more reliable and important in certain ways and instances than objectivity and reason—the mighty and strong in the world's eyes.

Indeed, the increase in skepticism since the Enlightenment and the Renaissance has become dramatic since the Restoration and seems to have undermined religious faith irreversibly, which some see as evidence of Satan's battle against the Restoration. But, on balance, I believe that this skepticism has been positive. There are of course a great many things toward which we should remain skeptical. Skepticism has undermined false religion and bad faith—all to the good. In fact, it can be read as a necessary part of the Restoration and preparation for the Eschaton, the final great drama. Though skepticism has sometimes destroyed true religion and good faith, when properly understood and used it reinforces the need for both religion and faith. It has, in the hands of faithful thinkers like Pascal, Coleridge, Kierkegaard, Karl Popper, and F. A. Hayek, undermined the excessive faith of many modern thinkers in such previously intimidating giants as Plato, Aquinas, Hegel, and Marx. It also has countered the modern tendency toward naïve faith in science as our savior. Skepticism has successfully refuted reductionism—the pervasive modern idea that all reality is matter and all theory of matter is reducible to physics. Skepticism has helped us rediscover the law of unanticipated consequences—that social experiments often fail, even when launched by moral truth and good intentions, because human nature is more complex than we have assumed. It is therefore dangerous to give great power to anyone on the basis of their claim to special truth or ways of knowing truth. In the perspective I am seeking here, skepticism leads directly back toward the balance of humility and fearlessness of true faith—that very thing that Latter-day Saints understand is among our chief purposes in life to develop.

Let me first establish my perspective from two basic Mormon texts, both from the Book of Mormon. The first gives the most challenging and yet satisfying basis I have been able to find for *ontology*: a concept of what the universe basically is. The second gives what I have found to be the most convincing and workable *epistemology*: a concept of how we know anything. In 2 Nephi, chapter 2, Lehi teaches his son that "it must needs be that there is an opposition in all things" (2 Nephi 2:11) and goes on to explain that this is not merely a descriptive statement about the divisions and conflicts of human personality and social interaction in history, but a proscriptive assertion about what the universe *must* be like, not only in order for righteousness and good to be brought to pass but in order for life, sense and sensibility, the earth, God, and even the universe itself to exist. The crucial thing this opposition at the heart of things makes possible is the creative activity and freedom of intelligences, initiated (at least in our sphere of present understanding) by God: "For if [opposition is] not there is no God. And if there is no God, we are not, neither the earth; for there could have been no creation of things, neither to act nor to be acted upon; wherefore, all things must have vanished away" (2 Nephi 2:13).

This crucial ontological point is reinforced in a revelation that was given to Joseph Smith three years after the Book of Mormon was published: "All truth is independent in that sphere in which God has placed it, to act for itself, as all intelligence also; otherwise there is no existence" (D&C 93:30). This scripture bridges ontology and epistemology because it not only suggests that the very existence of the universe depends on the dynamism of opposition and the perplexing, joy-bringing—but also pain- and sin-bringing—creative play of intelligences, including God. The passage also states that "truth," which we have been tempted to regard as static and permanently fixed, however elusive, is also inseparably connected to the creative activity of intelligences and relative to the sphere of existence where it is pursued. As the Lord told Joseph Smith in that same revelation, "Truth is knowledge of things as they are, as they were, and as they are to come." And knowledge, as we have learned so well since the Romantic revolution, changes as the knower changes. I believe that the second text I will use, Alma 32, gives us the best help both in understanding how the knower knows and what the process of change is. It also helps move us to engage in the process. Alma puts his finger on the essential dilemma of any epistemology. He points out that in his time, just as in ours, many start with a self-defeating condition before they will risk the search for truth and God: they say, "[i]f thou wilt show unto us a sign from heaven, then we shall know of a surety; then we shall believe" (Alma 32:17). Human beings *claim* they are perfectly willing to believe, if only someone will provide perfect knowledge—clear, rational argument and evidence—in advance. But Alma knows from experience that such a condition, such prior "knowledge," is a snare and a delusion, because "if a man knoweth a thing he hath no cause to believe"—that is, he will be satisfied with those static, unprogressive, essentially trivial aspects of existence which are available for perfect knowledge, and he will not be moved to change his life to conform to the active knowledge of self and God that comes only through faith. As Alma warns, "How much more cursed is he that knoweth the will of God and doeth it not" (Alma 32:19).

Alma is interested in something much more important than the knowledge available empirically and rationally. He is interested in *faith*, which he says is "not to have a perfect knowledge of things; therefore if ye have faith ye hope for things which are not seen which are true." In other words, we live in a universe (not of our making, nor ultimately of God's, but just irrevocably there) in which the most important spiritual realities and meanings are not empirically available to mortals. Some of those realities in fact seem to be merely potentials, yet to be built by beings willing to hope and to proceed without perfect knowledge. Truth is to be found in the process of *creating* the true realities possible in our universe. God is to be discovered as the being who guides and nurtures that process, but only as we create the beings we may become in that process.

How then are we to proceed in such a strange universe, so unresponsive to our desire for a sign, for perfect clarity and assurance? Alma is extremely fair; he asks the bare minimum required for the process to begin: "Awake and arouse your faculties, even to an experiment upon my words, and exercise a particle of faith" (Alma 32:27). This is *hope* being described, a motivating wish that certain things *could* be true, because he goes on to ask of us, "Even if ye can no more than desire to believe, let this desire work in you, even until ye believe in a manner that ye can give place for a portion of my words."

At this point alarm bells go off for skeptics, especially those aware of "cognitive dissonance" and the numerous ways mortals delude themselves. ⭢ Such are convinced that any tilt in the experiment, any emotional hang-up, any desire for social approval, even any desire to believe, destroys complete, disinterested neutrality—and thus the reliability of the experiment. They are right about the destruction of neutrality—but not about the value of the experiment: because all experiments *unavoidably* have *at least* those limitations, even the ones upon which apparent evidence is based. No human endeavor at all, including science, would be possible without some desire, some chance-taking, some hope and vision, some assumptions—if no more than faith in the reliability of our senses as they perceive and measure things. And there are some good safeguards against these minimal tilts, ones well-proven in science and ones that Alma not only accepts but firmly insists upon. He is perfectly aware that the process

⭢ Leon Festinger and others—notably in the book *When Prophecy Fails*—have documented this phenomenon well.

he is describing, central to the life of the universe, is a fragile one, much like the growth of a plant—the very metaphor he chooses. The process can be aborted by tilts in either direction: On the one hand the seed, even a "true seed," a "good seed," can be cast out by unbelief, by resisting the Spirit of the Lord. On the other hand the seed can be bad, and "if it groweth not, behold it is not good, therefore it is cast away" (Alma 32:32). That is, it *should* be cast away. But clearly Alma understands that some of us, because of cognitive dissonance, or pride, or fear, or some other weakness, may go on harboring bad seeds (whether false doctrine, Mormon mythology, or simply incomplete notions that need to be improved before they are planted and nurtured). And by sometimes not being skeptical *enough* at this point, we delude ourselves that these bad seeds are growing. Thus we invalidate the experiment and do real damage to ourselves and others.

But Alma realistically views even a successful experiment as only a beginning, though a crucial and rewarding step:

> Ye know that the word hath swelled your souls, and ye also know that it hath sprouted up, that your understanding doth begin to be enlightened, and your mind doth begin to expand. O then, is not this real? I say unto you, Yea, because it is light; and whatsoever is light, is good, because it is discernible, therefore ye must know that it is good; and now behold, after ye have tasted this light is your knowledge perfect? Behold I say unto you, Nay; neither must ye lay aside your faith, for ye have only exercised your faith to plant the seed that ye might try the experiment to know if the seed was good . . . And now behold, if you nourish

it with much care it will get root, and grow up, and bring forth fruit. (Alma 32:34–37)

This all strikes me as eminently reasonable and fair and modest, yet it does not shrink from suggesting how difficult and risky the business of learning to know through faith really is.

Though we may be blind and gullible pilgrims in a strange and deadly universe, assaulted on all sides by claims and counter-claims, there is an orderly way to begin to sort things out. We need only have the courage to hope, to desire a living and responsive universe no matter how responsible that makes us—and whatever increasing demands that places on us. If we refuse to begin or to continue the process, the judgment lies not on the universe—despite Albert Camus' pained and painful arguments—but upon ourselves:

If ye neglect the tree, and take no thought for its nourishment, behold it will not get any root; and when the heat of the sun cometh and scorcheth it, because it hath no root it withers away, and ye pluck it up and cast it out. Now, this is not because the seed was not good, neither is it because the fruit thereof would not be desirable; but it is because your ground is barren, . . . and thus, if ye will not nourish the word, looking forward with an eye of faith to the fruit thereof, ye can never pluck of the fruit of the tree of life. (Alma 32:39–40)

On the other hand, Alma's promise, which I have tested many times and found as true as anything I know about, is that

because of your diligence and your faith and your
patience with the word in nourishing it, that it
may take root in you, behold, by and by ye shall
pluck the fruit thereof, which is most precious,
which is sweet above all that is sweet, and which
is white above all that is white, yea and pure
above all that is pure; and ye shall feast upon this
fruit even until ye are filled, that ye hunger not,
neither shall ye thirst. (Alma 32:42)

No wonder that fruit was so desirable to Adam and Eve. I
mean that seriously, because I believe that was precisely the
fruit they learned to partake of in the Garden, through great
effort and moral anguish and courage. Their brave choice to
partake of the fruit of the Tree of the Knowledge of Good and
Evil began for us all the opportunity to engage in a similar
process of growth through faith. It is a process not available
in any other way and one that therefore our heavenly Father
and Mother, in great sorrow but in great hope, had to send
us forth to do—on our own, though with Christ's necessary
and sufficient help.

I know I have not pinned down precisely the only true way
for finding God and truth. But it is one way that I, your fellow
pilgrim in this lone and dreary world, can bear fervent witness
about. It may help to relate some contemporary ideas and
experiences to encourage understanding and a willingness to
try this approach to the fruit of knowledge. For instance, many
modern scientists and philosophers have carefully removed
any basis for undue pride or overconfidence in the once touted
powers of critical intelligence and the certainties of science.
In his essay "On the Uncertainty of Science," Lewis Thomas
argues powerfully for humble attention to our still mysterious but essential human gifts for ambiguity and for language:

"The culmination of a liberal-arts education ought to include, among other matters, the news that we do not understand a flea, much less the making of a thought." Another example is Alston Chase, who presents a striking description of what we have lost since the Renaissance by exalting knowledge over virtue and faith, not only in public and private evil committed by perfectly intelligent beings like the Nazis (who increased through science their power to do evil but not their will to avoid it), but also in educational disarray and general anxiety:

> The academic community, by putting schol-arly ideals above spiritual and moral ones, has forgotten how to make value judgments, and therefore does not know how to say what ought to be taught . . . Nuclear bombs, genetic exper-imentation, industrial pollution, carcinogens in processed foods are all products of our own inge-nuity and unlimited desire. In the end our fears remain because we have chosen neither to limit knowledge nor to rein in the human will. . . . Only in my lifetime have educators abandoned all pre-tense to limit reason by faith.

But, you may be saying, didn't you earlier praise desire and knowledge as parts of the process of finding truth? Yes, certainly, but only in the context of Alma's thorough and bal-anced treatment of the process of gaining faith. The process begins in a "hope for things which are not seen, which are true." But where do we get any idea about what Paul called "the substance of things hoped for" so that we can go on to develop (through Alma's process) some evidence for "things not seen"? Joseph Smith, in his *Lectures on Faith*, taught that three things are necessary for viable faith—that is, faith unto salvation: the idea that God exists, a correct knowledge of His attributes, and confidence that we are living in harmony with those attributes of integrity, charity, etc. The first two conditions are provided in history and revelation: God has assured us that He will not "leave us comfortless," and throughout the scriptures He both gives us the evidence and reminds us how important that evidence is to assure us of what Moroni calls, in the preface to the Book of Mormon, "what great things God has done for our fathers." But though God, through His loving watchfulness over human history, makes available to us all the essential knowledge on which hope and proper desire can be based, we must finally reach out to Christ for the power to repent and put our lives sufficiently in harmony with the divine nature that our hope can be properly directed and our knowledge sufficiently humble. Then, if our skepticism is adequately persistent, we can begin to develop a growing and saving faith.

I remember with continuing pain a conversation I once had with a fine young poet and thoughtful, sensitive husband and father. He and his wife had decided to no longer be involved with the restored gospel, not because it wasn't true but because they were afraid it *was*. He had considered the prevailing Mormon rhetoric about the celestial kingdom—apparently a place of organizational charts, high-powered administration, constant progress measured by graphs, assignments, and evaluations and constant cheer of the kind best imagined as a perennial missionary zone conference or an Amway sales force meeting. He had accepted the image as accurate and decided that he wanted no part of such a heaven, because there would obviously be no place for poets. Like Huckleberry Finn, he said, "All right, I'll go to hell," because his sound heart would not accept racist values—though he uncritically accepted them as true—of the imperfect society that had conditioned him. But my friend, right as he was to resist a false image of heaven, was wrong; his desire was not Christ-centered enough and his skepticism not persistent enough to help him beyond a community-taught "knowledge" that was flawed and limited, to help him move on to a growing and life-giving faith in the living God of the scriptures and of his own best imaginings—a God who, I believe, *is* a poet.

Besides the skepticism my friend needed in order to find faith, I mentioned another "weak reed." The first is "the null hypothesis," which refers to a process, familiar from algebra and used effectively by Hugh Nibley, by which the corrosive power of skeptical logic can be turned to the service of *affirming* propositions rather than constantly attacking them. For example, rather than merely pointing to logical and evidential weaknesses or problems in the claim that the Book of Mormon is of divine origin (a very easy thing to do) or trying to prove the claim directly (an impossible thing to do), we can make the "null" or negative hypothesis that the book is not divine, was written by Joseph Smith or some other early nineteenth-century person, and then apply all our skeptical, logical tools scrupulously to that proposition. The result, I believe, is a powerful argument that the null hypothesis is *not* true and by logical implication the opposite is true—the Book of Mormon is divine. In general, if we would be as rigorously honest and thorough in questioning our negative conclusions as we are our positive ones, we would find God and truth more easily. Skepticism should keep us from accepting inadequate answers and merely wishful hope—but also from accepting inadequate refutations and self-indulgent or cowardly despair. As Pascal taught, the possibility that God exists, the mere chance that he guarantees human immortality and joyful eternal purposes, is so stupendous a possibility that we ought to risk all for it, gamble everything, certainly time and intellectual persistence and "working out our salvation in fear and trembling," rather than getting lost in some absurdly fair or "objective" game of letting all the negative evidence overbalance the little, but sufficient, positive evidence. If I am marooned on a descrt island, absolutely dependent on finding another human being to comfort and perhaps save me, the one little swale where I find a single footprint is more important, more true, than the other hundreds of square miles where I find nothing.

I believe that the struggle to find truth is only really successful when united with the struggle to find God—and that the struggle is worth the pain and setbacks, worth enduring to the end. I believe the evidences God has provided in history and in the scriptures are adequate to show what great things he has done for our ancestors and can do for us if we will persist in the hope that such evidence provides. I believe His grace is sufficient, that He will visit us with assurance and spiritual confirmation from time to time—not as we demand it but as He knows we need it. And I believe the Church of Jesus Christ is the best context on earth in which to carry on the struggle—because it provides ways to know and serve Christ that can direct and discipline our desires and thus help us to hope genuinely in things that are real but not seen. And through the sacrificial service it requires and unconditional love it thus helps us learn, the Church can teach us to persist in humility—not to be consumers of truth but rather servants of truth and to affirm the struggle, becoming as little children; willing, as Joseph Smith the boy was, to ask and let it be given, to knock and let the door open.

Sterling McMurrin, one of the brightest people I've known and truly a post-Enlightenment rationalist, once bore his testimony as follows: "I came to the conclusion at a very early age, earlier than I can remember, that you don't get books from angels and translate them by miracles." I find that a remarkably unskeptical assertion, one that manifests much greater faith than I am capable of—a faith, that is, in a dogmatic and quite limited view of the world. I am inclined to believe what Shakespeare's Hamlet reminds us—that there are stranger things than are dreamed of in any of our philosophies. Joseph Smith was in one sense more skeptical than Sterling McMurrin, more willing to question the most basic assumptions and thus to make contact with the most basic, divine realities and learn basic truths about the universe. As we learn more about young Joseph as a practitioner of folk magic, one still in tune with forces and perceptions that had not yet been destroyed by Enlightenment rationalism and thus able later to look back to what he called "the ancient pattern of things," I hope we will not let our own rationalist limitations shock and disappoint us too much. We may even open up a bit ourselves. After all, it seems to me that the living God of the scriptures (the one whom I desire to love and serve and know) could make Himself known to a boy still capable of seeking treasures in the earth more easily than to someone who is certain you "just don't get books from angels."

Finally, let me say something about the role of the Church in our quest for truth. Not too long after that conversation with my young friend at Stanford who was struggling to get some divine confirmation, I heard President David O. McKay give one of his last addresses, one that was a little disturbing to those who thought the process of getting divine manifestations an easy one, especially for potential prophets. He told how he struggled in vain all through his teenage years to get God "to declare to me the truth of his revelation to Joseph Smith." He prayed, "fervently and sincerely," in the hills and at home but had to admit constantly, "No spiritual manifestation has come to me." But he continued to seek truth and to serve others including going on a mission to Britain, mainly because of trust in his parents and the goodness of his own experience in the Church. And finally, *during* that mission in England, while witnessing some remarkable spiritual out-pourings at a conference, including the presence of angels, he realized that "the spiritual manifestation for which I had prayed as a boy in my teens came as a natural sequence to the performance of duty." I have had many personal confirma-tions of that prophetic witness. Most of my profound spiritual manifestations that have confirmed and strengthened me in the struggle to discover and create truth and to find God—as well as my most soul-stretching moral challenges and my most precious though painful opportunities to learn how to love—have come "as a natural sequence to the performance of duty" in the Church.

I believe that, together with the scriptures which it plays a major role in preserving and teaching, the Church is one of the major gifts of grace God provides in His promise not to leave us comfortless in a difficult world. It is the most tangible, day-to-day reminder of "what great things the Lord hath done for [our] fathers," the chief way we "may know the covenants of the Lord, that [we] are not cast off forever." And accord-ing to Moroni, this is precisely the evidence of "how merciful the Lord hath been unto the children of men" and what we must "ponder" in our hearts in order to be *prepared* to know the truth of all things through the power of the Holy Ghost (see Moroni 10:3–5).

I know from experience that there are many ways to improve our receptivity to divine confirmation of truth. Pride and despair, seemingly opposite, are similar in their preoccu-pation with self, their inclination to put immediate success *or* failure in the quest for truth ahead of sacrificial love or even patience: "He that would save his life shall lose it." And a persistent inclination to extreme skepticism—or cynicism, whether intrinsic or adopted as a modern fad—can be a problem: "If ye do not cast [the seed] out by your unbelief, that ye will resist the Spirit of the Lord" is one of Alma's conditions for tasting the fruit of faith. But the essence of my wisdom is simply that one must keep trying, patiently and humbly, and that by far the best place to do that is within the bonds of brotherhood and sisterhood created by a covenant community; for all of us who have it available to them, the Church of Jesus Christ is that community. I just don't buy the objection that church participation is too stressful, too boring or painful or degrading or whatever. I have encountered most of those stresses quite directly and I'm not persuaded the price is too high, especially as I have found that the very problems and stresses that a demanding, authoritarian, but lay church places on us are a good part of its blessing to us in teaching us to love so that we can more ably create truth and find God.

Finally, I just can't accept the claim of some people (though I certainly feel the pain they reveal) that we must get on with our lives—that if there is no sure answer, fairly soon, to the question of Joseph's divine calling or the truth of the Book of Mormon claims, then we can't wait around but must try something quite different. This takes us back to Alma's condition of *desire*: What do we *want* to be true? The claims of the restored gospel, beginning with Joseph Smith and the Book of Mormon, are simply on the face of it the most intellectually and morally and spiritually exciting available on the earth. If it is true that we are eternal intelligences, gods in embryo who can fulfill our infinite potential only in an ever-ongoing process of perfecting the very best of what we know and find joy in—love, marriage, friendship, service, integrity, learning, pursuing beauty, creating—then it is worth every effort, every sacrifice, to engage in the process sufficiently to find out. Certainly, short of convincing evidence that such a possibility does not exist, we would be foolish to turn our energies to lesser options, especially those, however brave-sounding, that are content to limit our vision and responsibilities to this mortal—that is to say, material and doomed—life. So I encourage us to keep trying, however long and difficult the way.

It seems that all of us must go through some kind of Gethsemane, some version of Abraham's test when he was asked to give up his beloved son and his most cherished moral beliefs in order to know God. This may be the only way in the universe to be prepared to understand and accept for ourselves what Christ learned in the Atonement—and thus learn to forgive ourselves and others and develop faith unto repentance so we can be redeemed. For some of us that test may come in our challenge to keep trying, to keep planting seeds and nurturing them, without feeling any clearly recognizable swelling motions or spiritual confirmation, but simply enduring in desire and hope until, after long and patient service in love, the joyful taste of the fruit comes "as a natural sequence to the performance of duty." If my young friend from Stanford were here, this is what I would bear my own witness to—and hope for him.

A Thoughtful Love: Reflections on a Life of Faith as Commitment

DEIDRE NICOLE GREEN

God loves your critical mind," I reiterated to the students of my Global Women's Studies seminar on feminist theology at the end of our semester in 2020. One of my female students had lamented that in her lifelong experience in the church, this integral part of who she was seemed unwelcome. I could relate all too well and wanted to offer affirmation and hope gleaned from an arduous journey of attaining self-acceptance and a deep sense of divine acceptance amid an upbringing in a religious culture that too often devalues and dismisses critical thinking as unfaithful or unimportant. "Critical" is often set in opposition to loving, but I know that my own critical mind and my many questions lead me to love God and others more deeply. If my mind is one of the means by which God has endowed me with the ability to love God above all else (see Matt 22:37), then it stands to reason that God loves my mind, especially when used in a way that ultimately allows me to become more fully devoted to God.

The Church of Jesus Christ of Latter-day Saints proclaims itself to be the "only true and living church upon the face of the whole earth" (D&C 1:30), containing a fullness of truth. It also espouses the teachings of the New Testament, which claim that the first and great commandment is to love God above all else and with every part of oneself, and that the second commandment is like unto it, to love others as ourselves (Matt 22:37–40). The gospel teaches us that God's work and glory is to bring to pass the immortality and eternal life of human individuals—this is the ultimate manifestation of divine love. What we ought to mean, then, when we claim that the church has a special relationship to divine truth is that this religious institution bears distinctive resources to help God's children learn how to love as God loves.

Practicing Latter-day Saints speak comfortably about becoming like God and enjoying exaltation with those to whom they are eternally connected. Yet we rarely speak in this context of the ways we must struggle to practice the love we want to enjoy eternally. I believe that the difficulties and dissonance with which we must wrestle as both thinking and believing Latter-day Saints can prepare and strengthen us for the struggle of learning to love people vastly different from ourselves (as well as those who are altogether too much like ourselves).

I find that in my own life love breeds curiosity. I want to know the objects of my love, not in the two-dimensional way I know about facts, but in a dynamic, affected, and relational way. My reasons for being—and remaining—a member of the Church of Jesus Christ of Latter-day Saints present themselves in largely subjective ways. I trust the impressions I receive that come from God. My acute sense of divine presence in my life is more real to me than anything that is tangible in the world. Because I trust that relationship so deeply, I also trust the divine injunction that I have personally received to remain faithful to the restored gospel. This means I strive to continue to love and serve my coreligionists, however surprising and frustrating that injunction can be at times, given aspects of church culture that make it seem easier to walk away and disengage. I am inspired to stay by my own experience of God's relentless love for creation, which enfolds every individual in a care and affection for her specificity.

During my formative years, I sensed that divine love would embrace my inquisitive mind, but I struggled in a religious culture that did not appreciate my questions. As a young teenager, I vividly recall sitting in our family minivan parked outside our chapel. My mom and I waited for my father and brother so we could make our annual road trip back to southern Idaho to visit our extended family. I lamented to my mother that I feared I would never be able to make a decision about what we in those days called Mormonism. I *wanted* it to be true, I told her, and that meant I would never have the requisite objective stance to accurately assess its veracity. Paraphrasing Alma 32, my mother assured me that desire could be beneficial when making decisions about religious faith and knowledge. I felt somewhat reassured at this, but continued to crave something definitive that would allow me to ascertain both the truth and what religious affiliation God willed for me. Despite this struggle, I resolved that I would serve a mission if I was "still Mormon when I turned twenty-one," as I once proclaimed to a missionary dining with us one Sunday afternoon. This was only logical, I explained: If I believed something was universally true, and if I loved other people, I would want to share that truth with everyone.

That desire could support knowledge became more evident when my seminary class took up the study of the New Testament and I fell in love in a way I never had before; I knew that Christ was real and my Savior. Particularly while immersed in the Pauline Epistles, I felt that I had found a home. Paul spoke to me: he knew immense suffering and heartache due to the choices of other human beings and their rejection of goodness, yet he persevered and found meaning in the suffering and joy amid the sorrow. Most of all, he forged an abiding testimony of Christ and entered into a fellowship with him not despite but *through* the suffering and sorrow. I became more and more enamored with Christ and Christianity and knew that for me there would be no turning back. The testimony of Christ that came to me then has led me

to a persistent engagement with the Church of Jesus Christ
of Latter-day Saints, which I have found to be a means for the
transformation of my relationships with God, myself, and my
neighbors, as well as with scripture and the church. Through
this commitment, I have found distinctive ways to love.

During this same period of time of personal conversion, I
had a Sunday School teacher who changed the course of my
life in relation to the church. The patriarch of our stake, David
Ririe, was a retired agronomy professor from the University
of California at Davis. He was humble, unassuming, and
deeply intellectual. Unlike my peers, who were put off by my
questioning, my teacher welcomed my questioning—showing
me that at least one person recognized my mind as an asset
within my church community. I began to internalize the charitable message from my teacher that thinking and addressing
difficult questions were good and welcome in the restored
gospel. I started to feel at home in the church in a way I never
really had before. Although I was unresolved about identify-
ing myself as Latter-day Saint and was not yet ready to affirm
the uniquely LDS elements of testimony, I felt for the first time
that being a seeker need not bar me from my own community. Acceptance by my teacher and others helped confirm my
intuition that God accepted this part of me as well. My critical mind could be loveable, not just by other members of the
church but also by the divine.

I went to BYU at seventeen because I felt directed there
and because it seemed like the best place to determine if the
Church of Jesus Christ of Latter-day Saints was in fact God's
true church. I immersed myself in the Book of Mormon and
found that I was happy and peaceful as I read it. Admittedly, I
didn't much care for its narrative portions since I have always
preferred more didactic and propositional approaches to religious writing, which is perhaps to be expected of someone

studying philosophy. I increasingly felt comfortable with the Book of Mormon as a (possibly) divinely inspired text. Enter: David Paulsen. During my second year as a philosophy major dabbling in microbiology and psychology, I attended a university forum in the Marriott Center. Paulsen, a philosophy professor whom I had not yet encountered in the classroom, gave an address entitled "Joseph Smith and the Problem of Evil." I had what I would unreservedly call a conversion experience and knew that I wanted to do what he did—to use my educational training to illuminate the unique aspects of Latter-day Saint theology in ways that could contribute to wider discussions of vexing questions. I enrolled in his Philosophy of Religion and Mormon Philosophy of Religion classes, and later his courses on the Danish philosopher Søren Kierkegaard, for whom I developed a life-long regard; and I felt free. I could explore complex issues that fascinated me; more than anything, I watched as David exemplified and engendered a confidence that the restored gospel was strong enough to hold up under careful scrutiny. Questions and critical issues were not something to be evaded but embraced and examined. As I completed my studies, I followed through and embodied the logic I had unpacked for that unsuspecting missionary years earlier—since I was still a Latter-day Saint and approaching twenty-one years of age, I submitted my papers to become a full-time missionary and served in South Carolina. By that point, it was clear to me that I would be yoked to the Church of Jesus Christ of Latter-day Saints for the rest of my life.

Although I recognize the abundant goodness in other faith traditions and other worldviews, this is the religion that I love. Moreover, it is the religious community that I feel most called to love and serve within. My abiding faith in the restored gospel has not come easily. It has been a struggle in one way or another the whole way through. Fortunately for me, I see struggle as a virtue in most areas of life, certainly in matters of theological reasoning, spirituality, and religion. In the Hebrew Bible, Jacob wrestled with God for a blessing. The struggle continued throughout the night and was so vigorous that it knocked his hip out of joint, ultimately causing him to limp for the rest of his life. But he became a new being, the being God intended him to be—Israel, the one who struggles with God (see Genesis 32). I wholeheartedly believe that God loves me as a whole being, including my critical mind, which has drawn me into an intellectual struggle that has ultimately deepened my love for God. Just like Jacob, every one of us may at times experience the wounding, intellectual or otherwise, that occurs when the divine comes into contact with human life. We feel this wounding no less than Jacob did and yet this process presents us with a similar opportunity to become who the divine intends for us to be as we forge a new relationship with God—one fraught with both struggle and love. I am confident that I would not be the person I am today without the tensions and difficulties with which my faith has confronted me. Ours is not a facile faith but one that works to foster a profundity in my God-relationship, as well as a depth to my own character, that would be lacking otherwise. This enhanced capacity, I believe, engenders an ability to love more deeply and genuinely.

This indispensable process of becoming begs us to perpetually take on new questions in order to better come to know truth, God, and ourselves. Latter-day Saint scripture further provides beautiful models of this. Enoch questioned God directly about the way that God relates to the world. How is it that you can weep? How is it that you can respond to the world that you yourself created in such a way? God responds that he weeps over creation because God's children fail to love each other as God has commanded (Moses 7). If God can experience devastation in response to regrettable human actions, how could human beings be anything but immobilized and utterly undone by them? And if the most righteous people who ever lived, including Enoch and Christ himself, receive favorable responses when asking God questions, why should we shy away from asking too? Christ poses to God what is perhaps the most challenging question of all: "Why hast thou forsaken me?" (Mark 15:34). Can one challenge God any more polemically than that? Yet such questions, I submit, make possible greater union with God and in this way Christ's query stands as exemplary for all human beings. Further, the penetrating questions that Christ asks of his followers cut to the heart in order to determine how and how much we love.

When I first began living abroad while writing a dissertation on the limits of self-sacrifice in light of the commandment to love the neighbor as oneself, all of my scholarly work and my existential experience became focused on the complexities of scriptural teachings on love, selflessness, and how we might most productively live them out in the flesh. During this time, section 7 of the Doctrine and Covenants came to have a profound impact on me, helping me to sum up a major tension in my own life. In this section, Christ speaks to both John the Beloved and to Peter, asking them about the desires of their hearts. John receives the query: "John, my beloved, what desirest thou?" (D&C 7:1). John, rather resolutely, responds that his deepest longing is to receive "power over death" in order that he "may live and bring souls unto [Christ]" (verse 2). In answer to this yearning, Christ declares "Verily, verily, I say unto thee, because thou desirest this thou shalt tarry until I come in my glory, and shalt prophesy before nations, kindreds, tongues and people" (verse 3). John's restless love for the divine, for human others, and for the truth impels him to tarry upon the earth declaring the Gospel until the second coming.

Turning to Peter, Christ contrasts his desires to "speedily come" unto Christ in his kingdom with those of John (verse 4). Christ emphatically states that "this was a good desire; but my beloved has desired that he might do more, or a greater work yet among men than what he has before done" (verse 5). He continues that because John has "undertaken a greater work" Christ will "make him as flaming fire and a ministering angel" so that John can "minister for those who shall be heirs of salvation who dwell on the earth" (verse 6). Here, Christ lifts up the desire to remain among the living rather than enter into his eternal rest even though this means an extended separation between Christ and his beloved John. I see my life as constantly negotiating this tension: the yearning for death, rest, and close proximity with Christ and the impulse of love that drives life, perseverance, and a reluctant distance from the divine in order to minister within the (fallen) created order. It is the love that claims us, that possesses us, that demands that we remain amid the longing for a final rest. John forestalls his own comfort and blessedness in order to work for that of others, despite the risk that it could always be in vain. My life of faith and my religious scholarship demand postponing rest in order to work out of the relentless love modeled by God and Christ.

This tension further offers me a fruitful way to conceive of my relationship to the restored gospel. There arises at times the desire to capitulate to the longing for "death," for the need to separate from a community that I love and that as a result has the power to break my heart repeatedly and make me feel that rest is in order. Yet, my love for the restored gospel, which I understand to be a hard-earned love aimed at a subject with whom I share a dynamic, fluid relationship, always ultimately supersedes that urge. Moreover, I earnestly believe that it is in part the difficulty itself that makes remaining with the church spiritually efficacious. I understand the object of the life of faith to be the attainment of charity, the pure love of Christ (Moroni 7:47). I understand Latter-day Saint doctrine to call me and every other individual to live faithfully, hopefully, and charitably. I believe that not only our relationship to other fallible human beings but also our relationship to the institutional church can—in crucial, distinctive ways—foster the development of charity, fashioning us into individuals that better reflect Christ. Let me explain what I mean.

Because institutions provide opportunities and power that isolation does not, individuals often exist and interact within institutions. Hence Christian love and faith must direct themselves towards institutions as well as individuals. In our era where many are walking away from organized religion, this can be hard for people to fully grasp. Kierkegaard can help us. Pointing out the similarity between individuals and institutions, Kierkegaard intimates that institutions must work out their salvation just as individuals must (see Phil 2:12). Cautioning against any tendency to claim that an institution is complete or infallible, he asserts that the "deification of the established order is . . . perpetual revolt . . . continual mutiny against God." He observes that some people may believe that an institution has reached its zenith and as a result develop a complacency in the use of their own reason and agency. Exhorting Christians not to abdicate their responsibility to institutions in this way, Kierkegaard writes: "Every human being is to live in fear and trembling, and likewise no established order is to be exempted from fear and trembling." This is the case because the fear and trembling in which we live "signify that there is a God—something every human being and every established order ought not to forget for a moment."[1]

Humbled by their own imperfection before God, each individual as well as each institution is to recognize itself as being in a process of becoming. As Christians, we are enjoined to orient ourselves faithfully, hopefully, and charitably to institutions as well as individuals. Moreover, in order to influence an institution to become more faithful and more loving, we are required to enact neighbor love on a wide scale.

This conception of the individual's relationship to a religious institution strikes me as particularly relevant for the Church of Jesus Christ of Latter-day Saints, which explicitly takes itself to be in such a process of becoming. In January 2018, the Second Counselor in the First Presidency of the Church, Henry B. Eyring, stated in a press conference that Latter-day Saints (and others) would do well to remember this fact. He expressed that his hope for the press conference was to help others "see the church as we are, what we are determined to become, and why. This is important to us . . . but it is never easy." Even members of the church, according to Eyring, need to "work hard to see the church as it really is. It is even harder for those who are looking from outside." He continued, "It is also easier for us to describe what we are trying to become than it is for you to believe we really hold such lofty aims. The 'why' we aim so high and work so hard is more easily described by us but not, perhaps, easily believed." What LDS members and missionaries alike yearn to convey, as per Eyring, is the message of "who we are, where we are trying to go, and why it is worth it."[2] Here, a member of the highest governing body of the church makes plain that the church has not yet become what it is meant to be. This becoming, I believe, is largely a matter of expanding our notion of love. Perhaps one way this expansion—this working it out with fear and trembling—might play out is to teach people, particularly women, to love rather than fear their own capacity for critical thought. Moreover, we might see critical thought as one of the means by which we collectively urge ourselves on in this process of becoming. I suggest that some of Kierkegaard's insights about the nature of Christian love are instructive in terms of how individual members can help bring the Church's process of becoming to fruition.

An indispensable element of this kind of love is that it does not substitute an imaginary idea of another person—how we wish they were—for the actual person, in order to love them; rather, we love the person we see, as they are, with all of their imperfections.[3] True Christian love does not test the object of love in order to determine whether it is truly loveable, but remains enduringly loving despite changes and reasons not to love. Here, Kierkegaard offers a strong caveat:

> [This is not to] recommend a childish infatua-
> tion with the beloved's accidental characteristics,
> still less a misplaced sentimental indulgence. Far
> from it, the earnestness consists precisely in this,
> that the relationship itself will with integrated
> power fight against the imperfection, overcome
> the defect, and remove the heterogeneity. This is
> earnestness. . . ."[4]

Neither the beloved's imperfections nor her difference from the one who loves (heterogeneity) ought to be grounds for dis-tancing oneself from the beloved. Instead, the two individuals in the relationship are to "hold together all the more firmly and inwardly," that is, wholeheartedly, "in order to remove the weakness . . . when the defect or the weakness makes the rela-tionship more inward, not as if the defect should now become entrenched but in order to conquer it."[5] Only then does one truly love.[6] The faults of another person—or institution—are not to repel the loving subject, yet the subject neither blinds herself to the other's faults nor reduces them to a matter of indifference. Rather, love impels her to assist the beloved to become before God one who loves better and more Christianly.

For Kierkegaard, seeing the object of love as it actually is, is not a reason to attenuate one's commitment to the other but rather a reason to amplify the commitment. Continuing in relationship, and applying a redemptive honesty, empowers the one in the wrong to become better. Love does not delude itself by pretending to see love that is not present in the beloved, but actively engages the luminous vision of love, employing one's own "power to love forth the good in the impure," seeing "not the impure but the pure, which it loves and loves forth by loving it."[7] Through love, one labors to draw out love from the other. Here, love is a matter of the choice and capacity of the subject, independent of the object. An imperfect church provides ample opportunity to struggle to love—to work toward its improvement while becoming more loving individuals in the process. Moreover, by laboring to create a more loving church in which all feel both safe and welcome, one just is loving the neighbor. The remedy for doubt and death cannot be faith alone, any more than it can be certainty or objective knowledge. Effectively negotiating doubt calls for love, as well as faith, specifically the neighbor-love commanded by Christianity. This points to a notion of faith as fidelity—as remaining with the beloved in partnership and commitment—in, through, and despite faults in persons and the church.

It is our faithfulness to Christ that helps us and all those we relate to, including the institutional church, to be remade—even transfigured—by Christ's transformative love. This faith and love have the potential to transform our relationships to God, ourselves, and one another. The Book of Mormon, I believe, attests to this and offers illustrative examples. For me, the unique ways in which the Book of Mormon has taught me to live charitably, as well as faithfully, binds me to it and makes me cognizant of its relevance for my life in the twenty-first century. For example, in the Book of Jacob, we find the high priest rebuking the self-righteous Nephite men in the temple. He decries their arrogance, greed, oppression of others, and their practices that objectify and sexually commodify women, rendering them less than agents and subjects. In a moment of profound irony, Jacob turns on its head the self-righteousness and haughtiness of these people who pride themselves on their chosen status and their access to sacred texts, instructing them to look to the Lamanites to learn how to love (Jacob 3:5–6). Here, a Nephite leader affirms that the love that saves is that which regards and respects all others as equals and fellow members of God's creation, over against conformity and even covenant.

Pressing further, Jacob is unapologetic in holding up the Lamanites as exemplars of family love (verse 7), and then seeks to raze any remaining pride with this interrogation: "wherefore, how much better are you than they, in the sight of your great Creator?" (verse 7). Using the language of commandment, Jacob places an imperative upon the Nephites to no more revile against the Lamanites but instead to remember their own filthiness (verse 9). He further enjoins them to remember how they have grieved their children's hearts and may yet bring them to destruction through that filthiness (verse 10). Jacob reveals that the remedy for the various sins the Nephites embrace is love. They have forgotten to love their neighbors as themselves—not just the Lamanites, but the neighbors who are also their wives and children. Jacob insists that the Nephites must look to the very people they despise— those they regard as apostate, those they oppress due to racial

and class differences—to learn how to keep their own covenants, to learn how to love. This implies that what it takes to
be a teacher and example of Christian living is love—it is love
that gives us authority.

In this and other ways, my Latter-day Saint faith and the
scriptures unique to its canon have engendered in me a greater
capacity to love the neighbor. The Book of Mormon prophet
Alma, after giving one of his most stringent sermons, quali-
fies the rigor of his teachings. He declares: "I speak by way of
command unto you that belong to the church; and unto those
who do not belong to the church I speak by way of invitation,
saying: Come and be baptized unto repentance, that ye also
may be partakers of the fruit of the tree of life" (Alma 5:62).
Alma's mitigated stance towards those outside the church
models a softness—a way of being lenient in terms of our
expectations of those who do not share our faith. In order to
be neighborly, we can invite others to experience the restored
gospel for themselves, but we can never force them to comply
with our own standards of conduct. Again, reading this in
light of Jacob's sermon allows me to go further: while I cannot
require others to embrace my own standards of conduct, I can
learn from them how to better keep the spirit of those standards and even how better to reach their goal. I can recognize
my own nothingness and that as a human being I am just as
infinitely distant from God as every other human being. I can
let the other inspire me to live in a more godly way, even if
they do not regard their own lifestyle in these terms. These
insights illustrate how a true and living church distinguishes
itself by offering resources for, and greater commitment to,
loving the neighbor.

Just as the gospel, amid the dissonances of life, demands
that we be thoughtful about our faith, it also—in its gently
robust and complex way—invites us to be more thoughtful

about our love. It offers incisive teachings about how to love more fully and more liberally. The struggle that remaining faithful to the Church entails may actually be further productive of love, a deepening of our capacity to love. In this way, it affords ample opportunities to draw closer to Christ and to receive his image within ourselves. As we love and affirm the inquisitive, diverse, critical, and challenging minds and ways of ourselves and others, we further close the gap between the divine and a community that aspires to be in loving union with this divine. We also narrow the gap between that community and those who remain outside of it.

Critical thinking can thus support our efforts to become both more faithful and more loving. We can embrace such thinking—without ambivalence—when we allow it to be guided, above all else, by the love of God and by the authentic love of neighbor.

Our Eternal Round with the God Who Dances

STEVEN L. PECK

If you can't take a little bloody nose,
maybe you oughtta go back home and crawl under
your bed. It's not safe out here. It's wondrous, with
treasures to satiate desires both subtle and gross;
but it's not for the timid.
— *"Star Trek The Next Generation,"*
Q to Picard (Season 2, Episode 16: Q Who?)

God calls us to adventure. ☙ I believe that Earth life is not a test to separate the wheat from the tares. It is not a proof in the way that medieval villagers threw a witch into the pond to see if she would float. Not a simple assessment for placement in some grand hierarchy of prisons or resorts. It is an exam, rather, in the sense that we are learning the skills necessary for existence. Faith, hope, charity are attributes necessary to travel into the eternities. We are graced with a chance to set sail with God. We are learning to be shipmates on an adventure that requires certain tackle, knots, and such accoutrements that have been found useful for an eternal voyage into the unknown. I find the Greek word *techne* useful for framing the characteristic equipment we will need to manage our work travelling through an eternal existence. Existence is motion, nomadic. Nothing is ever set in stone, not even things really set in stone—even protons decay. This *techne* includes the idea of *arête*, skill, including some I would like to focus on:

☙ See Elder Uchtdorf's October 2019 General Conference talk, "Your Great Adventure," in which he uses J.R.R. Tolkien's book, *The Hobbit*, to frame our God's call in the preexistence to our current earthly adventure.

curiosity, generating novelty, and creativity. I cannot seem to bring myself to separate faith from these traits, which are necessary to equip us for an adventure that will never end. For example, can we really imagine that love and charity and hope and faith are being so ardently worked on here if it is not to continue their refinement as we journey on with God ⚜ in the eternities?

One of my earliest memories is of capturing bees foraging on dandelions in a grassy field behind our student housing complex at the University of Utah where my dad was going to school in Social Work. The trace impressions from those days are indistinct, and it is hard to form them into a visual picture that comes readily to mind. But one event stands out as if it were lived yesterday, and I can recapture the delightful attractiveness of the day quite clearly.

The sun is bright and the colors it discloses are not just instances of their usual hues. Rather they carry into my heart and mind an affective mood—a feeling that seems to define the long summers of childhood, when to play and explore was what it meant to exist. I must have been about four or five and my mom and I were in a grassy field behind a long building with blue wood siding. The greenness of the lawn, the light blue of the unsullied sky, and the billowy clouds are more distinct than anything I can recall of those early years. We were capturing bees in mayonnaise jars. I remember how excited I was to actually have one of these little creatures in the jar who moments ago had been visiting bright yellow dandelions. I was holding it in my hands! I put my ear up to its side and could hear the loud buzzing of the tiny prisoner proclaiming

---

⚜ By "God" in this braided essay, I mean to include variously, Heavenly Parents, Heavenly Mother, Heavenly Father, Christ, and the Godhead; and although I refer to God with the pronoun "He" as is traditionally used in our scriptures, I aim for it to be interpreted more resplendently in regard to gender.

its confusion and displeasure. I knew bees could sting, but I had no fear or apprehension about these—just a sense of triumph, delight, and elation.

I suppose that is why, after a lifetime, the event remains so clearly etched in my mind's eye, though the images have become a bit disjointed. I remember the bees in the jar. That I was not alone and that my mother was there guiding and helping me. The colors seem so clear. I'll never forget the grass and the dandelions and their contrasting treasure of emeralds and golds. There seemed to be so much freedom and gladness in watching a bee soar from the jar, its dangling legs laden with pollen under its heavy body, as it made a small slow circle before flying home. Since that time, these images have likely been reconstructed with bits and pieces of other memories, because the ways that memories are laid down and pulled up again are fraught and messy. Still, I'm convinced there is something of the visual essence of the recollection that remains true to the original event. But the mood! The feelings of delight and magic are so clear, so deep, that when I look back on that afternoon, I cannot help but long for such unassuming clarity of purpose and such untainted joy. I hope I get to be an untamed child again. Perhaps, it was in that jar of bees that a scientist was born. Curiosity was midwifed into the world. There were things to discover. The universe was infused with novelty and wonder.

I embrace a theology in which faith is a curiosity-based exploration of existence. A trust that God has graced us with equipment that will enable safe passage across fathomless seas.[1] Ours is not a static existence that follows well-worn deterministic paths of Einstein's or Augustine's block universe in which the whole course of existence is laid out—played in a cosmic film reel with fixed action sequences that cannot be changed or influenced by the projectionist from its deterministic order of scenes. I see the universe as one in which novelty emerges into new structures and forms—there is no set film that guides the sequences of adventure. Evolution's creative flourishing is part of my theology. As is astronomy, literature, geology, and all the ways humans have learned to engage with the manifest universe.

Given that the world demonstrably engenders new forms as it evolves, what does God mean when He says His course is "one eternal round?" Such a course seems to invoke a sense of repetition, as if existence circles back around and repeats endlessly. That doesn't feel right given what we know about eternal progression. What then could the Lord mean with this statement? The image occurs at many points in scripture: "For he that diligently seeketh shall find; and the mysteries of God shall be unfolded unto them, by the power of the Holy Ghost, as well in these times as in times of old, and as well in times of old as in times to come; wherefore, the course of the Lord is **one eternal round**" (Nephi 10:19).

Another example:

> And it may suffice if I only say they are preserved for a wise purpose, which purpose is known unto God; for he doth counsel in wisdom over all his works, and his paths are straight, and his course is **one eternal round.** (Alma 37:12)

Several things strike me in these passages. The first is that God's course is "one," and that course is an "eternal round." In addition his paths are straight. Both "straight" and "round?" Three other verses in the scriptural canon contain the phrase "eternal round":

> For God doth not walk in crooked paths, neither doth he turn to the right hand nor to the left,

neither doth he vary from that which he hath said, therefore his paths are straight, and his course is **one eternal round.** (D&C 3:2)

I perceive that it has been made known unto you, by the testimony of his word, that he cannot walk in crooked paths; neither doth he vary from that which he hath said; neither hath he a shadow of turning from the right to the left, or from that which is right to that which is wrong; therefore, his course is **one eternal round.** (Alma 7:20)

Listen to the voice of the Lord your God, even Alpha and Omega, the beginning and the end, whose course is **one eternal round,** the same today as yesterday, and forever. (D&C: 35:1)

In all of these, it appears that there is something God cannot get out of. Whatever this eternal round is, there are things He cannot escape. The path is set: no left turns, no right turns. The banks are too high to climb out, and He is stuck with the things He has embraced, as in the phrase "I the Lord am bound, when ye do what I say. . . ." (D&C 82: 10). Trapped in existence like a bee in a jar. But that makes no sense—God is creative. Inventive. A being that takes delight in novelty. Right?

Darwin[2]—"He who believes that each being has been created as we now see it, must occasionally have felt surprise when he has met with an animal having habits and structure not at all in agreement." Xenophon[3]—"With such signs of forethought in these arrangements, can you doubt whether they are the works of chance or design? No, of course not. When I regard them in this light they do look very like the handiwork of a wise and loving creator." Aristophanes[4]—"What is that thing crawling toward us? A scorpion or a spider?" Bergson[5]—"The universe endures. The more we study the nature of time, the more we shall comprehend that duration means invention, the creation of forms, the continual elaboration of the absolutely new."

There are several contradictions in thinking God is a creature of a fixed universe, locked in a cosmos of matter in motion, who, like Laplace's demon, ✦ knows the end from the beginning because He can calculate forward and backward the motion and trajectory of every particle and their interactions. What do we do with this, then? The Lord declares He is the beginning and the end, the Alpha and the Omega: "Listen to the voice of the Lord your God, even Alpha and Omega, the beginning and the end, whose course is one eternal round, the same today as yesterday, and forever" (D&C 35:1). He is embedded in an endless state, an eternal round, a circle in which there is no beginning and end. The scripture declares there is something about him that does not change. What is this unchangeability if novelty is a fundamental inhabitant of the universe which includes God?

God has agency. He is not such that his hand is forced; his actions in the world can be frustrated. Indeed, in light of some scriptures, God's aims are mostly frustrated. He can be talked out of things as He was with Abraham. He can issue commands that are never fulfilled.[6] Or see plans reorganized due to human actions. ✦ Given these passages, what can an "eternal round" possibly mean?

✦ Laplace, assuming a determinist universe, imagined a being who, knowing the position, momentum, and velocity of every particle of the universe, could predict all past and future events.

✦ For example, as the gospel topic essay, "Race and the Priesthood"[7] makes clear, there was never any revelation that supported the idea that the priesthood should be restricted to people of non-African descent. Rather, the restriction could have been based upon structural and cultural racism prevalent at the time, thus thwarting the Lord's work among black populations for many years.

"Eternal round" appears often in literature and discourse of the late 18th century. Joseph Smith and his associates would have likely been familiar with the phrase. It seems to make its first appearance in Edward Young's famous poem, "The Complaint, or Night Thoughts on Life, Death and Immortality," published in 1745:

> Man is the tale of narrative old time;
> Sad tale; which high as Paradise begins;
> As if, the toil of travel to delude,
> From stage to stage, in his **eternal round,**
> The Days, his daughters, as they spin our hours
> On Fortune's wheel, where accident unthought
> Oft, in a moment, snaps life's strongest thread,
> Each, in her turn, some tragic story tells,
> With, now and then, a wretched farce between;
> And fills his chronicle with human woes.[8]

Benjamin Stillingfleet, Young's contemporary, also uses the phrase in a set of theological poems on the economy of nature:[9]

> Their kindly influence; not there alone,
> Which strike ev'n eyes incurious, but each moss;
> Each shell, each crawling insect holds a rank
> Important in the plan of Him, who fram'd
> This scale of beings holds a rank, which lost
> Wou'd break the chain; and leave behind a gap
> Which nature's self would rue. Almighty Being,
> Cause and support of all things, can I view
> These objects of my wonder; can I feel
> These fine sensations, and not think of thee?
> Thou who dost thro' th' **eternal round** of time;
> Dost thro' th' immensity of space exist

Alone, shalt thou alone excluded be
From this thy universe? Shall feeble man
Think it beneath his proud philosophy
To call for thy assistance, and pretend
To frame a world, who cannot frame a clod? Not
to know thee, is not to know ourselves—
Is to know nothing—nothing worth the care
Of man's exalted spirit—all becomes
Without thy ray divine, one dreary gloom;

Emerson also claims the phrase in his sermon, *Wherefore let him that thinketh he standeth, take heed lest he fall (1 Corinthians 10:12)*, preached September 20th, 1829:

All these things speak to each of us—and command us every moment to feel that we are not creatures of necessity, but creatures of free will—improvable beings—not moving like the silent orb we tread upon, in **one eternal round,** but going backward or going forward in our mortal career, at our own free choice, and just as far and as fast as we will.[10]

In these poems, there is a connotation that the "eternal round" is not referring just to repetition, but to a mode of being. In the Young poem, it is describing human existence and its stages. In the Stillingfleet poem, the existential nature of the phrase is explicitly made in the line that follows, and Emerson's sermon is referencing 'free choice' and 'free will' as being part of our 'mortal' career.

These references shed light on an interpretation of our Latter-day Saint scriptures that suggests "eternal round" may not convey the sense that God is repeating the same thing over and over, but rather that God partakes of the same kind of existence that we enjoy. Or, to get the ordering right, we partake of the same existence that He enjoys. That like us, *He* exists in the forward movement of time inherent in things and from which not even He can escape: "neither doth He turn to the right hand nor to the left." Time unfolds. For us and the divine and all nature. God acts in response to the situation, which is not determined or orchestrated by divine decree or fiat. God is in motion in a call and response, like a jazz quartet. There is an action and reaction; the music is made when the players partake of the situation. Or like a dance—a round dance, say—in which, while there is music to set the rhythm and pace of the dancers, they are not locked into fixed courses like robotic automatons driven by fixed algorithms. There is play, agency, constant interaction. Existence is music, dance, and acting in concert with and in response to others.

Creation Always Begins with Chaos

turbulence, storms and lightning striking
willy-nilly through a lightless and angry
sky. It starts with monsters of the deep,
fierce beasts of mythic glance and terror.
Gods and Goddesses hover, unknowing
how to fly properly, brooding over the
waves cresting in a tumult of oceanic
turmoil, whispering to each other, trying
to find a way forward. Voids and emptiness
gather thick amid the crash and thunder of
matter run amok spilling over any bounds set
and framed to contain these raging waters.

With impatience the dancing deities
cry out, "Let there be light. Oh, please,
let there be light." And no one is more
surprised when it arrives, shining, brilliant,
as it pierces the clouds, and the storm abates,
and the monsters sink back into the deep unlit
regions from which they sprang. With the light

comes life, renewal, newness and novelty,
diversifying, emergent, swelling the waters
and world with activity and telos. And the
divine beings breathe a sigh of relief, and in
that breath, an agreement that this is good.

Time ticks.

And so it is with all beginnings, with all creations.

What at first seems like chaos, will open the door
to a place the Gods and us can grow, and breathe
and bask in the dawn light of brighter hope and
abundance, and the grace of new and better
things in a dazzling cosmos filled with radiant
wonder. Where time unfolds new universes.

The story of my faith is deeply embedded in agency interacting with matter in motion. Both gross and fine instantiations of matter. The music of existence emerges into the story in two senses, first in the way that matter itself is entangled in the world, and second in the way that our theological toolkits and concepts are enmeshed in this entangled world. It is a messy world. Not for the faint of heart.

Take the idea of triangles for a moment. Some of us are tempted by the idea that there is some perfect realm where triangles in their formalwear are eking out an eternal existence sitting beyond the ravages of time and circumstance. Plato laid this out nicely with his notion that there is a world of perfect forms that stamped as particulars the shape of things instantiated in this world. The form of the "good" stood as a form of forms. Plato considered God the form of all forms, existing up there (I'm pointing up) as the one pure being. A being beyond time, where time flows forward but which can be circumvented by this perfect being and who is its source rather than something embedded in it. Time is down here. With us. Not with him—the God of triangles. Oh, and these perfect ideal formal triangles escape time, just like all the Platonic forms. Unlike our conception of God who is embedded within time rather than above it. One who plans for a contingent future. And has memories of a lived past.

We lived in Winton, California, in a house along a country road that curved through an active San Joaquin Valley agricultural area. There were deep almond orchards to either side of the house and a sizable sweet-potato field directly behind us. We had citrus trees of various sorts scattered through the property. One in particular I remember grew bizarre fruits that looked like massive, thick-skinned grapefruits but that tasted like lemons. The skin was so loose it took only seconds to peel, but they were so sour I could only take a bite or two before my lips pursed so violently they could not be reformed into a more natural expression.

My most clear memory, however, was that I was in 7ᵗʰ grade and lived in fear every day. In the morning on the way to school, I would kneel down in the orchard and pray that the bullies would leave me alone. Sometimes it worked. Other times it did not. The thing that strikes me as odd now is that while school was terrifying, I loved the orchards, canals, fields, and semi-wild places that formed the demesne in which we lived. I felt safe when alone. The turbulent sound of water being whisked from the canal through diversion gates and into an orchard's irrigation network seemed magical and healing.

There were large pine trees to the side of the house that formed a windbreak and separated us from the rows of almond trees in the orchard adjacent. I would climb the tallest of these evergreens as a way to escape the fear I felt in school. I would scamper up into the very smallest branches at the tippy-top of the stately conifers and hang on tight, with my head nearly even with the top of the tree. The wind would blow, rocking me deliciously back and forth. I could see for miles, espying the fruit and nut orchards that seemed to run to the horizon, along with abundant vegetable fields scattered below. I felt safe. No one knew I was there. No one could see me (I supposed), and there was a security that seemed to run from the roots of the tree itself whispering that here, and in this moment, was where I belonged. I would get quite scratched up during my climb. The branches of these pines were small and close together, and I had to step right where the branch sprang from the trunk, or I would break it or slide down as it bent under my weight. A few did break and bend, but this never seemed like something to worry about. It was just one of the facts of climbing these pines. The scratches, the scramble to the top, and the swaying of the tree all combined to give me a sense of connection and value—a secure place in an uncaring world. I felt the tree liked me being there. Not that there was a conscious animism, but just a perception that both I and the tree were happy to be together. I belonged up there. The landscape below was tranquil and empty of malice, glowing. Even the sound of the occasional car or plane did not seem to interrupt my sense of wellbeing. I must have climbed after school because I remember the colors presented by a low sun, enhancing shadows and contrasts in the patchwork of fields below, giving depth and shape to the landscape that deepened its dimensionality and structure. The multitudes of greens added to the feelings of wonder and satisfaction. I learned to sway with the wind. To me it was the breath of God teaching me to join in the universe that moved with a music that could be heard in nature's ballet.

I longed for such peace as the view suggested was possible in a hurtful world. There was also a sense of mystery, the impression the world went on like this forever, with the numerous orchards of nuts and fruits; the calm and orderly layout of fields; the varied trees forming windbreaks and following natural waterways; the wide line of the canals and irrigation ditches disclosed occasionally among the quilted counterpane topology below; the scattered houses and outbuildings; the telephone wires, roads, and fences which marked the presence of other inhabitants—all these formed a horizon which stretched as far as my mind could take it. Even now, late in life, I wish I could recapture the sense I had, right then, in that tree, high above my fears, that the world was a kindly place that existed for my blessing and contentment.

There are reasons to rejoice. Unlike Plato's God, we are the stuff of time and rhythm. We are embedded in a universe with a God who dances. Who invites us to the dance in a free exchange of motion and movement into novelty and newness. Because we can join God in His life's purposes to make a place of safety and to fill the universe with the most unlikely thing of all: Love. This is God's project. So much so that the heavens suggest it is God's defining characteristic: "God is Love" (I John 4:8). In this I believe we see our hope. This is how we join the dance. We are involved in a project of agency beyond a simple test of obedience followed by a heroin-like eternity of full but meaningless joy. All of us are setting sail on an adventure with a deity dancing into a future that will never end. And no one knows where the experience will carry us and what music and meaning we will find. But by all indications love, society, and surprise will be our companions.

Push Me Higher

MELANIE RIWAI-COUCH

Church has not always been easy for me. As a woman, an indigenous person, and an academic, my mind and my church experience sometimes clash. I worry that things are moving too slowly or in directions that are different than I think they need to move. But I have been buoyed by undeniable experiences of priesthood power, the atonement, the temple, and kindness that solidify my testimony.

My great grandparents were Rina Puhipuhi Meihana, daughter of Meihana the paramount chief of Ngāti Kuia, and George Te Oti MacDonald, a descendent of Rangitane ki Wairau.

One of Rina Puhipuhi Meihana and George Te Oti MacDonald's eleven children was my grandfather George MacDonald, who married Kate Mahinaarangi Dawson. Together they had sixteen children. My father Dennis was the youngest and his parents died when he was very young.

My parents married in 1962, and had four daughters; we lived in Blenheim. I am the youngest in my family. My married name is Riwai−Couch, but my maiden name was MacDonald.

When I was four years old my parents separated, and then my sisters left for Church College of New Zealand, attending a Church boarding school in Hamilton. I was left at home to be raised by my dad.

When I was young the missionaries from the Church of Jesus Christ of Latter-day Saints would call over to our house and my dad would mostly turn them away. On a good day, they might get fed lunch, but dad would not go out of his way to make them feel welcome.

We could not afford to buy new things, but my father was very clever and figured out ways of fixing old stuff, and through his bartering or inventing we had what we needed to get by.

Between poverty, negative stereotyping of Māori people and struggling to get by, there were many challenges, including some abuse by an acquaintance. The Church became a safe place for me.

What I didn't know at the time was that my great grandfather George Te Oti MacDonald had been baptized a member of the LDS Church in 1894 when he was forty-one. His conversion trickled down through the generations and some of our family lines stayed close to the Church, but most of our family left.

When my dad was a boy, the missionaries used to come to our marae (tribal meeting house) at Wairau Pā and baptize the eight-year-olds in the Wairau River. In 1947 when my dad turned eight years of age, he hid up in a tree when the missionaries came—and he didn't join the Church until much later when he was an adult. What prompted him at the time was that my mother had left him and he thought maybe being baptized might win her back. My mother had already joined the Church several years earlier after having been taught by the missionaries.

My dad was an exceptionally good man—after all he raised four daughters alone, but at times it felt a little like we were left to fend for ourselves. He would never come into church for Sunday meetings—I would be dropped off in the car park and if I couldn't find a ride home I would either walk or phone Dad to pick me up. I wasn't baptized until I was ten, simply because no one knew that I hadn't been baptized already and I had no family with me. I never had family home evenings, scripture reading or seminary. My church experience consisted only of what I chose to do that I could get to unassisted.

At church I attended the children's primary classes and later youth classes. There I was taught that I was "a daughter of God." As members of the Church of Jesus Christ of Latter-day Saints, we believe in eternal families. We believe that before birth we lived with a loving Father in Heaven and that we chose to come to earth to gain a body and live our mortal lives. We choose to be baptized and to receive the constant companionship of the Holy Ghost. We have the opportunity to be obedient to the commandments of God. We can be kept together in eternal family units by making sacred covenants in holy temples. This means that marriage and families do not end at death, families are forever.

This doctrine, as true as it is, felt as far away from my reality as it could be. Despite this, I knew that when I was at Church I felt whole. Deep inside I started to understand that God wanted me to be okay, even though my situation then was not good.

The scriptures say that with God nothing is impossible, and as a teenager I decided that if anyone needed a miracle it was me.

A poster I had by my bed as a young teenager read, "Lord lift me up above my own narrow horizons, that I might fulfill your vision for me." This became my mantra. I began to believe in my own self-worth, and I started to feel that there might be something more to life for me.

When I was fifteen I was sent up to Church College of New Zealand in Hamilton. There I was taught by teachers who offered a spiritual edge to secular education. I felt safe for the first time in many years, and while I was in Form 6, my final year of school, I discovered that I was good at learning. My teachers inspired me—I wanted to be like them.

To get into university I had to make up for not completing high school. Fortunately my grades from Church College were good and I was accepted after completing some additional study.

No one in my family had ever completed a degree. University assignments often took me much longer than they took my fellow classmates. On top of my full-time study, I had to work twenty to thirty hours per week to pay my way through my studies and I was often exhausted.

It was hard staying active at Church as a young single Adult without any active family members. It was lonely and, like many others do, I chose to fall away from Church rather than stay.

It took me three years to build enough courage to walk back through the chapel doors. Perhaps one of the biggest things I debated was the fact that being in my twenties and returning to Church, particularly in Christchurch, meant that I needed to be prepared to be single for a very long time, given the small number of Church members in the area. But I knew that being obedient was more important—and so I returned.

I never really understood what it meant when people would say they had been saved by God, but I know now. Before, it felt like I was floating down a river being carried by the current and having very little control over the speed, the pace, the depths, or the obstacles. At one point I had to make a conscious decision to swim, and the direction I had to go was upstream, not down.

The more I swam the stronger and more confident I felt; I could lift my head, and I could make my own decisions. Through making and keeping covenants I gained spiritual strength, and I felt God's love.

I was able to advance my career while also having children, and also to complete my masters and doctoral degrees. I never expected to be a full-time working mum, nor, I think, did my husband, who has been a bishop and stake presidency member, expect to be a stay-home dad for a time while studying for his degree. But when we were about five years married, I met with my Stake President and asked him if I should be working or not. His counsel to me was, the question is not "should you work?" rather, the question should be, "are you doing what God wants you to be doing?"

The conclusion I came to is that women in the Church should not feel guilty for working, nor should we judge others who chose not to. We do what we have to do, and sometimes it is as simple as that. If we spend more time loving each other and less time judging, then it really won't matter.

If we believe in revelation, as we do, then we need to test the promise that God will help to direct our lives, and in so doing, we should not limit his range of possible answers for us. I ask God often what he wants me to be doing, and my commitment is to do those things. When you have that sort of confirmation then you do not need to worry about what people think, you just need to get on with doing what you need to do and to do the very best that you can at whatever it is God has lined up for you.

Victor Frankl, a psychiatrist who survived a Nazi concentration camp, concluded in *Man's Search for Meaning* that the meaning of life is found in every moment of living, and that life never ceases to have meaning. He said, "It did not really matter what we expected from life, but rather what life expected from us."

Sometimes life expects more from us than what we thought we could give, and we need to figure out how to step up. While visiting some friends in Pigeon Bay in 2015 our children took turns on a rope swing hanging from a large tree by the shore. As we pushed our twelve-year-old daughter more and more out over the water she found it thrilling. Arms out, soaring. I will always remember the way she squealed and yelled at us, "Push me higher!"

So I believe it is in life. If we want to experience something new and different we need to be willing to be pushed beyond our comfort zone, we need to appeal to Father in Heaven to "push us higher," and then we might be pleasantly surprised at what he has in store for us.

As it says in Matthew chapter 10, "[She] that findeth [her] life shall lose it: and [she] that loseth [her] life for my sake shall find it" (Matthew 10:39). We find ourselves when we surrender our will to God.

As I mentioned, Church has not always been easy for me. But my experiences have prepared me for this time. Now, as a multi-area manager for the Church looking after Church History in the Pacific, I feel that I can contribute and influence more to help the Church reconcile what it means to be global, inclusive of women and indigenous people.

My belief is that God wants me to be here, an active contributor to the Church, and He is the one who has blessed me with the insights, experiences, and qualifications that I have. Because of this God will find a way for me to participate as a member of His Church in a way that lets me feel whole. My challenge is to find ways of giving and helping to achieve the changes that Heavenly Father wants, in His time.

"Out of His Treasure Things New and Old"

FIONA GIVENS

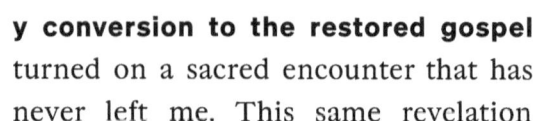

My conversion to the restored gospel turned on a sacred encounter that has never left me. This same revelation, however, also led me into a church and a canon that has on occasion perplexed me. Sometimes we Saints talk as though we have a monopoly on truth or are uniquely virtuous. In different quarters, God has been portrayed in contradictory ways and God's church and love cast alternately as constricted or expansive. In working through these thickets over the years, I have grown to view heaven's love as unbounded. I see my earlier Catholic faith as preparatory and complimentary and intrinsic, rather than as rival, to the restoration. I see God as welcoming all that is good, true, and edifying, no matter its source—just as our founding prophet taught. What follows are key strands along my path to this way of understanding the gospel.

Background

Anne Mary Martin was born in Tipperary in Southern Ireland, to a generationally strong Catholic family. Walter William Bulbeck was born into an Anglican family, whose forebears had resided for generations in Oxford. It is unlikely my father's family attended church except as a formality at Easter and Christmas. By the time Walter and Anne were married, he was no longer a believer. Their public union occurred at a time when the non-Catholic spouse was required to assure that the children would receive a Catholic education before the nuptials took place. Consequently, my brothers and I were educated in Catholic schools.

My high school years were spent at New Hall, a Catholic boarding school in Essex. Education was rigorous, and I loved my English and language classes in particular. Initially, however, it was not the education that endeared New Hall to me. It was the stables where I could ride every week. Most of my teachers were lay staff, but the school was home to the Community of Canonesses Regular of the Holy Sepulchre. Tradition has it that this order has existed since the 4th century, when Macarius, Bishop of Jerusalem, accompanied Helena, mother of Constantine the Great, in her search for the True Cross. The order eventually settled at New Hall in 1799. The Elizabethan manor was placed conveniently between London and Harwich and was home to a number of royals, including Henry VIII, who had procured the manor in 1517. The wall of the convent chapel still bore his coat of arms, HENRICUS REX OCTAVUS featuring among the inscriptions.

As pupils, the only services we were obliged to attend were Sunday mass and compline, after which the entire school retired to our separate houses. While the canonesses were not renowned for their singing, I was always moved to a peaceful stillness by the repetitive antiphons and responses. No matter how difficult the day had been, I returned to Campion House soul rested. While I frequently attended mass during the week, I particularly loved the Sunday service, perhaps because it was not followed by classes. The hymns and readings nourished my soul and mind and our parish priest, as I recall, always centered his homilies on the themes of a loving, kind, gentle and compassionate God and the beauty of the universe in which he resides.

The great gift of my convent school education was immersion in the sacred and the beautiful: the 16th century manor house, the creak and smell of ancient wooden floorboards, the evensong of the nuns, the equally ancient library and a curriculum saturated in the works of the most renowned literary minds. Summers I swam in the Indian ocean (my parents lived on Mahé, the largest of the Seychelles Islands). The other eight months I swam in the currents of Western art and literature.

Conversion & Perplexities

During my gap year in Germany I became friends with a young woman with whom I felt comfortable talking about things divine even though she was not Catholic. Intrigued by the similarity of our views on God, I accompanied her to church one Sunday morning at her invitation. As I stepped over an ordinary threshold into an unimpressive room, I experienced something beautiful and powerful. I had not experienced the Spirit in this way before and only on a few occasions since. I paid closer attention to what followed. What I remember from this ineffable conversion experience is fire and light. A few weeks later I rang my parents to share with them that I had decided to change my religious affiliation: I was going to join what we then called "the Mormons." I anticipated some hesitation, but not the devastation I saw in their response. My father wondered if I had joined the Baader-Meinhof terrorist organization, otherwise known as "die Rote Armee Fraktion." My mother stuttered, "What about Brigham Young and all those wives?" I knew of the former, as the Baader-Meinhof group was still active. As for polygamy, even though I was later taught that this practice was the order of heaven, I was surprised that it was not part of the missionary discussions.

My parents never recovered from my fateful decision. That they were not permitted to attend my wedding only aggravated my family's pain and profound sense of loss, which I share to this day. As my faith journey progressed, however, I came to see pain as a prelude to eventual healing. One Sunday I was approached by a Latter-day Saint friend who wanted to share with me a dream-vision she had had the night prior. The dream was related to me in a lady's bathroom at church, which is probably why the memory remains vivid. It seemed an odd place for the sacred. She was mother to three boys; the eldest had long, dark hair and my children called him Jesus. While I did not know this at the time, my friend was violated as a child, abandoned as a young mother, and left alone to raise her children, two of whom had special needs. Life had been one unremitting struggle to keep her head above the water that always threatened to submerge her completely in confusion and her pain.

In her dream-vision Jesus came to her. He called her by name and wept while repeating over and over the words: "I am so sorry for your life." No blame of any kind, for the way she had lived it, was laid at her door. When she awoke her pillow was bathed in her own tears—tears of healing. While the course of her life did not change much materially, she had experienced a deep-down change that would remain fixed in her soul. Her countenance had been suffused with holy light, which hinted to me that the agony of her mind and soul had been healed by divine and absolute love. I was moved by her transcendent experience, but at the same time troubled. This feeling of merciful comfort from the Son was consistent with what I had been taught as a child to hope for from both Father and Son, but I soon encountered, both in church and scripture, disturbing descriptions of God the Father with which I had to contend. Even while my conversion experience continued to animate me, mounting questions at times felt paralyzing.

For example, when I was called to fill the position of seminary teacher, I felt it incumbent upon me to search the scriptural texts more thoroughly. I became alarmed by the conflicting portrayals of the God of the Old Testament and the Christ of the New Testament (who in our theology are the same being). Jehovah is frequently portrayed as wrathful, vengeful and capricious—as in the story of the flood or the conquest of Canaan. And yet the Christ consecrates his time and effort healing the psychologically, emotionally, and physically wounded. Compounding the problem were Jesus's words: "Have I been so long time with you, and yet hast thou not known me, Philip? He that hath seen me hath seen the Father; and how sayest thou then, Shew us the Father?" (John 14:9), implying that God the Father's work and glory were identical to that of the Son's—our eternal as well as our mortal welfare. Yet, in the Doctrine and Covenants the Son pleads with the Father for clemency on our behalf: "Listen to him who is the advocate with the Father, who is pleading your cause before him—Saying: 'Father, behold the sufferings and death of him who did no sin, in whom thou was well pleased; behold the blood of the Son which was shed, the blood of him whom thou gavest that thyself might be glorified; Wherefore, Father, *spare these*'" (D&C 49:3–5, emphasis mine). His intercession is moving, but also very perplexing. It appears that two members of the Godhead, the Father and the Son, are working in contradistinction to each other; one has to plead with the other to be merciful. I was searching for confirmation of a unity of purpose and of personality between these two roles, these two depictions.

Reimagining Divinity

Years passed. Terryl and I were visiting Cedar Breaks in Utah. I remember a cloudless, "big sky" day. We pulled off the road and walked on soft, green grass to a pond. I was reminded of Switzerland. We stopped to sit on a bluff overlooking a valley far below and red mountains across. The place felt holy, untrammelled. It seemed natural to reach into our bag for the scriptures. The book fell open to Moses 7 and the account of the weeping God of Enoch. The air appeared to crystalize in front of us as I read, for which I had no explanation that would satisfy a scientist. The passage struck to our depths, a fresh revelation of an existing revelation.

Some time later, after a harrowing experience, I remembered the Moses 7 episode of Cedar Breaks and reached again for that text. And again the passage overwhelmed me. Had figures actually emerged in the marble for Michelangelo to sculpt, I experienced something very like it. Among those pages I read that God neither countenances nor orchestrates the agonies we experience individually or collectively in this world. Three times a disconsolate Enoch asks God, the Father: "How is it that the heavens weep, and shed forth their tears as the rain upon the mountains . . . How is it thou *canst* weep?" (Moses 7:28–29, emphasis mine). In his response, God inverts the order of the two great commandments: First: "Unto thy brethren have I said, and also given commandment that they should love one another [yet] they hate their own blood" and second: "that they should choose me" (Moses 7:33).

Always alert to hints that will lead to a deeper understanding of God's love, I have found language in Shakespeare's poetry that for me encapsulates beautifully the unwavering love of the Father—a love that is not to be purchased with obedience or which "alters when it alteration finds, / Or bends with the remover to remove. / O no! It is an ever-fixed mark / That looks on tempests and is not shaken (Sonnet 116). I hear that same message of absolute, uncompromising, eternal love in the words of Moses: "Wherefore should not the heavens weep?" God asks Enoch, "seeing these [my children] shall suffer." The emphasis in that vision concerns God's grief that we "suffer," rather than because we "sin." Such emphasis is a portentous revelation of his character and concerns, of his unwavering love.

This divine truth has altered the lens through which I view life and people, and comports with various texts I read, both old and new. In addition to Shakespeare's sonnet, these include theologian Nicholas Wolterstorff's writings, which suggest that we suffer because "we all prize and love; and in this present existence of ours, prizing and loving yield suffering. Love in our world is suffering love . . . Suffering is for the loving."[2] His words echo those of Dietrich Bonhoeffer who wrote that it is the Suffering God who has the power to draw all humankind to him because "The God of the Bible . . . wins power and space in the world by [this] weakness."[3]

This same God is also to be found in the book of Jacob, written by an unknown prophet and placed in the Book of Mormon. Jacob chapter 5 is a lengthy treatment of the suffering God who struggles to help each one of the trees in the olive grove reach the measure of his/her creation—particularly those that are beginning to decay. He expresses fear that his prodigious efforts might fail. "It grieveth me that I should lose *this* tree (Jacob 5:3, 7, 11, 13, 32, 46, 47, 51, 66). To my knowledge, these two passages in Jacob and Moses (Enoch) are the only ones to speak at length of the suffering of God the Father on behalf of humankind.

Contributions of My Early Catholic Faith

While these perspectives came as discoveries, they also felt familiar in some respects to the compassionate God I had encountered in my childhood. Further study brought further validation for the contributions of my Catholic faith to the building of God's kingdom—Zion. Re-reading Revelation 12 in preparation for my seminary class, I was drawn to a radically different interpretation of what my current faith tradition calls "the Great Apostasy." I discovered, to my great delight, that the ancient church of Christ, the "woman," did not die or remove herself from the earth. She was, instead, taken by the Spirit to "a place prepared for her." There she did not wither, but "was nourished of the Spirit" until she should burst out in full bloom once again. This reading was confirmed to my satisfaction by Joseph's own language, wherein he articulated a vision of restoration as that same woman reappearing as a new dawn, rising up "out of the wilderness—clear as the moon, and fair as the sun, and terrible as an army with banners" (D&C 5:14).

I was here presented with a template for a comprehensive revision of my earlier understandings of what conversion—and the restoration—entailed. I felt personal sanction to see my faith journey as continuous with my past, not disjunctive. Those worship forms of my childhood and adolescence, those devotions of the Canonesses of the Holy Sepulchre, the sermons by the parish priest on the beautiful God, together with the lovely and enriching voices of a thousand different texts, were not in conflict with the restoration. They were part of the Church of the Lamb.

One of the most compelling books on the authenticity of God's absolute love for each one of his children, and the most important to my theological understanding, is Julian of Norwich's *Showings*. It was in reading this book that I felt God's unequivocal love for me for the first time. The depth and breadth of his love permeate almost every line of the text. Julian's visions ring with an absolute authenticity.

We know almost nothing of the holy woman who wrote *Showings*. We have only approximate dates for her birth and death: 1342–c.1416. Even her name is unknown; we call her

Julian because that was the name of the church in Norwich to which she was attached as an anchoress. Her writings reveal her to be an educated woman, most likely a wife and mother. What we do know is that she lived through a period of unremitting suffering. Norwich, the second largest and richest city in England at the time, was first struck by the Black Plague in 1349, when Julian was seven years old. It returned off and on for decades, even into the fifteenth century.

It is a marvel, given the suffering and the constant death by which she was surrounded, that this book could have been produced at all. Yet it is these writings, in particular, that have been the most instructive in enabling me to see what I believe are God's true "character, perfections and attributes,"[4] though they have been slandered and distorted in the traditional Christian narrative.

In *Showings*, the parable of the Fall, for example, is not rendered as a fall into sin. Instead, God "beholdyth *synne as sorrow and paynes* to his lovers, in whom he assignyth no blame."[5] It is we, not God, who see ourselves as sinful. It is we, not God, who see ourselves as "so fowle." God, by contrast, perceives humankind as wounded, riddled with anguish and despair. It is we who have concocted God as "wroth." Julian states categorically that it is impossible for God to be angry because "anger and friendship are two contraries."[6] Love and anger, in other words, cannot co-exist in God. God's only joy is for the entire human family to become "lyke hym in hoolhood [wholeness]," restored to health and vitality. Indeed, God asks why his beloved servant should not be "highly and blessedly rewarded without end, [even] above that, which he should have received, had he not fallen, and to such an extent that his falling and the despair which he has experienced shall be alchemized into high, surpassing honour and joy everlasting."[7]

Julian helped persuade me that the reason the Father sent his Son was to heal us from our brokenness rather than to save us from our sins. God wishes, above all, for our wholeness—our healing, our perfection (Matt: 5:48). It is through the healing power of Christ that we may be "onyd [oned] and lyke to oure Lorde in althying [for] he wylle helpe us, and he shalle make it so."[8] Or, in the words of Moses, the "work and glory" of God, and presumably of the Godhead, is to bring to pass the "immortality" and "eternal life" of each one of the children (Moses 1:39).

Some Christians have been taught that God is God only of Christians and loves only the righteous. If humankind past, present, and future comprise the children of God, then why would our Heavenly Parents be so partial in their love? Do we cease to love some children when they choose not to follow our advice? Related questions inevitably follow: Is there a bar to which we must raise ourselves in order to win God's love? Is God's love to be purchased with obedience? A God of absolute love seems rather to contradict this over-nurtured theory.

The experience of reading Moses 7 and Jacob 5 confirmed to me that the restoration had corrected centuries of misconceptions about our Heavenly Father. I rejoice in the weeping God of Enoch—and I am anchored by this restored understanding of a God of absolute love, who grieves over and with us, who are children of Divine Parents and joint heirs with Christ (Rom. 8:17). I was fortunate in that many figures in my Catholic past taught a God of tender love, preparing me for the continuing revelation of God's additional "qualities, perfections and attributes" that I have come to recognize since becoming a member of the Church of Jesus Christ. It is in this gospel narrative that I have learned that the wrathful, vengeful god portrayed in portions of the Old Testament is an interloping imposter.

God's Universal Love

Another shaping event that opened up a new and wider perspective, allowing me to better see the large compass of God's
outreach, happened when I read Doctrine and Covenants 10—
and took notice of the date. In these verses, the Lord speaks con-
solation and reassurance to an audience potentially alarmed
by the looming Restoration. *Before* that seminal event—the
modern instantiation of the Church of Jesus Christ—Jesus
addresses words to a church—*his* church—already existing in
1829. In so doing, he emphasizes the universality of God's love,
the fact that the Restoration constitutes neither a monopoly
nor the entirety of truth, and affirms the value and inspiration of predecessor groups: "[B]ehold according to their faith
in their prayers will I bring *this part* [of my gospel] to the
knowledge of my people." God reassures them that he does
not bring his gospel to destroy that which his children have
already received but in order to build upon those inspired
foundations. Foundations that he owns and affirms. Those
who belong to this already existing church "need not fear, for
such shall inherit the kingdom of heaven" (D&C 10:52–55).

Here, once again, restoration thought bridges the centuries
to reconnect with a conception integral to the early church. The
sacrament prayer spoken over the emblems in the first extant
recorded version (the *Didache* of the first or second century)
are beautifully evocative of Christian hopes for a unified, if
scattered, body of Christ: "Even as this broken bread was scattered over the hills, and was gathered together and became
one, so let Thy Church be gathered together from the ends
of the earth into Thy kingdom."[9] Zion has commonly been
envisioned as a figurative conglomeration of celestial individuals—"every holy and godly person" who "is lifted above this
life," according to the Church Fathers.[10] That conglomeration

was called by early Christians "the invisible church," and I find in the restoration the same enduring principle called by other names: the church of Enoch, the Church of the Lamb of God, Zion, a place of joy for all those "who have published peace, who have brought good tidings of good" (Mos. 15:14).

In another instance of treasuring whatsoever is "of good report," I first encountered Zion not in scripture, but in Virginia Woolf's masterful novel, *To the Lighthouse.* There Zion is fully realized not on Sinai or in a tabernacle but in her home. The meal Woolf depicted is not a ritual offering, but a simple dinner, presided over by a different kind of high priestess—a mother who has, if only for a brief moment, gathered all and everyone in. "It partook, she felt, carefully helping Mr. Bankes to a specially tender piece, of eternity; there is a coherence in things, a stability; something [that] is immune from change, and shines out (she glanced at the window with its ripple of reflected lights) in the face of the flowing, the fleeting, the spectral, like a ruby; so that again tonight she had the feeling . . . of peace, of rest. Of such moments, she thought, the thing is made that remains for ever after. This would remain. 'Yes,' she assured William Bankes, 'there is plenty for everybody.'"[11]

Harvesting the True and Beautiful from Myriad Sources

By such threads as these I have come to realize that my personal spiritual quest has served me as preparation for, and as microcosm of, that quest in which I believe all Saints and people of good will are engaged: gathering from diverse inspired sources whatever is beautiful, true, and edifying, and then weaving those treasures into the common language and fabric of a people united by their desire to love and minister to the world's poor in spirit. I was rooted in Catholicism and nourished by an education centered on a magnificent literary heritage long before I was aware I was being nourished and sustained by my wider love of the beautiful, as such. I believe in the grand scheme of human origins and destinies laid out by Joseph Smith, and I have faith in the binding powers of the temple that sanctify and eternalize our relationships. The gospel as I understand it comprises whatever constitutes the transcendently beautiful, all things that affirm the "virtuous or lovely or praiseworthy." This canon was championed by our founding prophet and is as broad as God's reach to humanity, spanning centuries and cultures and genres.

Living Proof

JOSEPH M. SPENCER

*"I must remember that the gospel
is not on trial so much as the integrity
of those who can honestly testify of it."*
—Richard Lloyd Anderson

A Healthy Aid
to Honesty

For a scholar, writing a personal essay can be an act of self-honesty. The whole apparatus associated with scholarly writing—disciplinary jargon, citations and footnotes, stylized hesitance—too often becomes something to hide behind. The fact is that it is easier to pile up mere indications of authority than to actually risk attempting to speak authoritatively. It is in this way that the personal essay can be a healthy aid to honesty for the scholar. At the same time, however, asking scholars to write personal essays might wrongly convince them that their hard-earned knowledge amounts to a kind of wisdom. I am young, but I have certainly already learned that knowledge and wisdom are not the same. Study does not alone produce wisdom—and even knowledge, as Hugh Nibley used to say, is not bought as cheaply as we tend to think.

I am also mindful of the generational distance between me and the authors of essays in the original volume of *A Thoughtful Faith*, and I feel that distance with more humility than pride. I do not wish to have lived at another time than my own, but I do worry that I hail from a generation far too convinced of its own moral superiority. Young Latter-day Saint scholars can be tempted to believe themselves uniquely prepared to do things never imagined by their intellectual forebears. They (we!) often forget that they (we!) can only do what scholars before them (us!) have made possible. For me, then, this essay is partially an exercise in remembering—in remembering that I have only just started.

In light of all the above, to give structure to my reflections here I have decided to write in dialogue with an essay from the original volume of *A Thoughtful Faith*. And because I call home the same institution and even the same department that Richard Lloyd Anderson did before me, I have chosen to write in response to him. I present the following pages under a few headings, each a phrase drawn from Professor Anderson's essay. I mean to amplify moments in his wise words where I hear an echo of my own thoughts. Like he did before me, I find myself with a double commitment due to the academic position I occupy: a need to speak to average Latter-day Saints uninterested in specialized scholarship, and a need to do serious academic work on my faith tradition. I am convinced that such a double address needs to be heard more often—and more loudly.

A Generation without Moral Courage

I am a philosopher, so I will ask a philosopher's question here. *What does it mean to be thoughtful?* Or better, *What does it mean to think?* This question does not come from nowhere, but responds directly to the title of this book: *A Thoughtful Faith*. If we hope to articulate a faith we might call thoughtful, we ought to reflect carefully on what it means to think. We can eliminate cheap interpretations right away. Of course, we use the words "thought" and "thinking" unreflectively most of the time, as if they just named what Louis Althusser called our "spontaneous ideology"—whatever we "happen to think" about things. But I cannot believe that a thoughtful faith is that of someone just interested in expressing a point of view. We are all (symptomatically) interested in talking about our perspectives. There is nothing surprising or special about that. It is therefore wrong to associate thinking solely with the narcissistic pleasure of appreciating and expressing oneself.

So what does it mean to think? I will not lay out a long philosophical argument here, but, simply put, I would insist that thinking concerns itself with questions more than answers—with problems more than solutions.

What I have in mind here is this. It is far more difficult to discover and satisfactorily articulate a genuine question or a real problem than it is to provide possible or likely answers or solutions. Actually, that is probably too weak. It is far more difficult even just to *understand* a genuine question or a real problem than it is to provide possible or likely answers or solutions. A serious thinker does not read Plato or Aristotle to learn and then to assess their proposed solutions to obvious problems. Rather, a serious thinker reads Plato and Aristotle to riddle out the obscure problems they came to see with astonishing clarity. Similarly, it is an unserious or at least still maturing thinker who reads René Descartes's *Meditations on First Philosophy* and John Locke's *Essay Concerning Human Understanding* just to decide which of the two was right about the nature of knowledge. The philosophically mature thinker takes up Descartes and Locke primarily in the hopes of seeing the essential problem of knowledge that the *Meditations* and the *Essay* help identify.

A more recent historical example may be more illustrative. I have a soft spot for the work of Sigmund Freud, but I have learned how impolite it can be to bring up Freud or his disciples.

It is not that people are offended by the sometimes-lurid nature of Freudian work, nor that people think Freudians have too depraved a view of human beings. Sadly, Freud is too unpopular today even to elicit these kinds of worries. Instead, the objection I hear is usually that psychology and the brain sciences have both basically proved Freud wrong. That is probably fair (though I am neither a psychologist nor a brain scientist). For my part, however, I am uninterested in Freud's *solutions*. "Fine," I want to say, "but what's most interesting about Freud isn't his theories; it's rather the set of *problems* he identified and articulated. We're still grappling with those problems, and I've found that we often do so with less clarity about those problems than Freud and his associates."

Perhaps I am wrong about Freud. He may be less interesting than I think he is. And anyway, I might have made the same point with someone else—anyone whose answers and solutions are dated and who is therefore supposedly irrelevant today. For example, these days I hear people talk about Hugh Nibley this way, although I am convinced he is often closer to the real problems than are those who criticize his solutions. At any rate, I hope my point is clear. Thoughtfulness is an attentiveness to things that mutes the urgency of answering and solving because it is satisfied to sit with questions and problems themselves. Let the practical-minded produce answers and solutions (and let us thank them), but thinkers insist on attending to questions and problems. Do we even know what the problems are? Are we even sure we are asking the right questions correctly?

This is what I hear in the phrase "a thoughtful faith." In my view, a thoughtful faith is not necessarily informed or sophisticated, as we often assume. It is not a faith that is simply critical or hard-won or open-minded. It is, rather, a faith attuned to the fundamental problems that come along with faith—problems that are probably invisible *without* faith and perhaps invisible even to those *with* faith. A thoughtful faith is unafraid to postpone the practical work of solving problems so as first to probe the problems themselves.

The kind of patience required to be thoughtful in this way takes moral courage. I am convinced that this particular form of moral courage has become rare, that it is largely foreign to today's younger generations in so-called "developed countries" (that is, to *my* generation and others like it). Perhaps the internet is to blame, or maybe widespread prosperity in certain contexts. Whatever lies behind it, we are too impatient about problems and questions, too eager for solutions and answers. We lack the moral courage needed to be patient. Indeed, as often as not, what we call "questions" today ("I've just got a few questions about Church history") are not actually questions but demands for instant answers. In short, I hail from a generation too often lacking the moral courage to think.

Structural Intricacies

I have not yet clarified exactly what I mean by "questions" and "problems." I might work toward some illustrations by noting what French philosopher Gilles Deleuze says somewhere about "what every teacher knows." *Real* thoughtlessness, he says, does not show itself in a student's homework or exercises. There one finds just technical errors or impatience with the mechanics of finishing an assignment. Real thoughtlessness manifests itself in papers, presentations, and final projects, where it takes the specific shape of meaningless and ill-formed sentences, banal statements presented as profound truths, superficial articulations of genuinely deep problems, and substitutions of readier issues for those that are harder to comprehend. Thoughtlessness looks like failure to grasp real problems far more than it looks like failure to produce answers or solutions. This requires illustration.

The interesting historian is not the one who can identify names and places and dates, although that skill is crucial for doing good history. The interesting historian sees and can say something about the historical problems that make names and places and dates relevant. Similarly, the interesting student of the arts is not the one who can name authors and titles and successive periods, though, again, that skill is crucial for doing good work in the humanities. Instead, the interesting student of the arts sees and can say something about aesthetic problems, problems that repeatedly draw us to compelling art and literature. Yet again, the interesting scientist is not the one who can list theorems and observations and findings, though that skill is certainly crucial for doing good science. Rather, the interesting scientist sees and can say something about the scientific problems that call for ingenuity, showing why these problems deserve the immense investment science requires. And here is one more: the interesting person of faith is not the one who can quote passages of scripture, identify major events in the faith's history, list normative behaviors and ritual practices, and regale listeners with stories drawn from a life of service. Here once more, all of these skills are in fact crucial, but they are singly and collectively insufficient to make a person of faith thoughtful or interesting. Instead, the interesting person of faith sees and can say something about the central issues that scripture concerns itself with, about why the history of the faith remains relevant to the deepest concerns of the present, about how normative behaviors and ritual practices organize a rich life in contact with God, and about how a life of service reveals lastingly valuable examples of meaningful interaction.

Together these illustrations point to this formulation: A thoughtful faith looks for the *structure* of religious life. It sifts through experiences in serving others looking for patterns that suggest something about the nature of giving care. It ponders commandments and rituals hoping to discover the real obstacles to sensing the divine. It studies the past to see how now-latent but once-realized possibilities might show the enduring significance of a faith stretching into the future. It asks the scriptures to reveal their own questions and interests, their own projects and intentions, their own theological positions and doctrinal commitments.

Now, because it is what I spend most of my time studying, I want to say more about scripture. I have learned over years of study to privilege the structures that organize the text. In discerning the way a given book of scripture organizes itself, one comes up against what could be called "the real" of the text. To see how Genesis moves from a fundamental human problem through a divine solution to that problem and then to a reemergence of the same problem in a new way is to begin to allow Genesis to teach us about our dangerous tendencies as human beings. To see how Job organizes itself around a cycle of arguments with three distinct perspectives on suffering, tracking when these arguments are and are not interrupted by different kinds of discourse, is to begin to allow Job to teach us about God's nature as we work with suffering. To see how Isaiah begins with disasters that leave behind them just a small band of the faithful, and then how it continues by addressing a word of promise and hope to that same small band in the future, is to begin to allow Isaiah to outline the shape of covenantal history. To see how Matthew and Luke distinctly construct the life of Jesus, to see how Paul's letter to the Romans contextualizes what it says about Israel's destiny, to see how Nephi prepares his readers to read scripture through his visions, to see how Mormon sets historical events in contrasting parallels, to see how Joseph Smith's revelations shift from individual commandments to questions of ecclesiastical organization and then to matters of mystery, to see how Moses and Abraham provide different prefaces to a largely similar creation story—to see all this is to begin to allow the scriptures to teach us about the world. And *not* to see all this is to impose our own ideas on the scriptures, to make scripture just a mirror for our own interests and obsessions.

There is, I am convinced, something about structure that matters. It is in structure—the structure of experience, the structure of ritual, the structure of scripture—that we find God pushing back against us, revealing himself and his will to us. This is what philosophers (like Alma the Younger) call "the real." There is something indelibly real at work in the Restoration, something realer and more insistent than anything I bring to the Restoration. But the real of the Restoration reveals itself forcefully only after we have done serious work at discerning or reconstructing the material of religion.

The Tip of an Iceberg of Knowledge

This last point needs unpacking. I think it is best to do so by focusing again on scripture, and more narrowly on the volume of scripture I most often work on: the Book of Mormon. This seems to me timely because I have felt for a few years as if skepticism regarding the Book of Mormon is rising. I hear too frequently from believing Saints that the Book of Mormon is just a manifestation of Joseph Smith's early Protestant commitments, that it is not substantial enough to give us something to think seriously about. And so it seems to me worth clarifying exactly what is at stake here specifically in terms of that most remarkable of books.

I grew up thinking about First Nephi the way so many others seem to. Nephi is a model of obedience, unlike his brothers, but he fills his record with mysterious—incomprehensible—texts from Isaiah. In high school and then as a missionary, I scoured Nephi's writings looking to understand what it means to live obediently, and I struggled to discern meaning in Isaiah. During all those years, Nephi's text worked much like a mirror in my hands. In it, I could see my own world, the world *in front of* the text, albeit clarified by Nephi's story and example. I was not getting to Nephi himself, but I still felt like he was speaking to me.

Then there came a time when I learned to read the text for what lies behind it. I stumbled on Hugh Nibley's writings shortly after serving as a missionary, and I began looking for places in Nephi's writings that align with the ancient and the esoteric. I set aside the practical force of Nephi's story and looked for how it might exemplify primordial or eternal patterns that I could find in textbooks or the temple. I also began to read up on Isaiah, getting to know some history and context. And I started to feel as if I had actually begun penetrating the text, though I was ultimately looking *past* the text. That is, Nephi's text now functioned like a window for me. I could see through it to worlds beyond, as Nephi's story and discourses made them available. I still was not in conversation with Nephi himself, but I felt closer to his interests, or at least to something genuinely interesting.

Eventually, I stumbled on a passage in First Nephi where it seemed the prophet was actually trying to tell me something, to speak to me as his reader. In the first verses of chapter 19, I found him talking about distinct parts of his record. Some of these he described as particularly plain and precious—things he was commanded to write. Other parts he described as also sacred, but less central to the project he had apparently been instructed to pursue. This made me sit up and pay attention. For the first time ever, I had heard Nephi's actual voice. It was still distant, barely discernible in the cacophony of interpretations I had long imposed on the text. But I began to read Nephi in a new way, asking the text to tell me what it was up to, where it was going, what it might wish me to understand. And Nephi's voice has grown louder and clearer in the years since then, while the other voices—at first still dominant, to be sure!—have slowly fallen into the background. What has emerged as I have let Nephi talk is a convincing overarching *structure* for Nephi's record. It has taken me years to riddle it out in a way that is fully convincing, to me or to anyone else. But I believe I have come to see what Nephi's doing, why he makes the moves he makes, how he gets from point A to point B. I have become able to trace the contours of the real within Nephi's text. Nephi has finally pushed back against me hard enough that I think I have begun to let *my* interests go. I think I am at last sitting at Nephi's feet, ready to be taught.

Now, as I have come to see the scope and shape of Nephi's project, two things have struck me. First, I have been startled—shaken, really—by the complexity of Nephi's record. I do not have the space here to outline the structure of the text, ✦ but I am simply astounded that the real of Nephi's text is as real as it is, and that it is so much more interesting than anything I would have come up with myself. For that matter, it is a good deal more interesting and complex than anything I can imagine Joseph Smith coming up with in 1829. Simply put, even at the intellectual level alone, I frankly do not know how to make Joseph Smith the author of Nephi's record. It is carefully structured and artfully deployed. It is strikingly organized, consistently noting its central concerns and interests.

✦ I have spelled these details out elsewhere. See Joseph M. Spencer, *1ˢᵗ Nephi: A Brief Theological Introduction* (Provo, UT: Neal A. Maxwell Institute, 2020), 10–24.

It is filled with careful readings of texts, fully aware of the fragility of interpretation. It weaves complex narratives with consistent motifs and a strong sense of development. All this can be demonstrated. ⚐ But I am not talking about the text just keeping a few names and years straight, nor about doing a decent job of representing ideas from the ancient world. I mean that Nephi's project is systematic and self-aware, artful and hermeneutically savvy, in a way I cannot honestly attribute to Joseph Smith.

Now, lest I be taken here as just trying to add another brick to an old defensive wall (and without actually providing any details!), let me turn to the second thing that has struck me as I have worked on Nephi. What has *especially* impressed me is that all this complexity and artfulness, all the clear deliberation and thought traceable in Nephi's record—all this is basically invisible to most readers. The only way it becomes visible is if someone takes the kind of care to read that requires serious, years-long commitment. Here is a kind of learning that *cannot* be done without faith, without giving the record of Nephi the benefit of the doubt. And for that reason precisely, I doubt that I have discovered effective evidence to be used in an apologetic argument. The voice I have finally heard in Nephi's record can only be heard by a person of faith, a person of thoughtful faith. One has to assume that there is something more to the Book of Mormon than the semi-coherent ramblings of a frontier kid (however gifted). And then one has to attend to the development of a structural reading that requires extensive argumentation. The remarkable intentionality of Nephi's project is not a sign that the Book of Mormon or the Restoration is true. It is a reward for faithful and thoughtful reading—a sign, perhaps,

---

⚐ This is work I have also done elsewhere. See Joseph M. Spencer, *The Vision of All: Twenty-five Lectures on Isaiah in Nephi's Record* (Salt Lake City: Greg Kofford Books, 2016).

that *follows* faith. To take it and repackage it in an argument addressed to those without the patience to attend to the text is to put it to a purpose at odds with its very nature.

Intellectual conviction here looks something like the tip of a massive iceberg of study and careful reading. And what froze the iceberg in the first place was the kind of naïve or fledgling faith—"a particle of faith"—required to take the Book of Mormon seriously in the first place. But I am convinced that when that naïve faith works on the text long enough, then what I referred to earlier as the real of the text begins to speak. And at that point, the kind of knowledge often assumed to be cheaply bought can be had. Thousands of hours of study— some of it just reading, but much of it the kind of plodding and often trackless study required for serious comprehension of any text—have gone into sorting out Nephi's project. What I can share with others is only the tip of that massive iceberg. Hopefully, even just that is instructive.

Something More than Subjectivity

In the end, then, I want to say that the thoughtful person of faith worries less about showing off her conclusions than about sharing the nature of her commitments. She asks others to join in the careful and protracted study of the gospel, hoping for company as she searches for problems and questions worthy of sustained thought. Her gaze rests on scripture and ritual and history and tradition and even life, and in all these she seeks something more than subjectivity—she seeks the real. She looks to remove the mirrors that hide the material of religion. At first, such removal looks like a search for windows into the beyond, but eventually every thoughtful person of faith comes back to what is right in front of her: material, concrete religion. There she finds the real, irreducible to subjective interests. There, if anywhere, she finds truth, invariant and eternal.

In another vein, I might say that the thoughtful person of faith gives up fear, or maybe gives up shame. Or maybe she just finally musters moral courage. She sees that the gospel is not on trial because the gospel is itself a trial, the crisis of the whole world. To be tried by the gospel is to have one's patience and endurance tested. How long can I sit with Nephi before I want to scream? How long can I sit with *Isaiah* before I want to scream? How many times through the temple, how many sermons repeating the familiar, how many earnest prayers, how many phone calls to persons or families I have been asked to watch over? Am I patient enough to realize that the disquieting demand to answer and to solve is often a distraction? Can I tarry with the world long enough to hear what murmurs within it, to discern problems that might teach me what it means to mourn with others, what it means to live together in love?

At any rate, what is needed today is not *intellectual* proof or evidence of the gospel's *claims*. What is needed is *existential* proof or evidence of the gospel's *weightiness*. No one needs my arguments in defense of a few propositions. But so many need to see what it looks like to remain thoughtfully and carefully within the orbit of the gospel. They need to see illustrations of patient commitment, commitment of a sort that testifies that there is truth in the gospel worth sticking around for and giving serious effort to. They need to see that it is possible to believe—*really* to believe, right down to one's core—that the gospel will exhaust us long before we begin to exhaust it. They need to see that someone believes that the gospel will have proven us, never that we will have proven it.

The apostle Paul said that anyone who says they know something does not yet know what they ought to know, because we will ultimately come to see that it is God who knows us. I suppose I want to say that anyone who says they are proving the gospel has not yet proven what they ought to, because we will ultimately come to see that it is God who is proving us through the gospel. The gospel is a trial, a proof. I doubt it was ever meant to be anything else. But I worry that people too seldom see this because they too seldom see examples of patient adherence, born out of staid conviction that one can sense, track, and finally articulate real truths. Or, more accurately, I think people *often* see such examples, but it has become difficult to see such examples for what they are. People often dismiss such examples with facile critiques, claiming to see only ideological motivations for people's commitments to the gospel. But that is precisely why what is needed is existential proof—*convincing* demonstrations of lives genuinely lived in fidelity to the richness and depth of the gospel.

In that regard, I have long been struck by what might be called the "Hugh Nibley phenomenon." I seriously doubt that Nibley's arguments for specific propositions ever convinced more than a few people of the gospel's truth. But I am almost sure that Nibley's sheer existence as a thoughtful reader of history and scripture made many feel more sure that they should continue in the faith, *and* that they should work harder to be thoughtful. People bought his books and collected his articles—often enough unread—because they found something strengthening in the sheer fact that someone so astonishingly gifted in intellect found an unending store of things to study in the gospel. In short, it was not much of anything Nibley *said* that helped to keep people in the Church or that helped invite people to the Church. It was rather just that Nibley *existed*. Sadly, too many of Nibley's intellectual heirs emphasize his arguments for specific propositions, imitating his defenses of the gospel without reproducing the existential weight of his work. What is needed today is a host of Nibley-like thinkers, an army of people who model a thoughtful faith, and in such a way that neither their thoughtfulness nor their faith can be overlooked.

It is a Nibley-like testimony, at any rate, that I hope I have to offer. What is on trial, Professor Anderson says, is the integrity of those who can honestly testify of the gospel. I can honestly testify of it, most especially in a Nibley-like way. The Restoration, I am convinced, is real. The closer I get to it—that is, the more I let it speak for itself—the realer it gets. It resists my attempts to force it to say what I want it to say, and what it says when it speaks clearly is richer than anything I have come up with on my own. Frankly, the more honest I am with myself, with the sources before me, and with the very nature of reason, the more I am compelled to offer testimony to the world. It is true that my testimony often takes the shape of living in a certain way—an existential demonstration shown more than spoken. (It also takes the shape of spoken or written testimony when appropriate, to be sure!) But what I hope to give to the world over the course of a long career (fingers crossed) is a living testimony of the Restoration's truth. I wish to embody as an individual subject something much more than subjectivity.

A testimony of truth written right on the living flesh—that is what I hope others see in me, and it is what I hope to see in many others as well.

A Large and Reasonable Context

FRANCINE BENNION

Reprinted from the 1986 collection,
A Thoughtful Faith: Essays on Belief by Mormon Scholars.

At one point in my life, I thought I had become indifferent to matters of the intellect—academic or religious. I had seen too much collecting, collating, cataloguing, and cross-referencing by persons eager to reveal and defend a "new" insight, which as often as not had already been expressed in one form or another hundreds or thousands of years ago. I had seen long years, lives even, spent in "proving" the internal consistency and logic of systems based ultimately on unexamined assumptions. I had seen too much effort spent creating human ideas and cultures, including our own, which became the only reality experienced. I decided it would be better to start baking good chocolate cakes. Knowing the reality and goodness of God would be enough, and for some purposes it was.

But I found that though I can turn off academic game-playing, I cannot turn off lively seeing, analyzing, and questioning, or constructing sense, and making new (for me) metaphors. I cannot divorce thinking from religion, or from human relationships, or, for that matter, from taking a shower or doing the dishes. It is all very well to say that what matters is love, kindness, humility, and knowing God, but the fact is that none of these can be separated from what I think.

Those of us who have profound spiritual experiences continue to live, make decisions, and structure our worlds in part because of what we *think* about such experiences, not just because of our feelings or faith about them. Moses, Jacob, Isaiah, Nephi, Laman and Lemuel, Peter, Joan of Arc, Gerrard Winstanley, William Blake, Joseph Smith—all these and others who said they talked with God or angels make clear that a divine experience does not transform prophets or other persons into puppets with strings controlled by God: a human being thinks.

When a person with me shows tears, anguish, or confusion, or when I experience these things myself, or when I go out for the morning paper and see Mount Timpanogos all aglow, or for the evening paper and see richness of light on Dry Mountain, how can I pretend indifference to matters of the intellect, as though thinking is irrelevant?

Faith in God's ways, and commitment to them and to the people of my Church, are in my bones, at the core of who I am. So is knowledge that God is real, and good, and powerful. To abandon this faith, commitment, and knowledge would be to become a different person. To abandon them would be as difficult for me as to abandon thinking. However, the faith, commitment, and knowledge have not been matters of unconscious habit, or absence of seeing, hearing, and change.

As a child in Western Canada in the 'thirties and 'forties, I was among friends, neighbors, and schoolmates of diverse origins and religions. I heard from one friend that the Pope was infallible, and from others that God created us and the world out of nothing, that God was three in one and one in three, and when you prayed, He heard without ears and listened to everyone at once but wasn't a person. None of it seemed reasonable to me (a man who couldn't make a mistake? three and one at the same time? somebody who was nobody?), but they seemed satisfied. They prayed for help when they needed it, and tried to be good. Some of my schoolmates went to church when it wasn't Sunday, and some didn't go at all that I ever heard of, and others sang in Mrs. Cull's United Church choir all year and went to Bible school in summer but not to church in July because there wasn't any: it was vacation for everybody. There was more than one way to do things, and it seemed to me that while some choices mattered greatly, others mattered not at all.

Though vulnerable to many other personal hurts, I found no need to be defensive about my religion among friends in the United (Methodist-Presbyterian) Church, the Anglican Church, the Catholic Church, the Baptist Church, and the synagogue. Many of the people I knew were first generation immigrants, and few had grandparents born in Canada. A flood of displaced persons came from all over Europe after World War II, along with Australians and even an occasional American. I thought hardly anyone was particularly peculiar—or rather, everyone was, including me. I was aware of persons, not groups. Once when I cut through the back alley coming home from a piano lesson, a boy pointed his finger at me and stroked it with a finger of his other hand, calling, "Stinky little Mormon, stinky little Mormon," his voice rising and falling in singsong melody. I was hardly surprised—after all, it was Denny Burton.

Joseph Smith and Church history were not as important or as real for me then as Heavenly Father, Jesus, and the Holy Ghost. Till I was grown up, I had little awareness of my own pioneer ancestors: Pioneers and early Church leaders were another kind of creature, not like me. Stories I heard about their unqualified virtue didn't seem as real as stories about the Council in Heaven, or walking on water, or a little bread and fish fed to five thousand, or Christ's letting the children come to Him, or the decision of Eve and the struggles of Moses, Abraham, David and Jonathan, and Esther. My faith was in Heavenly Father; Church was where I learned and sang about Him and Jesus, and later the Holy Ghost, and where, as I grew, I saw my parents and other men and women building and worshipping together in His own church because they loved Him, and would give skin, muscle, life savings, and faith to Him.

Because of Him they also gave much to each other, teaching rowdy classes, mashing big pots of potatoes, and standing in long lines at receptions.

General authorities, who drove the long road from Salt Lake to Lethbridge Stake Conference several times a year, even in -40 degree blizzards, often ate in our home, and when they stayed with us we'd double-up on bedrooms so they could have one. I stood silently watching a presiding bishop play with my blond, dimpled little sister on his knee, and noticed that he seemed as delighted with her as my parents and everyone else did. When one apostle eating supper with us spilled crumbs on his tie, my sister observed, "You're as sloppy as I am," and when he took some berry jam from a crystal dish, my brother politely said, "When I take that much, I have to go without for a week." My mother blushed; Christ's apostle smiled. These authorities were fallible men, not infallible popes; not God Himself, but His dedicated servants. With no patina of perfection, they sacrificed, taught, and testified, at times lifting young and old alike in packed meetings, giving us awareness and courage. Whatever the topic, for me the cumulative song of their sermons was a state of being: Eternity, intelligence (the glory of God), joy, love, and height of soul.

Perhaps my physical landscape was important to my context for stake conference sermons. The sky was clear and the stars countless at night. Even now, when I visit that country and the wind blows so I must stand against it to keep my balance, the expanse in all directions invites to the ends of the earth beyond the prairie rim except to the West, where mountains loom a hundred miles away—not a barrier but a more visible invitation to explore and know.

Though our family at times had "home evening," or whatever it was called in the 'forties or 'fifties, I remember little about explicit instruction there or at regular Church classes, and there was no seminary. Far more important than lectures was the implicit framework my parents and teachers had for what they did. My parents didn't need to *tell* me about prayer or God, or *tell* me to give to the Church, or to set goals. These were self-evident parts of a whole. They didn't need to explain sacrifice and consecration. I saw theirs, and was involved in them. There were of course occasional lectures at home, but I don't remember systematic "religious" ones. I do remember my father sitting at the opposite end of the table in our small breakfast nook telling me—week after week, year after year—to sit up straight, put my shoulders back, and quit slouching. The fact that he had to keep telling me suggests something about the relative effectiveness of that kind of instruction.

Most important by far to my religious convictions was the quality of a few experiences that were not matters of teaching, authority, social habit, or abstract belief. They were not matters of so-called "faith" or "reason." They were matters of immediate, absolute reality. I knew about the fabrication of fairy tales and night or day dreams—I could create them all, and make them go as I wanted them to go. I knew that when my cousin, Tom, and I acted out stories, or the novel we were going to write, we were making up what we wanted to think and feel. But I knew my own imagination could not fabricate the astonishing transcendence I experienced when I was alone in the temple for a few minutes before baptism, or sitting on a folding chair far back in the recreation hall at a stake conference in my early teens, or receiving a blessing from David O. McKay, or in my middle teens knowing a few hours of absolute faith and almost immediate healing after long weeks of uncontrollable infection when I discovered the first part of D&C 88 one night while alone in a hospital far from home. I told no one of these experiences, because it seemed to do so would profane them, and because they are beyond the thousands of words I knew then and have learned since, and because there was no need: Anyone who had experienced such things didn't need to hear about them, and anyone who hadn't probably *couldn't* hear. Besides, I was a private person. I didn't talk about things most important to me.

Running through all my world, earlier than I can remember, were questions, and the lively searching they provoked—the most exciting kind of learning. The first "religious" (I made no such distinction then) question which I can remember came with a great shock a few weeks after I turned six. For the Dominion Day celebration in July, my parents and some friends arranged to meet in the afternoon for a picnic at Park Lake. My family and two others arrived first. Camp kitchens were filling fast, and we needed a stove for hamburgers and hotdogs. The men stayed at the entrance of the park to meet our other friends, and under a darkening sky the mothers and children walked some distance round the lake to a three-walled rectangular shelter complete with roof, two wooden tables, and a metal-covered cement stove for wood fires. A violent thunderstorm came up, splits and rumbles shaking the universe and us with light, sound, and finally a deluge. Under the sheltering roof we huddled in wonder, till an astonishing clap of brilliance, tingle, shaking, and smell came all together: Lightning down the chimney exploded our stove. Pieces of cement flew into bare arms, children were thrown against walls, purple-brown lines streaked down necks to ankles, and I ran out into rain and tall wet weeds screaming my question: "I thought Heavenly Father would take care of us?" No one was dead or permanently damaged, and my mother came into the rain answering me, "What do you think He did?"

What did I think indeed? Amidst crying children and frightened adults, I thought to myself about the meaning of "take care of us" and I later thought about it again. My fifth-year-thinking about God, myself, and the world hadn't taken into account complexities I met at six.

I've not had a chance since to assume I knew everything or could, though I kept trying. Years later, riding the train one hundred and forty miles home from a visit to the only orthodontist in the province, I saw a line of telephone poles getting smaller till they disappeared across the distant prairie, and that night in bed I thought about following such a line beyond the horizon, then around the earth till I came back to the beginning; or better still, taking such a line out past the stars to the end of space. But in space could there be an end? If there were, how could it be an end unless there were something "outside" it? And if there were nothing outside, *nothing* would then be *something,* wouldn't it? There couldn't be an end of space as I'd assumed, or, by the same reasoning, of time either. I glimpsed infinity then, without bounds, and in sudden terror looked to my own windowsill for familiar definition of glittering stars and black space beyond me.

Hearing in Church another day that the purpose of earth life is to get a body so we can be parents forever, I thought as I undressed that night that if I had come to get a body so I could have children, so they could get bodies so they could have children, so theirs could and theirs could—on and on in a chain through boundless eternity like paper dolls—then the whole business had no meaning. What was it *for?* Something was being left out. Then I heard in Church that we are here so God could test us, which suggested contradictions and more questions than it answered no matter how I interpreted it. Something was still being left out. How could my Catholic friend be satisfied with a catechism which supposedly gave her all the questions as well as all the answers?

From the time I started giving two-and-a-half-minute talks in Sunday School, scriptures were like a dictionary—a good reference book when there was a particular word I wanted to use. I'd look up *baptism* or *faith* in the index, find a verse, and make a talk around it without ever knowing or wondering who said it to whom, or when, or why. Verses of scripture, or even parts of verses, stood on their own.

The importance of context for a given scripture finally dawned on me one cold winter day when I was home alone practicing the piano and was interrupted by a knock on the door from a Jehovah's Witness whom I invited in. It was hardly a visit, but rather a matter of two persons thinking in mutually exclusive closed circles. The Witness did most of the talking, among other things proving to me from the Bible that we had no existence before birth. After two non-stop hours, as I finally ushered the earnest Witness out into arctic air, I thought, "One can probably prove almost anything with scripture if one is narrow, closed, and sure enough of being right." Then I thought, "A verse of scripture is in frameworks—several frameworks, the writer's and the reader's," and with new awareness I went back to the piano and my versions of Bach, Beethoven, Chopin, Prokofiev, and Pinto—each uniquely, himself, writing music both like and unlike the others.

That probably contributed to my decision to read the Book of Mormon right through instead of just picking verses from it. I'd begun several times, and knew "I, Nephi, having been born of goodly parents" by heart, but I'd never got past the first few chapters except to get a verse when I needed it. When my older sister came home for a few months and I saw her steadfastly studying the whole book, I decided to do it too. This time I was captured by the reading, which went quickly till I got to the chapters from Isaiah. They seemed to me the ravings of a madman. Why would scripture be so crazy? I put the book down. Later I hurried on to more straightforward chapters, got lost in the wars for a while, and finally finished the book quite unchanged. The good parts confirmed what I already thought, and I ignored Isaiah. You could say I consciously put it on the shelf, but the truth is I simply forgot about it for a while.

I can't ignore the Book of Isaiah now. None of it seems madness. Much of it exhilarates me, and after many readings, I still discover sudden illumination in an image here and there. But Isaiah also disturbs me. In more than one chapter, the writer(s) of Isaiah affirm human agency and divine justice and love, but in the same chapter give assurance that God manipulates human beings and then punishes or rewards them for the results of His own manipulation. Isaiah makes God a respecter of persons, who will not let His sun shine on both the good and the evil, i.e., Israelites and non-Israelites. Such a God is consistent neither with the Father of whom Christ tells nor with what some other scriptures seem to say. Like some other Old Testament scriptures, the Book of Isaiah seems to affirm some teachings of Christ and contradict others, and the mix causes confusion in some persons' relationships with God. I have not put the mix on the shelf, because the confusion has mattered much to persons I care about, and also because in context the mix and confusion make sense.

I am fifty now, and know both more and less than I did as a child. Tonight, coming up the stairs, I saw one of my scientific sons getting Snelgrove Canadian Vanilla ice cream out of the freezer. "I saw that," I teased. "How did you see it?" he answered, calmly putting cinnamon and applesauce on the ice cream. "With my eyes." "How did they do it?" Thinking of something else, I lost the connection for an instant, wondered who "they" were, and absently replied, "Why don't you ask them?" "They can't talk. You tell me." Remembering what our lighthearted exchange was about, and aware of research studies, quantum mechanics, and some ideas which have been around for hundreds and thousands of years, I said, "Well, that depends. Either some particles or some waves struck either some so-called matter or some so-called energy and . . . " "Don't get technical. Just tell me what happened." "I can't," I said.

Sometimes increased information and alternative theoretical approaches make simple accuracy hard to achieve, at least temporarily. But information, experience, and theories that are used as such can also make simplicity and accuracy easier to achieve. It is ignorance and inexperience, not a little knowledge, that make confusion.

A couple of years ago, I answered the phone. After some conversation, the voice at the other end shook and finally broke: "Does God love me? *Can* God love me?" "Why don't you try asking Him for yourself?" "I've tried. I try and I try, but I don't get any answer: I wonder if He's even there, or if He pays attention to me. *Can* He love me?"

It was not the time to talk about what prayer is, or why there might be no apparent answer. It was not the time to talk about important differences between feeling guilty and being evil. It was not time to say, "Well, let's just put this on the shelf a while. You don't have to get all heated up about it." It was certainly no time to refer to scripture.

Once, it had been profoundly comforting to this person to read

> But Zion said, The Lord hath forsaken me, and my Lord hath forgotten me.

> Can a woman forget her sucking child, that she should not have compassion on the son of her womb? yea, they may forget, yet will I not forget thee.

> Behold, I have graven thee upon the palms
> of my hands; thy walls are continually before
> me. (Isaiah 49:14–16)

But now, after reading in the Doctrine and Covenants about the wrath of God, and then going to Isaiah for comfort but instead chancing on verses about unforgiving divine vengeance, this person found scripture to be the problem, not the solution. Discussion of context would not erase deep despair at that moment, and any ignorant call to repentance for uncommitted sins would make it worse. What was needed was knowledge that God's love for a struggling human being is real—not just likely, logical, promised, or assumed, but real.

The voice on the phone came again: "Do you *know* He is real? Do you *know* He can love me?"

It is one of the few things I absolutely do know. Several years ago, while on a Church writing committee, I was asked to do a lesson on love for all persons. I wasn't qualified for the task. I myself didn't love everybody, didn't know what it felt like—not the all-encompassing, continuous state of being we wanted to teach. For several weeks I focused on learning. I cut out newspaper articles about loving persons and nasty persons and indifferent persons; I skimmed and reread assorted essays, discourses, biographies, autobiographies, short stories, poems, and sections of novels. I watched and listened; I consulted concordances for everything I could find in scripture (in context) on *love*, *charity*, other relevant words, and characters I remembered as loving or unloving. The scripture I found most powerful, Moroni 7:48, impelled me to pray with all energy of heart for the love I wanted to teach, and I did so at night and at assorted odd moments during the days. I was full of the search, and knew quite a bit.

One morning I took some clean clothes into my son's room. It smelled terrible. A search finally revealed the odiferous source: Several of Brett's dirty socks were in a heap with his cross-country running shoes. That night I reminded him to use the dirty socks basket outside his door by the washer. A few days later, the room stunk again, I found a pile again, I reminded him again, and a few days later again, and then again. Finally frustrated one evening, again, by the powerful air emanating to the hall from his room, I exploded (not my usual style).

In the middle of hot angry generalizations about his intractable laziness, I suddenly saw the great crack between how I'd been studying about love all afternoon and how I was feeling about my son now. What kind of person was I? In the middle of a word, in shame and despair of doing anything right that mattered, I went to my room, shut the door, and went to bed though it was hardly 9:00 P.M.—no toothbrushing, no prayer, no looking or analyzing. I slept deeply and blankly until just before morning, when I learned, to my astonishment, things I had thought I already knew about God, love, and human relationships.

When I was young, I dreaded becoming middle-aged and believing *all* to be just as I thought it was. When I was older, I had a period of wishing I might believe that *anything* was just as I thought it to be. One of many tensions in mortality is that between knowing and not knowing. We are likely to forget some things and remember others, to notice some things and ignore others, to assume some things and search for others. In all this mix, it is easy for most of us to trust ourselves too much or too little.

I know a little. I believe much and assume much—as most persons must do about anything. I know God now in ways enhanced by my questions and my experience. Though such knowledge does not solve all questions or smooth all hills and valleys, at the core of my context for current experience is the certainty I have about God and His relationship with us.

From the earliest years I remember, I have wanted a large and reasonable context—logical and internally consistent. I do not want it based only on human assumptions or second-hand reports, important though they be. I do not want my only realities to be those which I and others have created, important though they be. Though it is useful to know that someone says a thing is true, I want to learn whether it is true. I want to know reality beyond my own window sill. I want at least some acquaintance with ultimate, eternal truth—though I see it through a glass darkly till I die.

I need a reasonable context for diversity, suffering, confusion, sacrifice, and love; a context for delight and discovery, questions, and the lively exchanges repeated over and over for thousands of years without universally complete conclusions on everything, except those supposed by persons unwilling or unable to go beyond their own thinking. I need not only a good context of time, place, and circumstance for a given event or idea, but a large and reasonable context for looking at what scripture is, what humans are, who God is, what life is for, and how we do and don't make sense of things. Such a context is important for understanding not only answers, but also the questions.

From LDS scriptures I draw the basis for such a context. It certainly is not the only view which can be drawn from them, but is a framework which for me is logical, useful, and consistent with my experience with God and my fellow human beings—a framework different in important ways from traditional Christianity and many other religions and philosophies. My understanding is that God and His Son have given and continue to give the help we need to preserve our individual diverse wills and our capacity for both confusion and understanding, costly though that preservation be for us all. Otherwise, how could we continue to exist as individuals, capable of choice and change, capable of learning to deal with realities of personal relationships and natural "law" as He does, capable of rightness and truth without cracks or shadows if that is what we want, capable of knowing Him and ourselves, capable of joy and love, of choosing from all other possibilities to *be* as He is?

Last month our Sunday School class discussed D&C 132. One man was disturbed by language suggesting that women are property to be given to men, to be owned by them. Another man said that, personally, he puts his wife on a pedestal; in fact, he puts most women on a pedestal. A woman objected to that. A wonderful assortment of heads and faces responded to each comment, and a forest of lively but not hostile hands arose. Men and women talked about God, scripture, and men and women.

After the closing prayer, one man—who didn't get to speak before the teacher closed the discussion in time for sacrament meeting—said to another: "I don't know why anyone gets upset about men's higher position, their power over women. It's the way things were in the pre-existence, and it's the way God wants it. Women had just better obey and be happy about it." He was serious, and so was his neighbor, whose assumptions were different.

The two are friends. Both are committed to the Church and God, and both read scripture. Both have seen how men treat women, and each thinks differently about that and about other things. Each thinks his choices matter.

Who can say that faith and reason are separate categories? Those who have faith think about it. Those who reason, even (or especially) scientists, must begin with ultimate assumptions they cannot incontrovertibly prove, assumptions which they must rely upon with a degree of faith. It is not easy to define such complexities, or to be simple and accurate in expressing all the things important to us. Alive, we move in darkness and light, expressive and inarticulate, inventing and discovering. That makes sense to me, in context.

"The Lamanites . . . are More Righteous than You": A Believing Historian's Take on the "Curse" in the Book of Mormon

JENNY HALE PULSIPHER

When I was a young mother living in the San Francisco Bay area, I was asked to teach a sharing time lesson for a stake primary activity. I don't remember the topic, but I vividly remember the inept way I tried to make the point that Jesus loves everyone equally. Looking out at the children, who included both light-skinned descendants of Europeans and darker-skinned descendants of Pacific Islanders, I asked, "Does Jesus love people with brown skin as much as he loves people with white skin?" Perhaps some of the children raised their hands to answer, I don't remember. But I will never forget the slumped shoulders and defeated look of a Pacific Islander boy near the front of the room who bowed his head and said, "No."

I had assumed the only possible answer to that question was "yes." Frantic to do damage control, I spluttered that Jesus *did* love brown people as much as white, he loved *all* people equally, skin color didn't matter. I don't know if any of my protestations were enough to reduce the shame I had inflicted on him by asking the question. My heart still breaks every time I remember that day.

That child's lived experience made it possible for him to believe that he was inferior to the white children he worshiped with. The striking difference between his home community—a place blighted by a violent drug trade—and the exclusive surroundings of the ward he attended sent the message that his community was lesser. Unfortunately, he probably got that message at church too, from well-meaning but stumbling people like me, and from primary lessons and songs that characterized all the Indigenous people of the Americas and Pacific Islands as "Lamanites" whose ancestors were wicked and cursed with dark skin. Focusing on and connecting skin color with wickedness is both hurtful to Latter-day Saints of color and, as I will argue below, mistaken. ✦

Discomfort with how differences in skin color were interpreted in the Church has been a life-long concern for me, stemming from my own lived experience. My family participated in the Church's Indian Placement Program from the time I was seven years old. I was anxious for my Diné (Navajo) brothers to feel fully part of our family, ward, and community. I also identified strongly with my own Native American ancestors, Shoshones Sally Exervier Ward and her daughter Adelaide Exervier Brown, who were among the earliest Native converts to the Church. These connections sensitized me to problematic interpretations of skin color and made me feel discomfort on behalf of my brothers and my ancestors whenever I heard skin color or ethnic difference described as a sign of cursing or unrighteousness.

For the same reasons, I pay close attention to how skin color figures in the Book of Mormon. I love the Book of Mormon and have a spiritual witness that it is true. That witness dates from the first time I read it and prayed about it at the age of twelve, and it has been renewed through prayer and study during the dozens of times I have read it since then. While I approach the Book of Mormon as a sacred text, I also approach it through my training as a historian. This involves close reading, considering each writer's perspective and cultural context. My own context also matters. I, as a reader, am influenced by my

✦ I am grateful to Ignacio Garcia, Farina King, Cynthia Connell, Eduardo Pagán, and Mike Taylor for their helpful and insightful comments on an earlier draft of this essay. Ignacio Garcia notes that many who identify as Lamanite today focus on the blessings promised to Lehi's descendants in the Book of Mormon, rather than on skin color (personal communication).

own time and culture, which affect the assumptions I bring to my reading, what I see, and what I fail to see.

During my years of studying the Book of Mormon, I have come to believe that interpreting dark skin as a curse on wicked Lamanites is tragically mistaken. It confuses the prejudicial attitudes of some people in the Book of Mormon with God's will, and it ignores the revelations from God within the book itself that condemn such prejudice. Because of persistent assumptions and teachings that link dark skin with cursing and wickedness, many people within and outside the Church have felt shame, anger, or confusion surrounding the identity of "Lamanite." To lessen that pain moving forward and take up President Russell M. Nelson's challenge to "lead out in abandoning attitudes and actions of prejudice," we need to learn to read the Book of Mormon differently, paying attention to the divergences between the attitudes of the Nephite writers and God's direction to them.[1] The Book of Mormon reveals God's will for how people of different appearances and cultures *should* treat each other, but it also introduces us to a culture and people that, like our own culture, *needed* such teaching. Despite *and* because of the fallible people who appear in the pages of the Book of Mormon, it clearly speaks to the challenge of modern-day racism.

This essay represents how I have come to reconcile my conviction that the Book of Mormon is sacred scripture providing guidance on today's challenges with my recognition that interpretations of the book commonly used in the Church by lay members, policy makers, writers of manuals, and general leaders have at times fueled the fire of racial prejudice. I acknowledge the pain many have suffered because of discourses and practices surrounding skin color, even in the church that I love. I deeply regret times when I contribute to that pain. I hope that offering new ways to interpret the Book of Mormon will contribute to our shared effort to heal wounds and "root out racism." ⟡

1.   Our own time and culture influence how we interpret the Book of Mormon.

When the Book of Mormon was published in the nineteenth century, its readers assumed that the Lamanites who survived at the end of the book were the ancestors of the American Indians. Introductions to the Book of Mormon before 1981 said as much, and writings of nineteenth-century Church leaders and followers make it clear that they saw the Lamanites and the Native Americans as the same people.

Nineteenth-century white settler attitudes toward Native Americans were frequently negative, emphasizing their inferiority on the scale of civilization to the whites who steadily encroached on their lands. Some drew parallels between the Native Americans in their area and the "wicked" Lamanites of scripture in ways as painful to nineteenth-century Native people as they are to Indigenous people today. ⟡

The persistent association of Native Americans with Lamanites undoubtedly strengthened the popular view that the curse on the Lamanites was dark skin, and that when

---

⟡ In his June 2018 address at the Be One Worldwide Priesthood Celebration, Elder Oaks declared, "Racism is probably the most familiar source of prejudice today, and we are all called to repent of that."[2]

⟡ Michael Bennion notes the example of Nicaagat, who ran away from the Latter-day Saint home in which he was working because his employer "called his dark skin a curse and whipped him."[3] Admittedly, people like Brigham Young, who clearly saw the Native Americans as less civilized than the white settlers, also saw them as members of the House of Israel and spiritual equals of white church members.

the curse was lifted, the Lamanites/Native Americans would become white. An oft-cited scripture in support of that view appears in 2 Nephi 30:6, which states that "many generations shall not pass away among them [the "remnant" of Lehi's people], save they shall be a white and delightsome people." Joseph Smith changed "white" to "pure" in his 1840 edition of the Book of Mormon, as part of a general revision. All of his dozens of changes were carried over to the 1920 edition except for "pure" and two others. In that edition "pure" reverted to "white" and remained that way until 1981, when it was changed to reflect Joseph Smith's 1840 amendment.[4] The first decades of the twentieth century were the high mark of racial exclusivity in the United States, when the "one-drop rule" entered a number of state segregation laws. Perhaps that environment influenced the 1920 editors' choice to use "white" rather than "pure."

Race continues to be a divisive issue today, perhaps *the* most divisive issue. And the assumptions of our race-conscious society continue to affect the way we read the Book of Mormon. One example is the fact that few people question the label "three Nephites." The phrase does not appear in the Book of Mormon, which refers only to the "three disciples of Jesus" (4 Ne. 1:37; Ether 12:17). We know that just before the Savior's appearance, the church was "broken up in all the land save it were among a few of the Lamanites who were converted unto the true faith; and they would not depart from it" (3 Ne. 6:14).

 "The Lamanites, through transgression, became a loathsome, ignorant and filthy people, and were cursed with a skin of darkness. . . . yet they have the promise, if they will believe, and work righteousness, that not many generations shall pass away before they shall become a white and delightsome people but it will take some time to accomplish this, at best."[3]

 One-drop standards of racial purity were adopted in OK (1907), AR (1911), TN (1917), VA (1924), AL (1927), and GA (1927).[5]

Surely many of these righteous Lamanites were among "the more righteous part of the people" who survived the great destruction and welcomed the Savior at his appearance in the western hemisphere (3 Ne. 10:12). So why call the three disciples Nephites? It is undoubtedly because of the persistent, unjustified association of Nephites with righteousness and Lamanites with wickedness.

2. The perspective of the Nephite writers of the Book of Mormon influenced their negative view of the Lamanites.

We get *only* the perspective of Nephite writers in the Book of Mormon, so we should not be surprised that they so often depicted the Lamanites as unrighteous. They were almost constantly at war with each other. In every war, people describe their foes as evil aggressors and themselves as righteous defenders. ⚜

Writers in the Book of Mormon often characterized the Lamanites as wicked and barbaric, as when Alma described them as "a wild and a hardened and a ferocious people . . . who delighted in murdering the Nephites, and robbing and plundering them" (Alma 17:14–15). Similar passages appear in the writings of Nephi, Jacob, Helaman, Mormon and Moroni.[6] Admittedly, several Nephite writers did acknowledge the wickedness of their own people. Jacob declared, "Behold, the Lamanites your brethren . . . are more righteous than you" (Jacob 3:5). Alma said that "it shall be more tolerable for [the Lamanites] in the day of judgment than for you, if ye remain

---

⚜ Cynthia Connell observes that Lamanite and Nephite use of the term "brethren" for each other was a very accurate predictor of whether they were at war or at peace (personal communication). Notably, both Samuel the Lamanite and Moroni, who longed for reconciliation, used the term even during times of war (Hel. 13:30; Moroni 1:4).

in your sins" and added that, despite the Lamanites' sinfulness, "there are many promises which are extended to the Lamanites; for it is because of the traditions of their fathers that caused them to remain in their state of ignorance" (Alma 9:16; see also Alma 17:15). And Mormon's writings condemned the Nephites far more harshly than the Lamanites, going so far as to declare them "without civilization" (Moroni 9:9–21).

The common interpretive focus on Lamanite wickedness may lead readers to overlook these references as well as the Book of Mormon's many accounts of righteous Lamanites: King Lamoni and his father; their subjects who became the Anti-Nephi-Lehies and whose sons became the righteous "sons of Helaman"; Abish, the Lamanite woman whose father had been converted by a vision from the Lord; and the prophet Samuel the Lamanite.

There are also examples of prophets whose prejudice against the Lamanites—what we would call racism today—moderated over time. Nephi is one example. His early descriptions of Nephites as "white, and exceedingly fair and beautiful" and of the Lamanites having a "skin of blackness" and being "an idle people, full of mischief and subtlety" reflect his prejudice against them (1 Ne. 13:15, 2 Ne 5:21, 24). Years later, his farewell sermon made it clear that he had grown beyond this and all other forms of prejudice. He proclaimed again and again that Christ's gospel is for *all* people: "he manifesteth himself unto all those who believe in him, by the power of the Holy Ghost; yea, unto every nation, kindred, tongue and people" (2 Ne. 26:13); "he commandeth none that they shall not partake of his salvation" (v. 24); "he saith: Come unto me all ye ends of the earth"; "all men are privileged the one like unto the other, and none are forbidden" (v. 28). He then relayed God's command that "all men have charity," rebuked his people for their sinfulness (v. 30–32), and concluded with this transcendently beautiful passage: "For none of these iniquities come of the Lord; for he doeth that which is good among the children of men; . . . and he inviteth them all to come unto him and partake of his goodness; and he denieth none that come unto him, black and white, bond and free, male and female; and he remembereth the heathen; and all are alike unto God, both Jew and Gentile" (v. 33).

Nephi's sermon is a strong repudiation of the Nephite tendency to revile their Lamanite brethren for the color of their skin and their unrighteousness. It also declares that God, unlike the Nephites, does not disdain those born outside of the House of Israel: all are alike unto him. Nephi, who clearly displayed prejudice earlier, embraced the ideal of charity at the end of his life.

3. The curse mentioned in the Book of Mormon is not dark skin; it is being cut off from the presence of God.

A close reading of the Book of Mormon makes it clear that the "curse"—part of a blessing/cursing dyad repeated many times—was being cut off from the presence of God. The first appearance of the dyad appears in a revelation to Nephi while he was still in Jerusalem: "Inasmuch as ye shall keep my commandments, ye shall prosper, and shall be led to a land of promise. . . . And inasmuch as thy brethren shall rebel against thee, they shall be cut off from the presence of the Lord" (1 Ne. 2:20–21). Lehi's final blessings to his sons follow this same pattern: "Inasmuch as ye shall keep my commandments ye shall prosper in the land; but inasmuch as ye will not keep my commandments ye shall be cut off from my presence" (2 Ne. 1:20).

Neither of these passages mention skin color as part of the curse. Many generations later, Alma recalled Lehi's prophetic blessing and claimed it had been fulfilled: "Now I would that ye should remember, that inasmuch as the Lamanites have not kept the commandments of God, they have been cut off from the presence of the Lord" (Alma 9:13–14). Like Lehi, Alma said nothing about skin color.

So where does the idea that dark skin is a curse come from?

4.   **Dark skin may have been a natural result of mixing with people who were already in the Americas when Lehi's people arrived.**

The New World was already inhabited when Lehi and his family arrived. The Book of Mormon itself mentions the existence of some: the Jaredites who left the Old World at the time of the Tower of Babel, and the Mulekites who left Jerusalem around the same time as Lehi. Less overt references also appear: Nephi's brother Jacob made the offhand comment that "after some years had passed away, there came a man among the people of Nephi, whose name was Sherem" (Jacob 7:1). This Sherem did not seem to be a Nephite, and surely he would have been labeled a Lamanite if he were one, suggesting the possibility that he might have been from an entirely different group.

The Book of Mormon includes broader references to New World inhabitants before Lehi as well: Nephi declared that "the Lord God has led [people] away from time to time from the house of Israel, according to his will and pleasure" and mentioned that the isles of the sea "are inhabited also by our brethren" (2 Ne 10: 21–22). These passages clearly allow space for Indigenous people existing in the Americas before Lehi arrived—a view compatible with the Church's 2007 acknowledgement that the descendants of Lehi and Ishmael were "among" the ancestors of the American Indians, not their only ancestors.[7] Of course, archaeological evidence of such pre-Lehite peoples is abundant, as are Indigenous origin stories describing their creation on or connection to specific New World places. The Lord's declaration that "all nations of the earth" would record his words to them should make us open to the possibility of sacred traditions, stories, and writings from these Indigenous peoples (2 Ne. 29:12).

Lehi's people came into a land that was already inhabited with non-Israelites—a situation akin to the Israelites coming into the Land of Canaan. In the latter case, that cultural proximity led to strong proscriptions against intermarriage to prevent Israelites from abandoning their God and embracing the false religions of their neighbors. Lehi's people were heirs to this religious tradition, and the fear of cultural contamination from non-believers informs Nephi's account of the first years in the new land.

Consider the following events through the lens of Israelite proscriptions and fears: The first association of the "curse" with skin color comes after the arrival of Lehi's people in the New World. At this point, Lehi had died, and strife with Laman, Lemuel, and the sons of Ishmael led Nephi and his followers to flee to the Land of Nephi. From that place of exile, Nephi declared that "the word of the Lord was fulfilled which he spake unto me, saying that: Inasmuch as they [Laman and Lemuel] will not hearken unto thy words they shall be cut off from the presence of the Lord. And behold, they were cut off from his presence." Then Nephi made this startling claim: "as they [the Lamanites] were white, and exceedingly fair and delightsome, that they might not be enticing unto my people the Lord God did cause a skin of blackness to come upon them" (2 Ne. 5:20–22). What did Nephi mean?

I believe that the "Lamanites" had begun to intermarry and ally with the Indigenous people of the New World, leading to changes in cultural practices and, possibly, darker skin color among their children. ↰ Consider these circumstances: When Nephi fled into the wilderness, he took with him his friend Zoram, his brothers Sam, Jacob, and Joseph, and *his sisters*. The only sisters mentioned in the Book of Mormon were married to the sons of Ishmael who remained behind with Laman and Lemuel. These sisters likely took their children with them when they left with Nephi. So how did the Lamanites, bereft of half their population, become such a significant force that there could be "many wars" between the Nephites and Lamanites within forty years of their arrival in the Americas? (2 Ne. 5:34).

Intermarrying with the Indigenous people already in the Americas would have swelled Lamanite numbers, and it may have darkened the skin color of their children. Adopting Indigenous practices of tattooing or painting the skin may also have been seen as darkening the skin. Nephi's description of "a skin of blackness" may reflect his horror over his brothers' mingling with and adopting the traditions of non-Israelites. It is significant that Nephi and others also criticized other cultural practices of the Lamanites that were prohibited in the Old Testament, such as eating beasts of prey and cutting or printing marks upon the skin (2 Ne. 5:24).[8]

After describing the Lamanites' curse and their dark skin, Nephi declared God's will: "And thus saith the Lord God: I will cause that they shall be loathsome unto thy people, save they shall repent of their iniquities. And cursed shall be the seed of him that mixeth with their seed; for they shall be cursed even with the same cursing" (2 Ne. 5:22–23). Notably, the Lord's words—"thus saith the Lord"—did not refer to skin color.

↰ We don't really know what the skin tone of the ancient Israelites was like, but we should not assume that it was equivalent to what modern people call "white."

That was Nephi's interpretation. Instead, the Lord said that the Lamanites would be "loathsome" to the Nephites unless they repented, and he warned that intermarriage with the Lamanites would bring the same curse—being cut off from God's presence—upon their children.

The importance of avoiding intermarriage with unbelievers appears in the Book of Alma as well. Alma declared that "the Lord God set a mark upon them, yea, upon Laman and Lemuel, and also the sons of Ishmael, and Ishmaelitish women. And this was done that their seed might be distinguished from the seed of their brethren, that thereby the Lord God might preserve his people, that they might not mix and believe in incorrect traditions which would prove their destruction. And it came to pass that whosoever did *mingle his seed* with that of the Lamanites did bring the same curse upon his seed" (Alma 3:7–9).[9] It is worth noting that Alma did not define this "mark" as dark skin. In fact, he compared the mark on the Lamanites to other marks that distinguished believers from those in "open rebellion" against God, such as the red mark the Amlicites painted on their foreheads. Alma cites the example of the Amlicites as a fulfillment of Nephi's prophecy that God would "set a mark on them [the Lamanites] that they and their seed may be separated from thee and thy seed." If Alma had thought this mark was skin color, surely he would have said so, as there had been centuries of time for that to become evident. Instead, he declared that the Amlicites were "fulfilling the words of God when they began to mark themselves in their foreheads" (Alma 3:13–18).

5.   "Lamanite" is primarily a political designation.

Associations of dark skin with the "curse" are largely confined to the beginning of the Book of Mormon, after the division of

Lehi's people. A close reading of the term "Lamanite" in the rest of the Book of Mormon makes it clear that it is primarily a political designation indicating affiliation by choice.[10]

Alma explicitly defined Lamanites as a people "composed of the Lamanites and the Lemuelites and the Ishmaelites, and all the dissenters of the Nephites, from the reign of Nephi down to the present time" (Alma 47:35). Jacob also provided a political definition of Lamanite and Nephite: "I shall call them Lamanites that seek to destroy the people of Nephi, and those who are friendly to Nephi I shall call Nephites" (Jacob 1:14).

There are many examples in the Book of Mormon of people switching their affiliation from Nephite to Lamanite or vice versa. Alma said that the Zoramites (Nephite dissenters) "*became* Lamanites" (Alma 43:4). Later, Alma described a Nephite named Ammoron, who acknowledged that he was "a descendant of Zoram, whom your fathers pressed and brought out of Jerusalem" but then claimed a different identity: "And behold now, I am a bold Lamanite" (Alma 54:23–24). Helaman described such shifts in identity on a broad scale, saying that the Nephites "mixed with the Lamanites until they are no more called the Nephites, . . . even becoming Lamanites" (Hel. 3:15–16).

Political choice also went the other way, as in the well-known example of Ammon's converts who buried their weapons of war and "were no more called Lamanites" (Alma 23:17). Likewise, in the years just before the Savior's visit to the promised land, "all the Lamanites who had become converted unto the Lord did unite with their brethren, the Nephites. . . . And it came to pass that those Lamanites who had united with the Nephites were numbered among the Nephites" (3 Ne. 2:12–14).

In the era of peace after the Savior's visit political divisions disappeared entirely: "neither were there Lamanites, nor any manner of -ites; but they were in one, the children of Christ, and heirs to the kingdom of God." Then, after eighty-four years of peace, divisions reappeared. Notably, these were along lines of belief, not skin color. Nephi, son of Nephi, described "a small part of the people who had revolted from the church and taken upon them the name of Lamanites; therefore there began to be Lamanites again in the land" (4 Ne. 15–17).

The shifting composition of the Nephite and Lamanite groups even appears in prophecy. In the vision of the tree of life, God promised Nephi he would preserve "the mixture of thy seed [the Nephites], which are among thy brethren [the Lamanites]" (1 Ne. 13:30; see also 2 Ne. 26:15). Alma also prophesied that "those who are now, or the seed of those who are now numbered among the people of Nephi, shall no more be numbered among the people of Nephi. But whosoever remaineth, and is not destroyed in that great and dreadful day, shall be numbered among the Lamanites" (Alma 35:13–14). ⟡

Notably, Joseph Smith also acknowledged the blended, shifting, political nature of the term Lamanite, writing that in the last days the gospel would "come unto their brethren the Lamanites, and also *all that had become Lamanites*" (D&C 10:48).

6. God commands us not to judge each other— either by skin color or behavior.

The Book of Mormon offers us examples of people and even prophets who were guilty of prejudice against entire groups of people. But it also shows us that prejudice could coexist with revelations condemning it. Jacob, Nephi's younger brother, provides a striking example of both the disgust he and his

⟡ An intriguing example that skin color is not what distinguishes the warring groups in the Book of Mormon can be found in Alma 55, where a Nephite passes for a Lamanite.

people felt as the Lamanites became darker and the inspiration that told him that such attitudes were wrong.

Speaking to the Nephites, Jacob declared: "Behold, the Lamanites your brethren, whom ye hate because of their filthiness and the cursing which hath come upon their skins, are more righteous than you" (Jacob 3:5). Ironically, though Jacob believed that the Lamanites were more righteous than the Nephites, he also believed that their skin color was the result of a curse, and he associated that curse with sin: "O my brethren, I fear that unless ye shall repent of your sins that their skins will be whiter than yours, when ye shall be brought with them before the throne of God." Unless Jacob was speaking metaphorically, which seems unlikely given the specificity of what he thought would be "whiter" ("their skins"), he seemed to think that the righteous would be light-skinned and the wicked dark-skinned after the judgment. For him, dark skin had negative associations. His people clearly felt the same way; they "hated" the Lamanites both for their "filthiness and the cursing which hath come upon their skins."

But after all this evidence that Jacob and the Nephites despised dark skin, Jacob revealed God's startling revelation to him: "Wherefore, a commandment I give unto you, which is the word of God, that ye revile no more against them because of the darkness of their skins; neither shall ye revile against them because of their filthiness; but ye shall remember your own filthiness, and remember that their filthiness came because of their fathers" (Jacob 3:9).

As opposed to Jacob, God said nothing about the reason for the "darkness" of the Lamanites' skins. He simply commanded the Nephites to cease their prejudice on that account. He also commanded them to stop judging the Lamanites for their sins ("their filthiness") and focus on their own badly needed repentance.

The striking disjunction between Jacob's assumption about the meaning of dark skin and the Lord's message to him reminds me of times when I have sought guidance or comfort in prayer and, rather than receive the answer I had hoped for and half expected, I got a completely different message: You are thinking the wrong way. Think this way instead.

This account from Jacob provides readers with a clear view into the tension between cultural prejudice in the Book of Mormon and divine revelation about what is important: the Lord's commandment not to revile people because of the color of their skins or because of their sins.

Such nuance is everywhere in the Book of Mormon. It shifts from writer to writer, and it shifts within the teachings of the same writer over time, just as we should expect it to. We have seen such changes in the ways modern leaders of the Church of Jesus Christ of Latter-day Saints talk about race, even within the last few years, in response to President Nelson's prophetic call to repent and in their growing recognition of the deep wounds caused by racism.

In order to change our church discourse about race, we need to change the way we talk about the Book of Mormon. We need to shift from the perspective that everything in scripture (or in the modern Church) is just as God intended it to be, to the perspective that scripture is a record of God's dealings with his imperfect children. ⸙ When we read scripture, we learn from both the failures and the growth of ancient Saints. The Book of Mormon offers explicit examples of both, in the prejudice of Nephi and Jacob, in God's rebuke to Jacob and his

---

⸙ Church leaders continue to emphasize that the Restoration is an ongoing process, acknowledging the need for adjustments and refinements. See, for example, LeGrand R. Curtis Jr., "The Ongoing Restoration," October 2020 General Conference; and Dieter F. Uchtdorf, "Are You Sleeping through the Restoration?" April 2014 General Conference.

people, and in Nephi's transcendent sermon calling for radical inclusiveness. Few scriptural texts contain more hateful, divisive rhetoric than that flung between the branches of Lehi's family tree. Yet nowhere in scripture is there a more loving call to cast off the prejudices that divide us from each other and embrace all people as equally beloved children of God. I am grateful for what I have learned from both the examples of cultural prejudice and the divine direction to abandon it that appear in the pages of the Book of Mormon.

Why I Am a Believer

LEONARD ARRINGTON

Reprinted from the 1986 collection,
A Thoughtful Faith: Essays on Belief by Mormon Scholars.

**y path of commitment** to and belief in the Church of Jesus Christ of Latter-day Saints developed around four basic religious questions I encountered as I grew up. First, is there a living God? Second, was Jesus a teacher worthy to be worshipped? Third, was Joseph Smith a prophet deserving of allegiance? And fourth, is our Latter-day Saint culture meritorious—worth defending and working for?

As these questions may reveal, I believed the intellect to be enormously important—more important than the heart, more important than tradition. If my mind could not confirm the truth of my religion, I felt I would be unsettled and apprehensive. Nevertheless, I felt very comfortable with poetry, music, art, drama, testimony, ritual, ceremony, and other expressions of religious feeling and thought. I was also comfortable with people who contended that religion was a matter of spirit, not mind, and that testimonies could come only through the assurance of the Holy Ghost.

My struggle with the first question began when I was a freshman at the University of Idaho and continued until the third year of graduate school. I acted as a believer, willing to assume there was a loving and powerful Creator. But I was not satisfied until I had studied the matter through and came to a conviction that my intellect could defend. My first satisfying experience was with Lowell Bennion's *What about Religion?* This manual, used in the MIA, taught a crucial truth, namely that the restored gospel represents truth and enlightenment, not superstition and ignorance. Scholarship and education are part of the gospel; Mormonism undertakes to foster the discovery and spread of truth; God has commanded that we study and learn and become acquainted with all good books;

the glory of God is intelligence; and it is impossible for a man or woman to be saved in ignorance (D&C 90:15, 93:36, 88:118, 131:6). The manual also quoted with approval Brigham Young's statement in the *Journal of Discourses* that we accept truth no matter where it comes from, that Mormonism comprises all truth, and that there is an indissoluble relationship between religion and learning (JD 1:334, 11:375, 15:160). These became articles of my religious faith and continue to remain so.

When I went to the University, my roommate, anxious to test my mettle, provoked me into reading *Why We Behave Like Human Beings* by George A. Dorsey. This widely read treatise by a noted anthropologist and behavioral scientist gave a mechanistic interpretation of the ultimate questions—not intended to inculcate faith in religion. Man was viewed as little more than a complete biophysical machine. I vividly remember one phrase from it, suggesting that thinking was no more than "laryngeal itch." That stimulated me to read several books on evolution, including *On the Origin of Species* and *The Descent of Man* by Charles Darwin.

Dissatisfied with the superficial and uninformed views that were being conveyed in certain publications to which I was referred, I concentrated on the works of philosophers. First, I read *The Story of Philosophy* by Will Durant, which introduced to me the names of the most prominent persons who had pondered the great issues. I then systematically read some of the great thinkers—Plato, Aristotle, Thomas Aquinas, Spinoza, Immanuel Kant, Josiah Royce, and William James. I read some philosophical novels: Somerset Maugham's *Of Human Bondage* and George Santayana's *The Last Puritan* and *Reason in Religion*. I read the autobiographies of St. Augustine, John Henry Newman, and John Stuart Mill. I read several books that reviewed what the great thinkers had said about God, man, and the universe, and had personal experiences that confirmed their views in an intimate way. By the time I began my third year of graduate work, I had satisfied myself about the existence of God. And my religious experiences in my more mature years have merely served to corroborate what I had then come to believe. While philosophers have not always argued that the existence of God is demonstrable, they have presented arguments that have been persuasive to me. My experience suggests that Francis Bacon was correct when he contended that "a little philosophy inclineth man's mind to atheism; but depth in philosophy bringeth men's minds about to religion."

My conceptions of Jesus emerged when I was still in high school. I must confess that I read the Bible through when I was thirteen but, country boy that I was, I was turned off by the King James Version, which was to me a strange and unfamiliar idiom. When I went to the University, George Tanner, my LDS Institute instructor, gave direction to my search for Jesus as a person, as a leader. He introduced me to new translations of the Bible. These were helpful and I still often use them. At his suggestion I also read Shirley Jackson Case, *Jesus: A New Biography*; Ernest Renan, *The Life of Jesus*; Albert Schweitzer, *The Quest for the Historical Jesus*; and James E. Talmage, *Jesus the Christ*. I came away persuaded that Jesus was, indeed, a historical figure (some historians had expressed doubt on this point), that the values He taught were superior to anything mankind had ever devised, that Jesus was indeed a divine person, and that His life provided a model worth imitating in meeting today's difficult problems.

As to Joseph Smith, I hear many assessments that clash with the impressions I have acquired and confirmed in my years of research in the Church Historian's Office. Unquestionably Joseph had a marvelous intellect and also acute spiritual sensitivity. He honestly sought to resolve the many intellectual, spiritual, social, and personal problems that arose in his life-time. He was an imaginative thinker and leader. He accepted truth from many sources. And he had good values: people were more important than money, and the law of eternal progression pointed us all in the right direction.

What about the Prophet's accounts of his own experiences: the First Vision? the visit of the Angel Moroni to tell him about the golden plates? the return of John the Baptist to confer the Aaronic Priesthood and of Peter, James, and John to confer the Melchizedek? Can one accept all of the miraculous events that surrounded the restoration of the gospel? I was fortunate to have read George Santayana's *Reason in Religion* before confronting these historical problems. I do not say that I fully understood it or that I agreed with his basic premise, but the book gave me a concept that has been helpful ever since—that truth may be expressed not only through science and abstract reason, but also through stories, testimonies, and narratives of personal experience; not only through erudite scholarship, but also through poetry, drama, and historical novels. Santayana used the term "myth"—a term well understood in recent religious literature—to refer to the expression of religious and moral truths in symbolic language.

The word "myth" has some pejorative connotations in modern English. It can mean a story or belief asserted to be true but without any basis in fact. It can be an invented explanation of some natural or historical phenomenon or a wholly fictitious supposition or belief. However, this is not what Santayana had in mind. What he called myth was a traditional account of events and happenings that have religious significance. To say that something is a myth is not to say that it was deliberately fabricated, but to identify it as an account that may or may not have a determinable basis of fact or natural explanation. The truth of a myth is beyond empirical or historical accessibility. Examples are the Christian story of the Resurrection, the Virgin Birth, and the creation of the world as described in the Book of Genesis. These are ways of explaining events or truths having religious significance that may be either symbolical or historical.

To go one step further, even in a Shakespearean tragedy where, unlike the episodes of Mormon and Christian history, the characters and events are wholly fictional, one can find philosophical and religious truth. Examples of novels disclosing religious truths that I had read during the formative stages of my religious beliefs include: Dostoyevsky, *Brothers Karamazov* and *Crime and Punishment* and Tolstoy, *Anna Karenina* and *War and Peace*. Also, for that matter, the philosophical drama in the Old Testament, the Book of Job.

Because of my introduction to the concept of symbolism as a means of expressing religious truth, I was never preoccupied with the question of the historicity of the First Vision—though the evidence is overwhelming that it did occur—or of the many reported epiphanies in Mormon, Christian, and Hebrew history. I am prepared to accept them as historical or as metaphorical, as symbolical or as precisely what happened. That they convey religious truth is the essential issue, and of this I have never had any doubt. Ineffable experiences, messages, and value affirmations do not always lend themselves to scientific or literal or precise articulation. It does not bother me at all that, in describing a religious experience that transcends his ability to express it, a narrator, a testimony-giver, often resorts to traditional phrases in presenting it. Indeed, I do it myself, as those who have heard me speak in testimony meeting can vouch. The Italians have a useful expression for this sort of thing: "*Se non e vero, e ben trovato,*" which means, roughly: "Whether it is literally true or not, it's still true."

This brings me to my fourth basic question: Do Mormon values, policies, practices, and leadership justify a lifetime of devotion? Can one work as effectively in furthering the work of God through the church as through other causes? I came to the conclusion that Mormonism was indeed a positive influence worth contributing to and perpetuating.

In 1985, Alfred Knopf published my *Brigham Young: American Moses*. In preparing that biography, I learned that Brigham saw and read the Book of Mormon in 1830, when he was twenty-nine. Why then did he wait almost two years before joining the infant Church of Christ, as it was then called? When asked to explain this, he replied that he wanted time to observe the character of those who were leading the movement. "I watched," he said, "to see whether good common sense was manifest" (JD 8:38). After twenty-two months of observation and investigation, he decided that the movement did indeed manifest "good sense." He joined in 1832 and spent the rest of his life laboring on its behalf.

My examination of Mormon cultural institutions did not begin until 1941, when I was twenty-three and in my second year of graduate work. This study was the result of my surprising discovery at that time that there was a historically based Mormon culture, for neither I (raised in southwestern Idaho) nor my parents (who came of age in the south and midwest) had experience with the Mormon way of life.

After four years at the University of Idaho in Moscow, where I encountered only a few church members, I went to the University of North Carolina in Chapel Hill where I was the only Latter-day Saint in the University and in the community. So all these years I was outside the Mormon cultural community.

My major at the University of North Carolina was economic theory. While doing some teaching at North Carolina State University in Raleigh, I took a minor in agricultural economics and rural sociology. One day, as I was perusing some books for a class, I came across a description of the Mormon village in a new book on *The Sociology of Rural Life* by the young sociologist T. Lynn Smith. I did not know at the time that T. Lynn was a Latter-day Saint, but I was fascinated with his pages on the Mormon village—something I had never heard of before. I hunted for discussions on the subject in other texts and was delighted to find that Mormon rural life was of great interest to sociologists.

Partly as the result of the curiosity aroused by discovery that there was a recognized Mormon rural life pattern, I ran across an article by Bernard DeVoto in *Harper's Magazine*, which was about his grandfather—a Mormon farmer who had lived at Uinta, southeast of Ogden—and also two articles by Juanita Brooks, whom I had not heard of before. These introduced me to the literature on Mormon culture—something I had not been aware of because I had not grown up in Utah or in a Mormon village. I have spent the rest of my life trying to keep abreast of this literature and to contribute to it. Despite obvious critiques that could be offered from a later perspective, this literature persuaded me that Mormon culture was praiseworthy—that my people did indeed believe in education and were willing to sacrifice to put their children through college; that Mormon educators were loyal to the Church, were well respected, and sought to preserve the best values of the culture; that the people were not utterly provincial but, partly because of missionary contacts, had an interest in the peoples of the world; and that among the influential leaders of the faith were a number of impressive intellectuals. This was a great church, I came to believe. It perpetuated fine ideals of home, school, and community life; its approach and philosophy enabled its members to reconcile religion with science and higher learning; its strong social tradition taught its members to be caring and compassionate; and its strong organizational capability empowered its people to build better communities. As Brigham Young said, a central doctrine of Mormonism is that God's primary work is through people, and so our principal concern was with the here and now.

In short, despite flaws, this was a religion and a church worth working for. I went into the American armed services soon after reaching these conclusions, and upon my return at the end of World War II, I expected to live in a Mormon village to rear my children and to perform my life's labor.

After three years overseas in North Africa and Italy, I did return, obtained a professorship at Utah State University in the Mormon village of Logan, and remained there to rear our family in what Grace and I always regarded as sacred space, because in Logan we actually experienced the way of life we had read and dreamed about. Except for three sabbaticals, we did not leave our beloved Cache Valley until I was called to be Church Historian in 1972. In that capacity I was able to examine over a period of several years the most intimate records of the Church—records that are replete with faith-promoting incidents that served to strengthen my belief in the divinity of the latter-day work. Particularly meaningful to me was my private knowledge of the divine circumstances that led up to the announcement by the First Presidency that the priesthood might be conferred on all worthy males without regard to race or color.

Although later released from the position of Church Historian, I am still devoted to carrying out responsibilities which I trust continue to help build the Kingdom of God on earth. Many satisfying spiritual experiences, as well as my continued study of the Saints and their leaders throughout our history, have intellectually and emotionally validated my decision to serve the faith that I committed myself to many years ago, and that I believe to be based on true principles. "Blessed is he who has found his work," wrote Thomas Carlyle; "he needs to ask no other blessedness."

Questions at the Veil

PHILIP BARLOW

The twentieth-century Latter-day Saint teacher and humanitarian, Lowell Bennion, believed that we live in two worlds: the objective world of external reality and the inner, subjective world of values and meaning. My expansion of an implication he observed goes something like this: In the external world, I am small, of scant consequence, and subject to great forces beyond my control, including my own genetic and cultural inheritance. In the inner world of values, however, I play a significant role. I have a measure of choice in what I value and become. I help to fashion the lens through which I interpret the world.[1]

In this spirit, what follows is a personal meditation on one element of Latter-day Saint belief. This serves as a way of expressing my faith because the meditation illustrates how the gospel helps me make sense of life.

We might characterize my words as "an act of theology." By this I do not mean a pronouncement of official church doctrine, for which I am neither equipped nor licensed. Instead, by "an act of theology" I mean *the art and discipline of meaning-making at the junction of three primary influences: the religion I embrace; my personal experience and judgment; and the observable world.* By the "observable world" I mean "reality," to the modest extent that I apprehend it by attention to the persuasive findings of science, scholarship, direct surveillance, and the reports of thoughtful fellow travelers. My immediate theme is what we Latter-day Saints call "the veil," along with the questions we pose and receive through it.

Before turning to the veil, I offer comment on the first of the influences on my theological formation: my religion and its institutional expression, the church, which introduced me to the concept of the veil. Because the church sustains criticisms in our era as in earlier ones, it is worth noting, in passing, why it continues to nourish me. I have given fuller explanation of this in other forums.[2]

The Church

It is not lost on me that the church makes extravagant claims that seem unlikely from certain angles of vision. Yet the phenomenon persists. Despite its strangeness, in part *because* of its strangeness to modern sensibilities, the religion thrives, nourishes adherents, serves the world, challenges and is challenged by the wider culture, and perplexes its most thoughtful observers. It remains vital to me, for I see in the overall thrust of Joseph Smith's vision something grand, inspiring, and worth living toward. I find strength and productivity in the lay-oriented devotion of the organized Saints, their culture of saying "yes" to service and to looking after one another in the context of devotion to the divine. The church reinforces for me lovely, sacred commitments in the form of the sacrament, especially, and related ordinances. It fosters love of God and neighbor.

Because of our distinctive ways and beliefs, we can seem odd to outsiders. If one wishes to understand this curious religious movement, however, it helps to remember that *all* claims that grapple with the contours of reality may seem bizarre when extracted from their context, when superficially understood, or when viewed through the presumptions of another paradigm. This is so of a Buddhist's sense of recurrent birth, her highest aspiration to "cease to be"; or a Catholic's commitment to a mysterious Trinity and to a God enfleshed who walked on water, died, and came back to life; or an atheist's faith in a universe explained as fabulous accident (or, to the contrary, as cosmic inevitability). Unlike the early Christian apologist Tertullian (if we are to construe him literally), I am not a believer *because* the object of my faith is "impossible," but because the high claims of the gospel have not dissuaded me from rewarding participation and ongoing probing. In this respect the church parallels the universe itself. As geneticist J.B.S. Haldane observed, "The universe is not only queerer than we suppose, but queerer than we *can* suppose."[3] Despite this strangeness, I find myself a grateful participant in this implausible universe. This paradox holds promise, invites inquiry, and requires imagination if we are to navigate our world fruitfully. In the words of Annie Dillard, "our faithlessness is a cowardice born of our very smallness, a massive failure of imagination." Nature itself abounds in radicalism, extremism, and selective anarchy. Were we to judge nature strictly by our common sense, we could scarcely believe the world exists. "No claims of any and all revelations could be so far-fetched as a single giraffe."[4]

In the midst of the odd, unfathomable, tragic, and wondrous reality in which human beings find themselves, we Saints are "a peculiar people" in both modern and biblical ways. We are, first, *people*, which means it is not hard to discover among us, individually and corporately, wisdom and nobility as well as errors and foibles. As to foibles, we may all be honorary members of the fictional Chelm First Ward.[5] More gravely, like Job's friends, Christ's Pharisees, or Mosiah's Zoramites, we may sometimes grow too sure of ourselves, our religious paradigms, and our righteousness, thereby displeasing God. Despite our imperfections, however, we are a people trying together to respond to the divine, which we believe calls to us. We are a people composed of *persons*, and so we are diverse. In any given Sabbath meeting at which I find myself, I am surrounded by those I love and with whom I share much, but who also believe or reject things that I judge differently. So far, though, room has been made for me in the church's tent. In short, I am—quite happily—an eccentric member of a peculiar people on a strange planet.

The Veil: A Problem & A Tool

One entry into this peculiar people's sense of the human place in our bewildering universe—which thus functions also as one expression of my faith—is through the concept of "the veil." In Latter-day Saint parlance the veil refers to a barrier of memory and consciousness that separates humans from a wider reality. That reality is "eternity," which precedes or out-flanks our birth and the creation of our universe ("pre-existence"). It is that into which we shall enter upon death ("after-life"). Eternity is an enduring realm where God and all who are not in time, or our order of time, dwell ("the other side"). The veil, as the intangible barrier between the temporal and the eternal, is the bounds of our awareness.

Like all language, these terms belong to models that, even when apt, point to what likely are more complex and capacious actualities. Even our best conceptions probably resemble two-dimensional maps symbolizing multi-dimensional reality: white lies that tell the truth of the landscape.[6] They are highly impressionistic paintings that as a whole gesture toward something large. Viewed up close, however, the individual strokes may be crude, even errant and contradictory. Joseph Smith's strokes are often crude indeed—but crude in a profound way, like a Van Gogh painting.[7] Granting my assumption that external reality entails dimensions unsuspected by human thought and senses, I like the gospel metaphor of "veil" to describe something of the present human circumstance.

A veil is "something" rather than "nothing," suggesting a barrier but also a reality beyond this barrier. It is not a window, through which one casually discerns the transcendent "out there." Nor is it an impenetrable "wall." A veil may be thick and gauzy, and in this opaque form it may indeed be mistaken for a wall and have something in common with notions of thinkers and artists over the centuries who lament the vacuum of knowledge characterizing the human condition. This sense of "unknowability" inclines some to a resigned indifference to wider horizons for their actions, creating a class of the religiously tone-deaf. In more passionate souls, existential unknowing coupled with a sense of the incongruity of reality can drive one to bifurcation, as with Voltaire: "To believe in God is impossible; not to believe in Him is absurd."[8]

But on some occasions a veil is thinner, obscurely translucent. We have inklings of something beyond what empiricism allows. Perhaps the notion of the permeable veil that shrouds human minds has limited connection with Wordsworth's "intimations of immortality"—intimations which have thrived across diverse cultures, over millennia.[9] In several short parables, the ever-enigmatic Franz Kafka wrote of a haunting awareness of a message, a presence, a judgment, a *something* he found unshakable but maddeningly indiscernible because it is too peripheral to our predominant senses.[10] Latter-day Saint sensibility understands that the veil may even be parted: at death, in ritual, or by revelation.

I like the veil for more than its utility as a descriptive image for our mortal relation to a wider reality. I embrace it as a present and potentially useful fact. Unlike some of my fellow believers, I do not think of it as merely an obstacle to be punctured by revelation. I construe it, rather, as a phenomenon with a purpose, or to which I can assign a purpose: a pithy psychological or metaphysical "something" with which I am in creative and useful tension, like the friction I minimize when lubricating my car, but on which I depend when steering it.

Insufficient regard for the veil can be problematic, even dangerous. We Saints are sometimes blithe about our revelations. While I prize curiosity, imagination, and the written and unwritten inspiration that points to eternal aspirations and horizons and sometimes helps me pick my way through thickets, I do not believe in encouraging adult naiveté, Freudian projection, superstition, or fanaticism—under the sovereign notion that "more faith is always good." Suicidal and homicidal terrorists are also possessed by extraordinary faith. For Christians, the scriptural mandate is that we be "wise as serpents and harmless as doves," not harmless as doves and just as dumb.[11]

Nor do I believe in spending much time elaborating the unknown. Every time I hear confident and comforting explanations of "the way things are," I am apt to think, "This doesn't go far toward explaining crocodiles, flesh-eating bacteria, babies born with two heads, or a tsunami that may obliterate thousands of people at a time." Nor does it account for the conflicting inspirations that various people sometimes profess. My impression is that, informed and animated by a thoughtful faith in a wider horizon, the veil should funnel the bulk of our attention to the here and now—on the time, people, problems, and opportunities of this day, at this moment, in this world. Despite the grace offering glimpses of eternal purposes, my life unfolds in tremendous, all-but-complete ignorance of our mysterious universe. The merest dabble into quantum physics, black holes, dark matter and energy, interstellar wormholes, or the Higgs-Boson particle reminds me of that fact. There is no proving God to others. Ultimate reality is not something I *know*; it is something in which I put my trust.

In gospel understanding, the veil is necessary to our stage of progression as beings. While we search, listen, and pray for comfort and direction beyond our sphere, the veil—the necessary epistemic distance from this "beyond"—affords us a freedom for independent action not otherwise possible were we literally and readily able to see God smiling or frowning at each move. The freedom independently to discern and choose between good and evil (morality) and good and bad (quality) is at the core of our purpose.

Although Joseph Smith taught that we are in but one stage of a broader evolution, we are invited through mortal experience to discover, forge, claim, and realize—to make real—our highest identity and character. In Latter-day Saint belief the potential of that character for degradation or exaltation is scarcely bounded, and it yields a unique construction of two dimensions of Christ and his atonement: "The potential *evil* of human beings is of such a depth that the Son of God died in the flesh to confront it; the potential *good* of human beings is of such a height that the Son of God lived in the flesh to reveal it."[12] On the latter point, distinctively emphasized in the Restoration, the gift of self-knowledge offered is something in the spirit of Disney's animation, "The Lion King," in which the deceased King Mufasa speaks from the Beyond to his exiled, befuddled, uncoronated, but coming-of-age son: "Simba, you are more than you have become."

Questions Posed at the Veil

Be-veiled as we are—in our confusion and unknowing, our curiosity and vulnerability, our passions, agonies, delights, yearning, choosing, and wonder—we humans ask questions. We are hardwired to do so: both our circumstances and our natures require it. Unless this impulse is unnaturally driven from us by excessively efficient teachers, overly worried parents, or our own cowardice, sloth, or distractibility, we are intrinsically interrogative beings. And therein lies a crucial tale: we are clues to ourselves. That is, our native curiosity itself provides an inkling of our intended response to the experience of being human on this earth.

This curiosity can be distorted. I recall taking my one-year-old nephew, David, out for walks in the forest that lay behind our family home in Utah. Together we marveled at most everything: the November air, crisp as an apple; red ants and black ants resolving some dispute; three distinct trees somehow grown together as one; blue-brown beetles visually as formidable, up close, as any dinosaur. As we walked, we named things. I would say "blue jay" or "lily" or "dirt" and David would approximate the sound. I cheered and hugged; David was reinforced. He learned language.

In time, though, I noticed a change. The focal point of his attention, with my reinforcement, subtly shifted: from the bird or the flight of the bird or the smell of the lily, to his own ability to attach conventional sounds to these—to name them. The acquisition of language is essential, but in the process of becoming himself in this way, David diluted—distorted— another part of himself: his unfiltered sense of relation with the world. Over time, and in his case, I am happy to say, temporarily, he learned less about curiosity and experiencing the universe and more about getting A's in school.

Despite these dangers of distortion, we are, again, natively interrogative beings. We ask questions of life, of the cosmos. We ask questions of the God we believe in, the God we rail against, or the God we do not believe in because we see other people's superstitions, or because God seems inaccessible, or because of the world's hurt, and our own.

Our questions to this God form themselves variously. Among the most common is "Why *me?*"—a protest posing as query. Among them also are "Why, God, don't you show yourself?" And "What does life mean?" "Where do I fit?" "Who am I?" And "What will become of me?"

Many of the most poignant questions present themselves classically in the Bible and other Restoration scriptures. Fueling our awareness of injustice, the scriptures ask, "Why do the wicked prosper?" In excruciating (literally: *crucifying*) times, it may come to "Why hast thou forsaken me?" As a cluster, the questions represent the human search for God or meaning or ultimacy or relief. Sometimes they signify despair; sometimes, human outrage at what humans must endure.

Such questions are understandable, legitimate, perhaps even necessary for a season. Pursued relentlessly and with vehemence, however, they can cripple our radar. We may rage until we lose hearing. We may forget our station. If this attitude continues, our purchase will not be sweet illumination, but only gall.

Questions Received at the Veil

It helps me at times to shift my perspective: *Our interrogation of God may be fruitfully inverted.* Through this means, the questions may be read not as the human search for God, but as God's search for humanity.[13] Here, the answers to the questions we ask of God, through the veil, come back, through the same medium, as counter-questions—queries put to our souls by God. Latter-day Saints know sacred queries in their temple ritual, but other queries that haunt the human soul, or ought to, are widely accessible. Developing an ear for these soul-queries alters our ordinary preoccupations and our natural but sometimes self-centered questions. It puts us, rather than God, in the witness stand. *Absorbing questions rather than inexorably posing them may, at times, be a more promising avenue of inquiry.*

Such questions have their archetypes in scripture. Some might be put to us as a people: "Have you become of one heart and one mind, with no poor among you?"[14] Others, on which I focus here, come to us as individuals. God asks, "Adam, where art thou?" as if to say, "Man, Woman, where do you stand? What ground do you inhabit? What have you been about?"[15] Or, more explicitly, God might ask us to ponder, "What manner of men—of women—ought ye to be?"[16]

We have Christ's inquiry of Peter, posed by implication to us as well: "Lovest thou me?" And to the disciple's perhaps too-ready answer, the question recurs and recurs, implying an underlying question: *"Really?"*[17]

Alma the Younger in effect expounds upon Christ's query to Peter by asking, "Can ye look up, having the image of God engraven upon your countenances?"[18]

While we march to our jobs and to our churches and sports arenas and homes, perhaps oblivious to the wounded and bereft around us, Christ may ask, "Have I been so long with you, and yet thou hast not known me?"[19]

To our questions-become-accusations against the Divine, in the midst of our pain, comes the divine question to Everyman, embodied in Job: "Who is this who speaks with words devoid of knowledge?"[20]

To our moral or situational quandaries, perhaps the best question is not "What would Jesus do?" (a rather sentimental and unscriptural presumption), but rather, as Dostoyevsky transposed the query, "What will I do, with only His image before me?"[21]

On a stormy sea, the Lord asks, "Why are ye fearful, O ye of little faith?"[22]

Before a dreaded task, a cup we would have pass from us, comes Mordecai's godly challenge to Queen Esther, whose life and people are in peril: "Who knows but that you have come to your . . . position for such a time as this?"[23]

When in our preoccupations we seek more to be comforted than to comfort, seek compassion only from, and not toward, God, we are asked, "Could you not watch with me one hour?"[24]

It may be that "Christ the Word," as the Gospel of John casts him and as the Greek "*logos*" connotes, is indeed the "word;" that is, the "reason," the "mind," the "logic" and "expression" of God. But it may also be that Christ is, at last, God's interrogative syntax, embodied: "Whom do men say that I am?" "Whom do *you* say?" And implicitly: "So what?"[25]

The Question that Will Not Cease

I value my life in the church. I value also the life of the mind. In some ways my religious practice and professional efforts are independent spheres. But who I am (and how I answer questions put to me by experience and scripture) conditions how I construe and go about all my tasks.

My personal, Latter-day Saint-inflected rumination has it that we are natively question-asking beings, that our loving God, in whose image we were fashioned, is complementarily a question-asking God, and that the veil through which we and God inquire of one another is fundamentally an interrogatory medium. Life itself is inherently interrogative and, like Wordsworth, I embrace rather than lament the veil that makes it so, even as I am intrigued and grateful for intimations and prophetic glimpses beyond it.[26]

To whatever religion we subscribe, the limits of our knowing, and the human ability and instinct to ponder those limits, implies an ultimate Question that looms behind all else. Although it may be submerged, the Question is never extinguished, not in any day or moment. Even for those who hold to no God, even to those in the most dire of circumstances, and even to those who cannot hear or articulate the inquiry, it abides: Life itself asks of us a Question from which there is no escape. Viktor Frankl discovered that the question need not be extinguished, short of death, even in the vice of a concentration camp.[27] But for me, the ultimate author of the Question that life poses is the Author of creation. Our inescapable reply, the way that we reply, the quality and content of our reply, is that which creates the meaning of our lives—and forges the caliber of our souls. We *become* the answer to life's query.

Life, then, is a question, posed by God, through a veil.
How shall we respond? ⚘

⚘ Philosopher Dennis Rasmussen, through rather a different path, asks a related question at the beginning of *The Lord's Question: A Call to Come Unto Him.*[28] While the seeds of my own thought were planted long ago by an encounter with the work of Viktor Frankl, Rasmussen and I share interests. His book poses a series of questions asked by an all-knowing God to fallible man. If an omniscient and omnipotent deity asks a question to which He already knows the answer, wonders Rasmussen, what response does man actually have? Is the question posed by God more accurately considered a question posed by ourselves, since God knows better than we what the answer ought to be?

ACKNOWLEDGMENTS

Faith may be a gift, as Paul declares with power in I Corinthians and elsewhere, but for other writers of scripture and for many of the authors in the preceding pages, faith is also a choice. Like love, it is a gift that requires cultivation to thrive across time—cultivation in the form of attention, rumination, prayer, and responsive, generous living. I am grateful to the women and men who have leveraged and cultivated their gifts in these and other ways, and who forged the essays that constitute the volume you hold. Finding the words publicly to share their hearts and heads in a sometimes critical world can be an act of courage and generosity.

I would have been fortunate to be able to include many others, equally gifted and willing, in this project. While factors such as timely availability, the need to represent diverse constituencies and issues, and others contributed to the final shape the collection has assumed, I am in joyful awe at the range and caliber of thoughtful, faithful colleagues both at Brigham Young University and around the globe for whom scholarship is, in Elder Neal A. Maxwell's phrase, "an act of worship." This disciple-scholarship is particularly rich—and transparent to me on a daily basis—among my friends at the Maxwell Institute for Religious Scholarship at BYU, whose support has supplied me with the time, collaboration, and nourishing ambiance to shepherd this work to completion.

Among its other imaginative initiatives, I am grateful to the Faith Matters Foundation for its interest in publishing these essays, in particular to Bill Turnbull. I am equally grateful for the hands-on skills of Zach Davis, Cole Melanson, Jessica Sarah Beach, Mark Melville and especially Lori Forsyth, whose friendship, patience, and tenacity have been perfectly pitched to lure me at last through my tangles.

The wise counsel, grace, and tolerance of Deborah Barlow and others of my family during the course of large projects affects, for the better, everything about everything.

Our widest thanks to the thousands of Saints who respect the life of the mind as well as the spirit—those who labor each day, in our imperfect ways, to make the *trueness* of the church *real*.

PHILIP BARLOW

THE WRITERS

LEONARD ARRINGTON (1917–1999) structured his adult faith around four basic questions he encountered while growing up: whether God exists, whether Jesus is a divine teacher worthy of our worship, whether Joseph Smith was a prophet, and whether Latter-day Saint culture bears fruit worth defending and supporting. From the origins of the Mormon History Association (1965) to the closing years of the twentieth century, Arrington was the patron of virtually all scholarship focused on Restoration history. He taught and wrote principally at Utah State and Brigham Young universities, surrounding a term as Director of the History Division of the Church. Among his most impactful books are *Great Basin Kingdom: An Economic History of the Latter-Day Saints, 1830–1900* and *Brigham Young: American Moses*. An abbreviated version of his essay first appeared in *Sunstone* magazine.

PHILIP BARLOW, editor of *A Thoughtful Faith for the Twenty-First Century*, has here contributed a different essay than the one included in the original *Thoughtful Faith* collection. The new essay, adapted from one first published in *Dialogue: a Journal of Mormon Thought*, is "Questions at the Veil." It speaks of the importance to our faith of absorbing, rather than merely posing, a certain class of questions. Barlow is a Senior Research Fellow at the Neal A. Maxwell Institute for Religious Scholarship at BYU. His latest book is *Time*, a volume in the "Themes in the Doctrine and Covenants" series (Maxwell Institute and Deseret Book, 2024).

An informed and authentic faith is not always reducible to tidy theological structures. For **FRANCINE BENNION** (1935–2024), faith and thought were an organic part of her being. In this essay she gives them a "large and reasonable context." Bennion taught at Ohio State University and Brigham Young University in what were, to her, the complementary fields of English, piano, and scripture. She served on the Young Women's General Board, the Relief Society General Board, and the Church Writing Committee.

A physician-scientist focused on finding and testing treatments for life-threatening infections and a more compassionate way to practice intensive care medicine, **SAMUEL MORRIS BROWN** is also a religious humanist who works in intellectual history and theology, with a half-dozen books published in those fields. As his essay explains, he is a lapsed atheist whose faith puts him in an advantageous position to censure the cynicism he left while acknowledging the limitations of the faith community he embraces and loves.

One of America's most accomplished historians and one of the Church's finest intellects here argues for the final "irrelevance" of the intellect in certain aspects of faith. **RICHARD L. BUSHMAN** is known to many Latter-day Saints as Joseph

Smith's preeminent biographer and is esteemed by his professional peers as a path-breaking scholar of diverse dimensions of colonial America. The first of his many books, *From Puritan to Yankee: Character and the Social Order in Connecticut, 1690–1760*, earned the history profession's Bancroft Prize. Bushman is the Gouverneur Morris Professor of History emeritus at Columbia University.

Few minds have ranged so broadly and deeply as **EUGENE ENGLAND's** in probing the profundities of the gospel and in successfully relating these to both philosophical inquiry and to everyday Christian living. England *(1933–2001)* taught literature at Brigham Young University and was the founding editor of *Dialogue: A Journal of Mormon Thought*. He championed literature in the Restoration and was himself a master of the personal essay. Some of his best are gathered in the book *Dialogues with Myself*. He described the ideal modern Mormon scholar as "critical and innovative as his gifts from God require, but conscious of and loyal to his own unique heritage and nurturing community, and thus able to exercise those gifts without harm to others or himself."

For more than two decades, **J. SPENCER FLUHMAN** has worked with students to wrestle with questions raised by history and faith, treasuring both realms and seeking to integrate them. Trained in history at the University of Wisconsin, Fluhman has published on Latter-day Saints and American religion. His *"A Peculiar People": Anti-Mormonism and the Making of Religion in Nineteenth-Century America* was published by the University of North Carolina Press in 2012. Formerly the executive director of the Neal A. Maxwell Institute for Religious Scholarship, he teaches history at Brigham Young University.

FIONA GIVENS's faith odyssey inclined from Catholicism to the Restoration, in which she finds a gospel vision embracing all truth and beauty, regardless of their source. Her published work has investigated antecedents to the Feminine Divine in ancient traditions and has construed "wound" to be a more apt term than "sin" in diagnosing the human condition. With her husband Terryl, she has co-authored, among other volumes, *The God Who Weeps* and *The Christ Who Heals*.

To **TERRYL GIVENS,** real discipleship requires risk, a "holy danger" combining steadfast commitment to Christ and courageous confrontation with institutional realities. That was the experience of Eugene England, whose life and legacy, in relation to faith, Givens surveys in this essay. Givens is a Senior Research Fellow at the Neal A. Maxwell Institute for Religious Scholarship at BYU. Among his many books are *Wrestling the Angel* and *Stretching the Heavens: the Life of Eugene England and the Crisis of Modern Mormonism*.

MICHELLE GRAABEK–WALLACE has experience navigating faith, church culture in international contexts, unanswered questions, and trust in God. She completed her PhD at the European University Institute in Florence, Italy, specializing in the intersection of migration, women's, and religious history. Prior to her graduate studies she managed education and events programs at various historic houses in London. Michelle is now a historian at the Church History Department.

DEIDRE NICOLE GREEN is Assistant Professor of Latter-day Saint/Mormon Studies at the Graduate Theological Union centered in Berkeley, California, from which she also took her Ph.D. in 2012. She is the author of *Jacob: a brief theological introduction to the Book of Mormon* and *Works of Love in a World of*

Violence: Kierkegaard, Feminism, and the Limits of Self-Sacrifice. Her essay argues for the primacy of love in our attempts to live the gospel, noting that we are in need of "a thoughtful love" as much as we are "a thoughtful faith."

With research interests that include the history of women and children in American religions, the intersections of religion and capitalism, and the intellectual history of nineteenth-century America, **KRISTINE HAGLUND** here explores beauty not as mere decoration, but as an expression of holiness. A former editor of *Dialogue: A Journal of Mormon Thought*, she is also the author of *Eugene England: A Mormon Liberal*, published as the inaugural volume in the University of Illinois Press's *Introductions to Mormon Thought* series. She is currently pursuing doctoral studies in American Studies at St. Louis University.

DAVID F. HOLLAND teaches American religious history at Harvard Divinity School, where he is the Associate Dean for Faculty and Academic Affairs. In his view, an expanded canon and continuing revelation bring together the scriptures, doctrines, and cultures of diverse times and places. The resulting "collision" has the capacity to knock the human chaff from enduring divine truth. Holland is the author of *Sacred Borders: Continuing Revelation and Canonical Restraint in Early America* and *Moroni: a brief theological introduction.*

A scholar of Chinese history and global religious movements, **MELISSA WEI-TSING INOUYE** (1979–2024) completed both undergraduate and graduate degrees at Harvard. She was a senior lecturer at the University of Auckland in New Zealand before working for the Church History Department. Her memoir, *Crossings*, was co-published by the Maxwell Institute and Deseret Book. Her book *Sacred Struggle* was released six months before her death in 2024.

Widely celebrated meditation guide **THOMAS WIRTHLIN McCONKIE** explores our journey of growth in intelligence, consciousness and light through contemplative practice, developmental psychology, and the power of the Wisdom traditions, especially Buddhism and Christianity. Having returned to the restored church from which he once retreated, McConkie is founder of Lower Lights School of Wisdom, a community of practice dedicated to training contemplatives. He is studying transformative spiritual practice and frameworks in a master's program at Harvard University. His book *At-One-Ment* was published in 2023.

STEVEN L. PECK explores how randomness, evolution, and time are the root of the universe's engine generating the novelty we see all around us. Creativity is the defining characteristic of God. Peck is a biology professor at BYU, trained in quantitative ecology but enjoys creative writing and, best of all, watching birds. He has been a fellow of the Maxwell Institute for Religious Scholarship. For the body of his literary work, he received the 2021 Smith-Pettit Foundation Award for Outstanding Contribution to Mormon Letters.

Based on his extensive experience with the reach and limitations of the field of population genetics, molecular biologist **UGO A. PEREGO** has offered his perspectives on issues pertaining to DNA studies and the historicity of peoples of the Book of Mormon. He also considers the ancestry of Joseph Smith Jr.'s family, discussing what information genetic data can and cannot offer on the matter. He earned his doctorate from the University of Pavia in Italy.

Historian **RICHARD D. POLL** (1918–1994) first offered the theme of his essay in a sacrament meeting in Palo Alto, California in August 1967. It was later published in *Dialogue: a Journal of Mormon Thought*. His now classic images of the "Iron Rod Saint" and the "Liahona Saint" illuminate contrasting understandings of the nature of scripture and related dispositions undergirding their respective loyalties to the church. Poll was a professor of history at Western Illinois University and lectured on American history at Brigham Young University. With Eugene Campbell he co-authored *Hugh B. Brown: His Life and Thought*.

JENNY HALE PULSIPHER, a historian at BYU, has written that faith is sometimes a gift and always a choice. She studies Indigenous people of North America and their interactions with early settlers. She received her PhD from Brandeis University and is the author of *Subjects unto the Same King: Indians, English, and the Contest of Authority in Colonial New England* and Swindler *Sachem: The American Indian Who Sold His Birthright, Dropped Out of Harvard, and Conned the King of England*.

MELANIE RIWAI-COUCH believes that in testing God's promise to direct our lives, we should not limit his range of possible answers for us. She is a Multi-Area Manager for the Church History Department over the Pacific Area and the Matthew Cowley Pacific Church History Centre in Hamilton, New Zealand. An author and educator, Riwai-Couch has served as a school principal and as Senior Adviser to the New Zealand Ministry of Education. She received her PhD in Education from the University of Canterbury in Christchurch.

As an openly gay Latter-day Saint, **BEN SCHILATY** sits—precariously, by his account—amidst the strong and often contrasting beliefs motivating his communities. He authored *A Walk in My Shoes: Questions I'm Often Asked as a Gay Latter-day Saint*, published by Deseret Book, and with Charlie Bird co-created the podcast "Questions from the Closet." Formerly employed in the Honor Code Office at BYU, he teaches social work at Utah Valley University.

Philosopher **JOSEPH M. SPENCER,** who teaches in the Department of Ancient Scripture at Brigham Young University, urges a fresh approach to the Book of Mormon, one less preoccupied with its historical or literary dimensions in favor of a specifically theological reading of the text as we have it. Spencer stresses the value of recognizing and formulating problems worthy of study rather than haste in listing solutions to quandaries only superficially grasped. Spencer's recent books include *1st Nephi: a brief theological introduction* and his two-volume work: *The Anatomy of Book of Mormon Theology.*

In prose that is half-poetry, **EMMA LOU THAYNE** (1924–2014) describes a faith so naturally integrated with the fabric of her life that she finds it unrewarding to separate them for analysis. Widely anthologized, Thayne published nine books of poetry and wrote the lyrics to the beloved restoration hymns "Where Can I Turn for Peace" and "I Wonder When He Comes Again." Her career included activism against nuclear arms and efforts to support the arts in Utah communities. She received the Gandhi Peace Award in 2013. Her essay is reprinted by permission from *Exponent II.*

World traveler, political scientist, and Utah Valley University president **ASTRID S. TUMINEZ** thinks of faith as an adventure. Her journey from village slums in the Philippines to the mountains of Utah is a chronicle of belief, doubt, despair, hope, and love as she has striven to reconcile her faith with her experiences as a woman, wife, mother, leader, and child of God. Her quest for self-discovery in an imperfect world bristling with questions illuminates lessons about approaching life with humility, curiosity, and awe. Among other works, she is the author of *Russian Nationalism Since 1856*.

Historian **LAUREL ULRICH's** essay borrows an image from Emily Dickinson to help us see the perils of harboring a brittle, misplaced faith. Ulrich is the 300th Anniversary University Professor emerita at Harvard University. She has been a MacArthur Fellow and received both the Pulitzer and Bancroft prizes for her history, *A Midwife's Tale*. Other scholarly works include *A House Full of Females: Plural Marriage and Women's Rights in Early Mormonism, 1835–1870* and *Well-behaved Women Seldom Make History*. She was one of the founding editors of *Exponent II*, where this essay first appeared. It is reprinted by permission.

Throughout her life and as a therapist **BONNIE YOUNG** has learned that our hunger for perfection can make it difficult to connect with God. Young is pursuing a PhD in psychology at Utah State University and is a marriage and family therapist specializing in anxiety-related disorders and sexual issues. She is the author of *Sex Educated: Letters From an LDS Therapist*.

ENDNOTES

PREFACE

1. Dawn Hall Anderson, "Seasoned Saints," *Dialogue: A Journal of Mormon Thought 21*, no. 2 (Summer 1988): 159–61.

MELISSA WEI-TSING INOUYE

1. M. Russell Ballard, "The Trek Continues!," *Ensign*, November 2017, 104–6.

2. "Plural Marriage in Kirtland and Nauvoo," Gospel Topics Essays, The Church of Jesus Christ of Latter-day Saints.

KRISTINE HAGLUND

1. Genesis 4:3–5; 1 Samuel 15:22; Psalm 51:16; Doctrine and Covenants 97:8.

DAVID F. HOLLAND

1. See Margaret Fuller, *Women of the Nineteenth Century*, ed. Larry J. Reynolds (Norton, 1997); Charles Capper, *Margaret Fuller: An American Romantic Life* (Oxford University Press, 2010).

2. See Theodore Parker, *Theodore Parker's Experience as a Minister* (Rufus Leighton, Jr., 1859); Dean Grodzins, *American Heretic: Theodore Parker and Transcendentalism* (University of North Carolina Press, 2002).

3. Theodore Parker, *A Discourse of Matters Pertaining to Religion* (Little and Brown, 1842), 187–88, 192.

THOMAS McCONKIE

1. Acts 17:28, New International Version (NIV).

2. Moses 1:33–35.

3. For additional insights, see "'Nones' on the Rise," Pew Research Center, October 9, 2012.

4. Joseph Smith, *The Words of Joseph Smith*, ed. Andrew F. Ehat and Lyndon W. Cook (Grandin Book Company, 1991), 183–84.

5. See Dieter F. Uchtdorf, "Come, Join with Us," *Ensign*, November 2013, 21–24.

6. *The Cloud of Unknowing*, 14th century, trans. Ira Progoff (Dell/ Doubleday, 1983).

7. Isaiah 55:8.

8. Mark 1:14–15.

9. Jalal al-Din Rumi, "A Community of the Spirit," in *The Essential Rumi*, trans. Coleman Barks (Castle Books, 1997), 3.

10. "Letter to William W. Phelps, 27 November 1832," 4, The Joseph Smith Papers.

BONNIE YOUNG

1. Psalm 57:1; Luke 13:34; Isaiah 27:1.

2. Moses 1:18.

3. Psalm 66:16.

J. SPENCER FLUHMAN

1. See Robert Orsi, *History and Presence* (The Belknap Press of Harvard University Press, 2016), 4.

2. "My Belief," chapter 8 of the present volume: Philip L. Barlow, ed., *A Thoughtful Faith for the Twenty-First Century*. See also Richard Lyman Bushman, "After the Golden Age," *Journal of Mormon History* 38, no. 3 (Summer 2012): 225–31.

3. Stuart Parker, "The Hermeneutics of Generosity: A Critical Approach to the Scholarship of Richard Bushman," *Journal of Mormon History* 38, no. 3 (Summer 2012): 12–27.

4. Jana Riess, "Richard Bushman and the Future of Mormon Teaching," in *To Be Learned Is Good: Essays on Faith and Scholarship in Honor of Richard Lyman Bushman*, ed. J. Spencer Fluhman et al. (Neal A. Maxwell Institute for Religious Scholarship, 2017), 155–66.

5. Richard Lyman Bushman, "Finding the Right Words: Speaking Faith in Secular Times," in *To Be Learned is Good*, 295–306.

6. Joseph Smith Jr. to the Church and Edward Partridge, March 20, 1839, The Joseph Smith Papers. Spelling, capitalization, and punctuation modernized.

7. Thomas W. Simpson, *American Universities and the Birth of Modern Mormonism, 1867–1940* (University of North Carolina Press, 2016).

8. Email exchange with Kathryn Lofton, January 9, 2009.

9. Oliver Wendell Holmes, as quoted in Richard J. Mouw, *The Smell of Sawdust: What Evangelicals Can Learn from Their Fundamentalist Heritage* (Zondervan, 2000), 151.

10. Orsi, *History and Presence*, 29.

BEN SCHILATY

1. Sharon Eubank, "By Union of Feeling We Obtain Power with God," *Ensign*, November 2020, 55–57.

2. Jeffrey R. Holland, "'Lord, I Believe,'" *Ensign*, May 2013, 93–95.

3. Kenneth Agutamba, "Genocide and the Power in Forgiveness," *The New Times*, October 27, 2018.

MICHELLE GRAABEK-WALLACE

1. Lars Bjørnsten, "H.C. Andersen: 'Er Du i Verden Vide.' 1867," H.C. Andersen Information, accessed April 11, 2022, https://www.hcandersen-homepage.dk/?page_id=59777. Translation is my own.

2. Erastus Snow journals, 1847 December–1850 September, n.d., 111, MS 1329, Church History Library, The Church of Jesus Christ of Latter-day Saints.

3. C. C. Shaw, "Some of Our Composers: Hans Henry Petersen," *Juvenile Instructor*, March 15, 1902, 168–69.

4. "I'm a Pilgrim, I'm a Stranger," in *Hymns of The Church of Jesus Christ of Latter-day Saints* (The Church of Jesus Christ of Latter-day Saints, 1985), no. 121.

5. Thomsen Josephine Hyrumine Hansen, "Sketch of the Life of Anne Katrina Hedvig Rasmussen," 1926.

6. "Secret Prayer," in *Hymns*, no. 144.

7. 1 Nephi 11:17.

8. C. S. Lewis, "On Obstinacy in Belief," in *The World's Last Night and Other Essays* (HarperCollins, 2017), 25–26.

UGO A. PEREGO

1. Lawrence E. Corbridge, "Stand Forever," BYU Speeches, January 22, 2019.

2. Lynn B. Jorde and Michael J. Bamshad, "Genetic Ancestry Testing: What Is It and Why Is It Important?," *JAMA* 323, no. 11 (2020): 1089–90.

3. A recent comprehensive and well-written treatise on this subject and a great resource to learn more about the genetic evolution of hominids, including modern humans, is David Reich's *Who We Are and How We Got Here: Ancient dna and the New Science of the Human Past* (Oxford University Press, 2018).

4. "What Does the Church Believe About Dinosaurs?," *New Era*, February 2016, 41; and "What Does the Church Believe About Evolution?," *New Era*, October 2016, 41.

5. Ugo A. Perego and Jayne E. Ekins, "Is Decrypting the Genetic Legacy of America's Indigenous Populations Key to the Historicity of the Book of Mormon?," *Interpreter: A Journal of Latter-day Saint Faith and Scholarship* 38 (2020): 355–90.

6. "Book of Mormon and DNA Studies," Gospel Topics Essays, The Church of Jesus Christ of Latter-day Saints.

ASTRID S. TUMINEZ

1. Friedrich Nietzsche, *Thus Spake Zarathustra* (The Macmillan Company, 1896), 27.

2. Shunryu Suzuki, *Beginner's Mind* (Shambala Publications, 2011), 1.

3. Timothy Keller, *The Prodigal God* (Random House, 2008), xiv–xv, 1.

4. William James, *The Varieties of Religious Experience* (The Modern Library, 2002), 327.

5. Stephen Blackmer, "Staying Put," Letters from Church of the Woods, Kairos Earth, June 12, 2020.

TERRYL GIVENS

1. Marcelino D'Ambrosio, *When the Church Was Young: Voices of the Early Fathers* (Franciscan, 2014), 21.

2. Minutes, April 4–5, 1860, President's Office Journal, Brigham Young office files, CR 1234, Church History Library, The Church of Jesus Christ of Latter-day Saints.

3. See Terryl L. Givens, *Wrestling the Angel: The Foundations of Mormon Thought: Cosmos, God, Humanity* (Oxford University Press, 2015), 112–16.

4. Eugene England, "Perfection and Progress: Two Complementary Ways to Talk About God," BYU Studies 29, no. 3 (Summer 1989): 31. The original talk was given at BYU in 1979.

5. Eugene England, "Are All Alike unto God? Prejudice Against Blacks and Women in Popular Mormon Theology," Sunstone 14, no. 2 (April 1990): 13.

6. England, "Are All Alike unto God?," 14.

7. Eugene England, "On Finding Truth and God," in Why the Church Is as True as the Gospel (Bookcraft, 1986), 111–12. First delivered at the 1985 Sunstone Theological Symposium.

8. John Milton, "Aeropagitica," in The Prose Works of John Milton (W. Ball, 1838), 113.

9. "Revelation Book 1," 31, The Joseph Smith Papers.

10. David Whitmer, An Address to All Believers in Christ by a Witness to the Divine Authenticity of The Book of Mormon (David Whitmer, 1887), 30–31.

11. "History, 1838–1856, volume C-1 Addenda," 20, The Joseph Smith Papers.

12. "History, 1838–1856, volume D-1 [1 August 1842–1 July 1843]," 1555–57, The Joseph Smith Papers.

13. Hyrum L. Andrus and Helen Mae Andrus, They Knew the Prophet: Personal Accounts from over 100 People Who Knew Joseph Smith (Bookcraft, 1974), 140.

14. Michael Massing, Fatal Discord: Erasmus, Luther, and the Fight for the Western Mind (HarperCollins, 2018), 674.

15. Martin Luther, The Bondage of the Will (Hendrickson, 2008), 33.

16. Collected Discourses Delivered by President Wilford Woodruff, His Two Counselors, the Twelve Apostles, and Others, ed. Brian H. Stuy (BHS Publishing, 1999), 4:72–73.

17. Darius Clement to Warren Foote, April 20, 1894, in Warren Foote, Autobiography, 3:14, Washington County Historical Society, available online at http://wchsutah.org/people/warren-foote-journal1.php.

18. Clement to Foote, April 20, 1894, 3:14.

19. "Remarks," Deseret News, April 19, 1866, 154.

20. Collected Discourses Delivered by President Wilford Woodruff, 4:71.

21. Lorenzo Snow, "Opening Address," in Seventieth Annual Conference (Deseret News, 1900), 1–2.

22. Robin Scott Jensen et al., eds., Manuscript Revelation Books, facsimile ed., 1st vol. of the Revelations and Translations series of The Joseph Smith Papers, ed. Dean C. Jessee et al. (Church Historian's Press, 2009).

23. "Discourse by Elder George Q. Cannon," Deseret News, May 19, 1880.

24.John Henry Evans, "Bishop Spalding's Jumps in the Logical Process," *Improvement Era* 16, no. 4 (February 1913): 345.

25.J. M. Sjodahl, "The Book of Abraham," *Improvement Era* 16, no. 4 (February 1913): 326–27.

26.B. H. Roberts, "A Plea in Bar of Final Conclusion," *Improvement Era* 16, no. 4 (February 1913): 309–25.

27.Junius W. Wells, "Scholars Disagree," *Improvement Era* 16, no. 4, (February 1913): 341–43.

28.David Barber, "An Interview with Eugene England," *Student Review*, April 10, 1998, 10.

29.Philip L. Barlow, foreword, in *Leonard J. Arrington: Faith and Intellect: The Lives and Contributions of Latter-day Saint Thinkers*, ed. Gary James Bergera (Signature Books, 2019), viii–ix.

30.One witness to such a fireside recounts the unsettling but transformative experience in Boyd Petersen, "Eugene England and the Future of Mormonism," *Dead Wood and Rushing Water* (blog), January 28, 2016.

31.Ronald W. Walker, Richard E. Turley Jr., and Glen M. Leonard, *Massacre at Mountain Meadows* (Oxford University Press, 2011).

32.*Saints: The Story of the Church of Jesus Christ in the Latter Days* (The Church of Jesus Christ of Latter-day Saints, 2018–2024).

33.D. Todd Christofferson, "The Doctrine of Christ," *Ensign*, May 2012, 88.

34.Dieter F. Uchtdorf, "Come, Join with Us," *Ensign*, November 2013, 21–24.

35.Cited in Dian Saderup Monson, "Eugene England—Master Teacher: The BYU Years," *Sunstone* 121 (January 2002): 26.

36.Monson, "Eugene England," 26.

EUGENE ENGLAND

1.The essay has been edited lightly for space considerations.

DEIDRE NICOLE GREEN

1.Søren Kierkegaard, *Practice in Christianity*, ed. and trans. Howard V. Hong and Edna H. Hong (Princeton University Press, 1991), 88.

2.From personal transcription of Henry B. Eyring's opening remarks at First Presidency News Conference, January 16, 2018, The Church of Jesus Christ of Latter-day Saints, available on YouTube.

3. Søren Kierkegaard, *Works of Love*, ed. and trans. Howard V. Hong and Edna H. Hong (Princeton University Press, 1995), 164.

4. Kierkegaard, *Works of Love*, 166.

5. Kierkegaard, *Works of Love*, 167.

6. Kierkegaard, *Works of Love*, 167.

7. Søren Kierkegaard, *Eighteen Upbuilding Discourses*, ed. and trans. Howard V. Hong and Edna H. Hong (Princeton University Press, 1990), 61.

STEVEN L. PECK

1. See Daniel O. McClellan, "2 Nephi 25:23 in Literary and Rhetorical Context," *Journal of Book of Mormon Studies* 29 (2020): 1–19.

2. Charles Darwin, *On the Origin of Species by Means of Natural Selection, or the Preservation of Favoured Races in the Struggle for Life*, 1859, in *From So Simple a Beginning: The Four Great Books of Charles Darwin*, ed. Edward O. Wilson (W. W. Norton & Company, 2006), 568.

3. Xenophon, *Memorabilia. Oeconomicus. Symposium. Apology*, trans. E. C. Marchant, rev. Jeffrey Henderson, Loeb Classical Library 168 (Harvard University Press, 2013), 57.

4. Aristophanes, *Clouds. Wasps. Peace*, ed. and trans. Jeffrey Henderson, Loeb Classical Library 488 (Harvard University Press, 1998), 413.

5. Henri Bergson, *Creative Evolution* (Palgrave Macmillan, 2007), 7.

6. See Doctrine and Covenants 57.

7. "Race and the Priesthood," Gospel Topics Essays, The Church of Jesus Christ of Latter-day Saints.

8. Edward Young, *The Complaint: Or, Night-Thoughts on Life, Death, and Immortality*, rev. ed. (Peter Wilson, 1766).

9. Benjamin Stillingfleet, *Miscellaneous Tracts Relating to Natural History, Husbandry, and Physick [...]* (R. and J. Dodsley, S. Baker, and T. Payne, 1762).

10. *The Complete Sermons of Ralph Waldo Emerson,* ed. Teresa Toulouse and Andrew Delbanco (University of Missouri Press, 1990), 2:52.

FIONA GIVENS

1. Matthew 13:52, KJV.

2. Nicholas Wolterstorff, *Lament for a Son* (Eerdmans, 1987), 89.

3. Dietrich Bonhoeffer to Eberhard Bethge, July 16, 1944, in Larry L. Rasmusssen, *Dietrich Bonhoeffer: Reality and Resistance* (Westminster John Knox Press, 2005), 17.

4. *Lectures on Faith* 3:2–4.

5. Julian of Norwich, *Showings* (Norton, 2005), 12.40, 54.

6. Julian, *Showings*, 14.49, 67.

7. Julian, *Showings*, 14.51, 71 (bracketed translation mine).

8. Julian, *Showings*, 13.42, 58.

9. "Teaching of the Twelve," 7.9.4, in *The Ante-Nicene Fathers*, ed. Alexander Roberts and James Donaldson (Eerdmans, 1977), 7:380.

10. Chrysostom, *Proof of the Gospel*, 6.24, in *Ancient Christian Commentary, Hebrews*, ed. Erik M. Heen and Philip D. W. Krey (InterVarsity Press, 2005), NT 10:223.

11. Virginia Woolf, *To the Lighthouse* (Harcourt, Brace, Jovanovich, 1989), 105.

JENNY HALE PULSIPHER

1. Russell M. Nelson, "Let God Prevail," *Ensign*, November 2020, 92–95.

2. Dallin H. Oaks, "Love Your Enemies," *Ensign*, November 2020, 26–29; and Dallin H. Oaks, "Racism and Other Challenges," BYU Speeches, October 27, 2020.

3. Michael Kay Bennion, "Captivity, Adoption, Marriage and Identity: Native American Children in Mormon Homes, 1847–1900" (master's thesis, University of Nevada, Las Vegas, 2012), 96.

4. "To the Saints," *Deseret News*, March 4, 1852.

5. Peggy Pascoe, *What Comes Naturally: Miscegenation Law and the Making of Race in America* (Oxford University Press, 2009), 119.

6. 2 Nephi 5:24; Jacob 3:9; Helaman 3:15–16; and Mormon 5:15 (here Mormon is referring to the combined "remnant of the seed of Jacob," the Lamanites and the Nephites who allied with them [Mormon 5:8–24; 6:15]).

7. Peggy Fletcher Stack, "Single Word Change in Book of Mormon Speaks Volumes," *Salt Lake Tribune*, November 8, 2007.

8. Enos 1:20–21; 2 Nephi 5:24; Leviticus 11; Leviticus 19:28. I am indebted to Eduardo Pagan for his incisive thinking about the "skin of blackness" in the Book of Mormon.

9. Italics added. For another scripture that suggests that change in skin color was a result of intermarriage, see 3 Nephi 2:15–16.

10. P. Jane Hafen made this point in her 1998 essay "The Being and Place of a Native American Mormon," in *New Genesis: A Mormon Reader on Land and Community*, ed. Terry Tempest Williams et al. (Gibbs Smith, 1998), 38.

PHILIP BARLOW

1. Lowell L. Bennion, *The Things That Matter Most* (Bookcraft, 1978), 19–22.

2. For example, in the original collection, *A Thoughtful Faith: Essays on Belief by Mormon Scholars* (Canon Press, 1986), 235–58, and "Questing and Questioning," *Sunstone*, November 26, 2014.

3. J. B. S. Haldane, *Possible Worlds, and Other Papers*, Essay Index Reprint Series (Books for Libraries Press, 1971), 286.

4. Annie Dillard, *Pilgrim at Tinker Creek*, 1st Perennial Classics ed. (HarperPerennial, 1998), 146.

5. See the insightful, amusing parody of Saintly folkways in James Goldberg, Nicole Wilkes Goldberg, and Mattathias Singh, *Tales of the Chelm First Ward* (By Common Consent Press, 2024).

6. Mark Monmonier and H. J. de Blij, *How to Lie with Maps*, 2nd ed. (University Of Chicago Press, 1996), 1.

7. Philip L. Barlow, *Mormons and the Bible: The Place of the Latter-day Saints in American Religion*, updated ed. (Oxford University Press, 2013), xxxiii.

8. While widely attributed to Voltaire, there seems to be no publication bearing the philosopher's name in which this statement appears as recorded. Nonetheless, its pervasive usage in modern literature suggests some degree of authenticity in origin.

9. Terryl Givens, *When Souls Had Wings: Pre-Mortal Existence in Western Thought* (Oxford University Press, 2010).

10. Franz Kafka, *The Basic Kafka* (Washington Square Press, 1979), 159–60, provides an example. More broadly, one can discern in Kafka's "The Castle," "The Trial," "The Burrow," and elsewhere a persistent struggle not merely with his illness, his pathologies, his cloudy relations with his father and with women, his Jewishness, and his entanglement as an employee of the modern bureaucratic state. One can discern beyond all this the grappling of a tortured prophet of "the modern mind" that "knows two things at once: that there is no God, and that there must be God." This God, for Kafka, need not be personal, to be sure. See Roberto Calasso's brilliant interpretation of Kafka: *K.* (Vintage Books, 2006).

11. Matthew 10:16.

12. Philip Barlow, "Unorthodox Orthodoxy: The Idea of Deification in Christian History," *Sunstone*, September–October 1983, 18.

13. Abraham Joshua Heschel, *God in Search of Man: A Philosophy of Judaism* (Farrar, Straus & Cudahy, 1955).

14. Moses 7:18; Deuteronomy 15:4.

15. Genesis 3:9.

16. 3 Nephi 27:27; see also Lynn G. Robbins, "What Manner of Men and Women Ought Ye To Be?," *Ensign*, May 2011, 103–5.

17. John 21:17.

18. Alma 5:14.

19. John 14:9.

20. Job 38:2.

21. Fyodor Dostoyevsky, *The Brothers Karamazov: A Novel in Four Parts and an Epilogue*, trans. Constance Garnett (Macmillan, 1922), 269.

22. Matthew 8:26.

23. Esther 4:14.

24. Matthew 26:40.

25. Mark 8:27.

26. William Woodsworth, "Ode: Intimations of Immortality," in *The Oxford Book of English Verse*, ed. Christopher B. Ricks (Oxford University Press, 1999), 349–55.

27. Viktor E. Frankl, *Man's Search for Meaning* (Beacon Press, 2006), 108–9.

28. *The Lord's Question: A Call to Come Unto Him* (Keter Foundation, 1985), 4.

COLOPHON

The text of the book is typeset in William, a modern interpretation of William Caslon's historic typeface, crafted by Maria Doreuli to honor tradition while meeting the demands of contemporary design. The writer's names and the footnotes are typset in Söhne, designed by Kris Sowersby and engineered by Noe Blanco.

Cover illustration, chapter title page backgrounds, drop caps and other illustrated details by Jessica Sarah Beach.

Book design & typography by Cole Melanson.